New Insights into Language Anxiety

SECOND LANGUAGE ACQUISITION

Series Editors: **Professor David Singleton**, *University of Pannonia, Hungary* and Fellow Emeritus, *Trinity College, Dublin, Ireland* and **Dr Simone E. Pfenninger**, *University of Salzburg, Austria*

This series brings together titles dealing with a variety of aspects of language acquisition and processing in situations where a language or languages other than the native language is involved. Second language is thus interpreted in its broadest possible sense. The volumes included in the series all offer in their different ways, on the one hand, exposition and discussion of empirical findings and, on the other, some degree of theoretical reflection. In this latter connection, no particular theoretical stance is privileged in the series; nor is any relevant perspective – sociolinguistic, psycholinguistic, neurolinguistic, etc. – deemed out of place. The intended readership of the series includes final-year undergraduates working on second language acquisition projects, postgraduate students involved in second language acquisition research, and researchers, teachers and policy-makers in general whose interests include a second language acquisition component.

Full details of all the books in this series and of all our other publications can be found on http://www.multilingual-matters.com, or by writing to Multilingual Matters, St Nicholas House, 31-34 High Street, Bristol BS1 2AW, UK.

SECOND LANGUAGE ACQUISITION: 114

New Insights into Language Anxiety

Theory, Research and Educational Implications

Edited by
Christina Gkonou, Mark Daubney and Jean-Marc Dewaele

MULTILINGUAL MATTERS
Bristol • Blue Ridge Summit

Library of Congress Cataloging in Publication Data
A catalog record for this book is available from the Library of Congress.
Names: Gkonou, Christina, editor. | Daubney, Mark, editor. | Dewaele, Jean-Marc, - editor.
Title: New Insights into Language Anxiety: Theory, Research and Educational Implications/Edited by Christina Gkonou, Mark Daubney and Jean-Marc Dewaele.
Description: Bristol; Blue Ridge Summit: Multilingual Matters, [2017] | Series: Second Language Acquisition: 114 |
Includes bibliographical references and index.
Identifiers: LCCN 2016053136| ISBN 9781783097715 (hbk : alk. paper) | ISBN 9781783097708 (pbk : alk. paper) | ISBN 9781783097722 (Pdf) | ISBN 9781783097739 (Epub) | ISBN 9781783097746 (kindle)
Subjects: LCSH: Language and languages–Study and teaching–Psychological aspects. | Second language acquisition–Research. | Anxiety.
Classification: LCC P53.7 .N39 2017 | DDC 401/.9–dc23 LC record available at https://lccn.loc.gov/2016053136

British Library Cataloguing in Publication Data
A catalogue entry for this book is available from the British Library.

ISBN-13: 978-1-78309-771-5 (hbk)
ISBN-13: 978-1-78309-770-8 (pbk)

Multilingual Matters
UK: St Nicholas House, 31-34 High Street, Bristol BS1 2AW, UK.
USA: NBN, Blue Ridge Summit, PA, USA.

Website: www.multilingual-matters.com
Twitter: Multi_Ling_Mat
Facebook: https://www.facebook.com/multilingualmatters
Blog: www.channelviewpublications.wordpress.com

Copyright © 2017 Christina Gkonou, Mark Daubney, Jean-Marc Dewaele and the authors of individual chapters.

All rights reserved. No part of this work may be reproduced in any form or by any means without permission in writing from the publisher.

The policy of Multilingual Matters/Channel View Publications is to use papers that are natural, renewable and recyclable products, made from wood grown in sustainable forests. In the manufacturing process of our books, and to further support our policy, preference is given to printers that have FSC and PEFC Chain of Custody certification. The FSC and/or PEFC logos will appear on those books where full certification has been granted to the printer concerned.

Typeset by Deanta Global Publishing Services Limited.
Printed and bound in the UK by the CPI Books Group Ltd.
Printed and bound in the US by Edwards Brothers Malloy, Inc.

Contents

   Contributors   vii

1 Introduction   1

Part 1: Theoretical Insights

2 An Overview of Language Anxiety Research and Trends in its Development   11
Peter D. MacIntyre

3 On the Misreading of Horwitz, Horwitz and Cope (1986) and the Need to Balance Anxiety Research and the Experiences of Anxious Language Learners   31
Elaine K. Horwitz

Part 2: Empirical Investigations

4 Anxiety and L2 Self-Images: The 'Anxious Self'   51
Erdi Şimşek and Zoltán Dörnyei

5 Are Perfectionists More Anxious Foreign Language Learners and Users?   70
Jean-Marc Dewaele

6 Social Anxiety and Silence in Japan's Tertiary Foreign Language Classrooms   91
Jim King and Lesley Smith

7 Do You See What I Feel? An Idiodynamic Assessment of Expert and Peer's Reading of Nonverbal Language Anxiety Cues   110
Tammy Gregersen, Peter D. MacIntyre and Tucker Olson

8   Towards an Ecological Understanding of Language Anxiety   135
    Christina Gkonou

9   Exploring the Relationship between Anxiety and Advanced
    Hungarian EFL Learners' Communication Experiences in the
    Target Language: A Study of High- vs Low-Anxious Learners   156
    Zsuzsa Tóth

Part 3: Implications for Practice

10 Anxious Language Learners Can Change Their Minds:
    Ideas and Strategies from Traditional Psychology and Positive
    Psychology   177
    Rebecca L. Oxford

11 The Links Between Self-Esteem and Language Anxiety and
    Implications for the Classroom   198
    Fernando D. Rubio-Alcalá

12 Conclusion   217
    Christina Gkonou, Jean-Marc Dewaele and Mark Daubney

    Index   224

Contributors

Mark Daubney is a teacher, teacher trainer and researcher at the School of Education and Social Sciences, Leiria Polytechnic Institute, Portugal. Presently, he is an adjunct professor in the Department of Languages and Literatures at the same institution, where he is the coordinator of the English Department and the Chinese-Portuguese-English Studies first-degree course. His research interests broadly focus on teacher training and the influence of affective factors on classroom interaction, especially the interface between emotions, such as anxiety and motivation, and teacher identity. His PhD was a longitudinal study of anxiety experienced by trainee teachers on their teaching English as a foreign language (TEFL) practicum.

Jean-Marc Dewaele is Professor of Applied Linguistics and Multilingualism at Birkbeck, University of London. He does research on individual differences in psycholinguistic, sociolinguistic, pragmatic, psychological and emotional aspects of second language acquisition and multilingualism. He is the author of a monograph, *Emotions in Multiple Languages*, published in 2010 (2nd edn in 2013). He is president of the International Association of Multilingualism, Convenor of the AILA Research Network, Multilingualism, and former president of the European Second Language Association. He is General Editor of the *International Journal of Bilingual Education and Bilingualism*. He won the Equality and Diversity Research Award from the British Association for Counselling and Psychotherapy (2013) and the Robert C. Gardner Award for Excellence in Second Language and Bilingualism Research from the International Association of Language and Social Psychology.

Zoltán Dörnyei is Professor of Psycholinguistics at the School of English, University of Nottingham. He has published extensively on various aspects of language learner characteristics, second language acquisition and language teaching methodology, and he is the author of over 20 books, including *The Psychology of Second Language Acquisition* (2009, Oxford University Press), *Motivating Learners, Motivating Teachers: Building Vision in the Language Classroom* (2014, Cambridge University Press, with M. Kubanyiova), *The Psychology of The Language Learner Revisited* (2015, Routledge, with

S. Ryan) and *Motivational Currents in Language Learning: Frameworks for Focused Interventions* (2016, Routledge, with A. Henry and C. Muir).

Christina Gkonou is Lecturer in teaching English to speakers of other languages (TESOL) and MA TESOL Programme Leader at the Department of Language and Linguistics, University of Essex, UK. She convenes postgraduate modules on teacher training and education and the psychology of language learning and teaching. Her main research interests are in all areas of the psychology of learners and teachers, but more specifically in language anxiety and emotions, teacher identity and agency and emotion-regulation strategies for language learning. She is the co-editor of *New Directions in Language Learning Psychology* (2016, with Sarah Mercer and Dietmar Tatzl).

Tammy Gregersen received her MA in Education and PhD in Linguistics in Chile, where she also began her teaching and researching career. She is currently a professor of TESOL and teacher educator at the University of Northern Iowa (USA). She is the co-author, with Peter MacIntyre, of *Capitalizing on Language Learners' Individuality*, and co-editor with Peter and Sarah Mercer of *Positive Psychology in SLA* (both published by Multilingual Matters). She is currently working on two other titles, one on nonverbal communication in the language classroom and the other on innovations in teacher education. She has published extensively in peer-reviewed journals and contributed several chapters to applied linguistics anthologies on individual differences, teacher education, language teaching methodology and nonverbal communication in language classrooms. Tammy is passionate about traveling, and has presented at conferences and taught in graduate programmes across the globe.

Elaine K. Horwitz is Professor of Curriculum and Instruction at the University of Texas at Austin, United States. She teaches courses in second language acquisition, language teaching methodology, language testing and programme evaluation and second language research methods. She is well-known for her pioneering research on language anxiety and beliefs about language learning. She is the author of *Becoming a Language Teacher: A Practical Guide to Second Language Learning and Teaching* and co-editor of *Language Anxiety: From Theory and Practice to Classroom Implications*.

Jim King is Lecturer in Education at the School of Education, University of Leicester, UK. Before gaining his PhD in Applied Linguistics from the University of Nottingham, Jim taught in various higher education, English as a foreign language (EFL) and English for academic purposes (EAP) contexts around the world, including spells in Japan, Australia, Poland, Hungary and Italy. His research interests focus on the issue of silence in education and on psychological aspects of second language learning and teaching. His publications include the 2013 monograph *Silence in the Second Language Classroom* and the 2015 edited volume *The Dynamic Interplay between Context and the Language Learner*, both published by Palgrave Macmillan.

Peter MacIntyre received his PhD in psychology from the University of Western Ontario (now Western University) in 1992 with R.C. Gardner and is now a Full Professor of Psychology at Cape Breton University. His research examines emotion, motivation and cognition across a variety of types of behaviour, including interpersonal communication, public speaking and learning. The majority of Peter's research examines the psychology of communication, with a particular emphasis on second language acquisition and communication. He is co-author of both *Capitalizing on Language Learners' Individuality* and *Optimizing Language Learners' Nonverbal Behavior: From Tenet to Technique* with Tammy Gregersen, co-editor of *Positive Psychology in SLA* (with Tammy Gregersen and Sarah Mercer) and co-editor of *Motivational Dynamics in Language Learning* with Zoltán Dörnyei and Alastair Henry.

Tucker Olson is a research assistant at the University of Northern Iowa, where he studies Spanish and global studies. He recently began serving as a primary literacy volunteer for the Peace Corps in the Dominican Republic, along the Haitian border. He plans to continue his academic interests in Hispanic linguistics, with an emphasis on queer sociolinguistics in transnational contexts.

Rebecca L. Oxford holds a doctorate and a master's degree in educational psychology and two degrees in languages. One of her greatest interests is how psychology and language learning intertwine (as in her chapter in this book), and other interests are strategic self-regulation, spirituality in education and the intersection of peace communication and positive psychology. She led language teacher education programmes and taught graduate courses for several decades at the University of Alabama and the University of Maryland. At these institutions, she received multiple awards for teaching and had numerous opportunities to mentor younger faculty members and doctoral students in research and publication. At the University of Maryland, she received the most prestigious faculty honour, the Distinguished Scholar-Teacher Award. She received a lifetime achievement award from Heinle & Heinle publishers stating that her research on learning strategies changed the way the world teaches languages. Having retired from the University of Maryland, she is currently teaching again at the University of Alabama and continues to mentor other scholars. She has presented her research in more than 40 countries, published more than a dozen books with several more underway, co-edited three book series and eight journal special issues and authored approximately 250 articles and chapters.

Fernando D. Rubio-Alcalá is a professor of applied linguistics at the University of Huelva, Spain. He holds a PhD in Language Anxiety and his main area of research interest focuses on foreign language teaching and learning, especially affective factors, and plurilingual education. He has authored numerous scholarly texts such as *Anxiety and Language Learning* (2004; in Spanish), *Self-Esteem and Foreign Language Learning* (2007; Cambridge Scholars Publishing) and 'Self-Esteem and Self-Concept in Foreign Language Learning' (2014; in S. Mercer and M. Williams; Multilingual Matters). He has been a plenary speaker at many academic events in Europe, North America and South America.

Erdi Şimşek is a PhD candidate at the University of Nottingham, UK, under the supervision of Professor Zoltán Dörnyei. He holds an MA in Applied Linguistics from the University of Nottingham, with his dissertation entitled *Insights into Situated Classroom Anxiety*. His current research interests include foreign language anxiety; second language (L2) persona, vision and mental imagery; stage fright and narrative identity.

Lesley Smith currently teaches English language courses at the University of Notre Dame, Indiana. Prior to this, she worked as an assistant language teacher at the Université de Technologie de Troyes, France, before going on to complete a postgraduate degree in TESOL from the University of Leicester, UK. She is particularly interested in social anxiety in adult English language learners and group dynamics in L2 and general education contexts.

Zsuzsa Tóth is a senior lecturer at the Institute of English and American Studies, Pázmány Péter Catholic University, Hungary. She is an EFL instructor and teacher trainer. She holds a PhD in Language Pedagogy (Eötvös Loránd University, Budapest) and an MSc in Applied Linguistics (University of Edinburgh). Her professional interests include individual differences in L2 learning, teacher education issues and EFL teaching methodology. Her main research area is the study of foreign language anxiety. She has authored the book *Foreign Language Anxiety and the Advanced Language Learner* (Cambridge Scholars, 2010).

1 Introduction

Mark Daubney, Jean-Marc Dewaele and Christina Gkonou

Preliminary Thoughts on Language Anxiety and the Focus of this Anthology

This anthology focuses on the topic of language anxiety (LA), a complex emotion that, for approximately four decades, has consistently attracted the attention of second language acquisition (SLA) researchers, teacher educators and teachers across the globe. In turn, this interest has led to substantial, diverse and exciting contributions to the literature in the field. In their recent publication on learner characteristics, Gregersen and MacIntyre (2014: 3) describe LA as reflecting 'the worry and negative emotional reaction when learning and using a second language and is especially relevant in a classroom where self-expression takes place'. Within the classroom, it has been found to subtly and pervasively shape the thoughts, feelings and actions of those engaged in the teaching and learning of a foreign or second language (L2). As a rule, LA research has focused on learners, yet teachers have also been shown to be susceptible to the nervous reactions anxiety arouses (Daubney, 2010; Horwitz, 1986). In L2 classrooms across many different settings, research has established that LA is a relatively common but largely unwelcome emotion, due to its potential to impact negatively in a myriad of ways on the language learning experience.

Indeed, contemplating the potential fallout from LA makes for fascinating yet unnerving reading. Among other things, it can impede the learning of the target language and hinder academic success; lead learners to abandon their studies; engender negative attitudes towards the target language and its respective culture(s); diminish the willingness to communicate; create counterproductive tensions among a class of language learners; sow the seeds of self-doubt in the minds of learners regarding their identity, feelings of competence and degree of self-esteem; and have a corrosive influence on the very lifeblood of L2 learning itself – the enthusiasm and motivation necessary to engage and embrace another language other than one's own.

Such a list helps to explain why LA continues to resonate with researchers and practitioners alike and why the ongoing fascination with this affective variable is both relevant and understandable. It also underpins our desire, as editors of this volume, to bring this collection of chapters to fruition in order to achieve a more up-to-date understanding of this emotion.

It has been nearly 40 years since Scovel's (1978) review urged greater scientific and methodological rigour upon SLA researchers investigating affective variables. In the ensuing years, much research has been undertaken, and LA is now indisputably part of the SLA landscape. Presently, the influence it is deemed to exert within the complex network of factors impacting on the degree of success of language learning is such that it is rare indeed to encounter publications in SLA focusing on individual differences or affective factors that do not refer to it. In fact, when SLA scholars ponder these characteristics, anxiety is often the first to be discussed (see Gregersen & MacIntyre, 2014). Arnold and Brown (1999: 8) believe it to be the most influential affective factor 'obstructing the learning process', while in terms of interest generated, Scovel (2001: 127) ranks it as 'second only to motivation'.

The present volume focuses on some of the most recent developments in LA theory and research as well as the implications these have for classroom practice. Further, it does so in the light of an increasingly influential paradigm shift currently shaping the field of SLA, a *dynamic turn*, which currently positions research as 'situated and process-oriented, which means that learners attributes are neither stable nor context-independent, but interact with the context and over time' (Dewaele, 2012: 43). An important driver of this perspective is *dynamic systems theory* (DST; de Bot *et al.*, 2007; Larsen-Freeman & Cameron, 2008), also known as *complex dynamic systems theory* (CDST; MacIntyre *et al.*, 2015), which we will consider further in the following sections.

Why an Anthology about Language Anxiety?

As editors, we are all of the firm conviction that the current climate shaping SLA research is a most propitious one for re-evaluating LA. When positioning the present volume in this landscape, one of the key considerations that has influenced our thinking is that, given the remarkable interest in LA over the last 40 years, accompanied and driven by what MacIntyre (1999: 24) referred to, at the advent of the 21st century, as 'a virtual explosion' in research, interestingly, only two bespoke volumes on LA have been published over the same period.

The first was Horwitz and Young's (1991) landmark collection, which itself included reprints of key papers on the topic. The second was Young's (1999), which, like the first, brought together theoretical, empirical and practical contributions, and whose subtitle – *A Practical Guide to Creating a Low-Anxiety Classroom Atmosphere* – gives a clear indication of the overarching goal that preoccupied – and continues to preoccupy – researchers and practitioners when addressing LA. A 17-year hiatus, then, between Young's and the present volume, would suggest a reassessment, including new insights, is somewhat overdue.

Further, the aforementioned paradigm shift and growing influence of DST, together with the flourishing field of language learning psychology (Gkonou *et al.*, 2016; Mercer *et al.*, 2012; Williams *et al.*, 2015) means the absence of such a volume at this important juncture in SLA research would leave LA somewhat under-represented when considering learner characteristics. This is of particular concern when LA, according to Dörnyei and Ryan (2015: 176), can be regarded 'as a kind of bellwether of various theoretical and methodological changes occurring in the field of L2 individual differences'.

So while this anthology comprises contributions on theory, research and practice, and is therefore organised in a similar vein to that of the two aforementioned volumes, we are also keenly aware of the flux and complexity presently characterising the field and the need to consider anxiety within this emerging and increasingly influential paradigm shift, including the attendant calls for researchers to explore different and more dynamic conceptualisations of the affective dimension (see Gregersen *et al.*, this volume; MacIntyre, this volume; Pavlenko, 2013; Şimşek & Dörnyei, this volume). Thus, Dörnyei and Ryan (2015: 180) suggest that future research into LA 'will need to foreground a more dynamic conception of anxiety, highlighting aspects of change as well as types of adaptations that can lead the behavioural outcomes of anxiety both in the positive and negative direction'. We see the present volume as dovetailing with these recommendations, thereby constituting a current and thought-provoking pool of knowledge and ideas from which both researchers and practitioners can draw for their own present and future projects.

All three editors share a common interest in LA research and the need to bring about a greater and more nuanced understanding of this emotion. We are also equally aware of the applied nature of our field and how this understanding should be factored into further investigation, teacher training and pedagogy, contributing, ultimately, to both effective language learning and teaching characterised by engagement and enjoyment.

Issues of Change and Challenge: Language Anxiety in a Landscape of Increasing Complexity

The aforementioned calls for anxiety to be conceptualised and researched from more dynamic perspectives reflect the underlying changes in the SLA field and the challenges arising from these. Generally speaking, LA has been conceptualised as a single, powerful and negative influence residing within the learner, and therefore a force to be reduced or, better still, eliminated from individuals and the classroom, although some researchers have questioned the wisdom of this view (see Scovel, 2001). Shaped and influenced by cognitive psychology, approaches to LA research have shifted from seeing this emotion as a transference to the L2 domain of other types of anxiety, such as test anxiety or communication apprehension, to the now prevailing notion that it is in fact unique to L2 learning itself, and therefore a situation-specific anxiety (Horwitz *et al.*, 1986; MacIntyre, 1999). Having taken on board Scovel's recommendations by fine-tuning definitions and developing more sophisticated instruments, LA research has, until very recently, settled into somewhat insistent patterns of investigation, the thrust of which has been to first measure levels of anxiety with self-reports – the Foreign Language Classroom Anxiety Scale (FLCAS; Horwitz *et al.*, 1986) being the best known – then to identify causes of the anxiety, followed by the application of strategies to reduce it. Over two decades ago, calls (see Skehan, 1989) were already being made to move away from this somewhat limited methodological, and largely quantitative, research framework. Indeed, the aforementioned shift towards complexity and a move away from seeing learner characteristics as stable aspects of the learner has only served to highlight the need for new and creative approaches to LA research. The challenge, then, is to find new ways of researching anxiety in the changing L2 landscape.

In fact, some of the previous and overriding concerns in research, including the somewhat sterile and circular arguments attempting to ascertain whether LA is a cause or effect of L2 performance, have gradually given way to a greater interest in the broader experience of anxiety as lived by learners (see Horwitz, 2001; King & Smith; MacIntyre; Oxford; Tóth, this volume) as well as its impact on classroom interaction and learning. This represents a recalibrating of perspective, with the focus now squarely on how the learning process as a whole is affected, as opposed to a narrower focus on measurable outcomes. In fact, recent LA research (e.g. Gregersen *et al.*, this volume; MacIntyre & Gregersen, 2012; MacIntyre & Serroul, 2015) has resorted to more innovative methodologies in order to investigate anxiety over varying timescales, thereby reflecting a concern with exploring the fluctuating and dynamic natures of individual differences rather than conceiving and investigating them as stable traits. However, Dewaele and Al-Saraj's (2015) recent work alerts us to the danger of dismissing the influence of psychological traits on anxiety and, by extension, on other learner characteristics.

Nevertheless, given the growing influence of the view of learner psychology as an interdependent network of aspects shaped by context and time, it is no surprise that anxiety, with its intimate connections to motivation, risk-taking and other affective variables, presents L2 researchers with fascinating challenges.

To start with, LA may be conceptualised as a trait or a situation-specific anxiety, that is, an emotion which is either stable across both time and contexts, or specific to one domain only. Can a learner experience both trait and state anxiety? Can the learner experience both at the same time? Further, are the underlying causes of anxiety to be found in the learner, the teacher or the communicative environment or the subtle interplay of all of these? Yet another conundrum is whether anxiety may be conceived as *facilitating*, a helpful anxiety leading to greater attention, effort and performance, or *debilitating*, that is, a downward spiral of negative thoughts and feelings, leading to diminished attention and poorer performance. Presently, researchers (see Horwitz; Rúbio, this volume) largely view LA as a debilitating, unhelpful emotion. Yet recent research (Dewaele & MacIntyre, 2014) has looked at enjoyment and anxiety and how these two emotions interact within learners, highlighting how positive and negative emotions may mutually shape one another. Novel in its approach, such research should see greater caution exercised regarding the somewhat simplistic binary conceptualisations that may unnecessarily constrain our view of learner characteristics and hence our vision for research frameworks.

It is our opinion that the present anthology rises to the challenge of conceptualising, investigating and addressing anxiety from fresh perspectives, through different lenses and in relation to areas that have been little studied, and opens up exciting paths to further explore this multifaceted emotion.

The Organisation of this Anthology

The anthology itself is divided into three sections. Part 1 focuses on theoretical insights, with Chapters 2 and 3 exploring how LA has been theorised and researched up to the present time, thereby providing solid theoretical and conceptual foundations which underpin, inform and interconnect with the subsequent chapters. Further, these first two chapters – written by the prominent LA scholars, Peter MacIntyre and Elaine Horwitz – also discuss key issues, misconceptions and controversies that, over the years, have left and continue to leave their mark on the field. Part 2 (Chapters 4–9) is concerned with the empirical study of LA. The body of research represented in Part 2 not only details a concern with anxiety in L2 contexts that include European, North American and Asian settings, but also reveals the rich conceptual frameworks and methodological instruments which researchers are working with and applying to LA research. Part 3 (Chapters 10 and 11) centres on thinking about LA in educational settings and how practitioners might consider addressing it in their own contexts. Finally, we conclude the volume (Chapter 12) by drawing together the key themes arising from the previous contributions, and look towards possible paths that might be forged and explored by future LA research.

The Target Audience

We think the scope of the anthology is likely to capture the interest of a range of interested readers. Firstly, researchers in the field of SLA – both established and less experienced – will find that the chapters provide exciting and fresh perspectives on LA as well as rich possibilities for future research. Those on undergraduate, master and doctoral programmes, and likely to be among the less-experienced researchers, will also benefit. Teacher trainers, teachers and language students will encounter much to reflect on, including guidance on how to identify and address anxiety – including its alleviation – in classroom practice (see Oxford; Rúbio, this volume). Finally, we hope those engaged in the wider field of applied linguistics, as well as general psychology, will find bridges, interconnections and points of interest that will allow them to reflect productively on their own particular areas of specialisation and expertise.

Acknowledgements

Our sincere thanks go to all the contributors for their willingness to come on board this rewarding project and for having done so much to bring about this anthology. Much of the groundwork was laid in informal conversations that took place at the international conference, Matters of the Mind: Psychology and Language Learning, held in Graz, Austria, in May 2014. Thanks also to the contributors to this volume who reviewed the chapters and to Sarah Mercer and Stephen Ryan for their insightful feedback. Finally, our gratitude goes to David Singleton, who was such an enthusiastic supporter from the start, and to Multilingual Matters, especially Laura Longworth, for being a supportive and professional publisher.

References

Arnold, J. and Brown, H.D. (1999) A map of the terrain. In J. Arnold (ed.) *Affect in Language Learning* (pp. 1–24). Cambridge: Cambridge University Press.
Daubney, M. (2010) Language anxiety in English teachers during their teaching practice. Unpublished PhD thesis, University of Aveiro, Portugal.
de Bot, K., Lowie, W. and Verspoor, M. (2007) A dynamic systems theory to second language acquisition. *Bilingualism: Language and Cognition* 10, 7–21.
Dewaele, J.-M. (2012) Personality: Personality traits as independent and dependent variables. In S. Mercer, S. Ryan and M. Williams (eds) *Psychology for Language Learning: Insights from Research, Theory and Practice* (pp. 42–57). Basingstoke: Palgrave Macmillan.
Dewaele, J.-M. and MacIntyre, P.D. (2014) The two faces of Janus? Anxiety and enjoyment in the foreign language classroom. *Studies in Second Language Learning and Teaching* 4 (2), 237–274.
Dewaele, J.-M. and Al-Saraj, T.M. (2015) Foreign language classroom anxiety of Arab learners of English: The effect of personality, linguistic and sociobiographical variables. *Studies in Second Language Learning and Teaching* 5 (2), 205–228.

Dörnyei, Z. and Ryan, S. (2015) *The Psychology of the Language Learner Revisited.* New York: Routledge.
Gkonou, C., Tatzl, D. and Mercer, S. (eds) (2016) *New Directions in Language Learning Psychology.* Cham: Springer.
Gregersen, T. and MacIntyre, P.D. (2014) *Capitalizing on Language Learners' Individuality: From Premise to Practice.* Bristol: Multilingual Matters.
Horwitz, E.K. (1996) Even teachers get the blues: Recognizing and alleviating language teachers' feelings of foreign language anxiety. *Foreign Language Annals* 29 (3), 365–372.
Horwitz, E.K. (2001) Language anxiety and achievement. *Annual Review of Applied Linguistics* 21, 112–126.
Horwitz, E.K and Young, D.J. (eds) (1991) *Language Anxiety from Theory and Research to Classroom Implications.* Englewood Cliffs, NJ: Prentice-Hall.
Horwitz, E.K., Horwitz, M.B. and Cope, J. (1986) Foreign language classroom anxiety. *Modern Language Journal* 70 (2), 125–132.
Larsen-Freeman, D. and Cameron, L. (2008) *Complex Systems and Applied Linguistics.* New York: Oxford.
MacIntyre, P.D. (1999) Language anxiety: A review of the research for language teachers. In D.J. Young (ed.) *Affect in Foreign Language and Second Language Learning: A Practical Guide to Creating a Low-Anxiety Classroom Atmosphere* (pp. 24–45). Boston, MA: McGraw-Hill.
MacIntyre, P.D. and Gregersen, T. (2012) Affect: The role of language anxiety and other emotions in language learning. In S. Mercer, S. Ryan and M. Williams (eds) *Psychology for Language Learning: Insights from Research, Theory and Practice* (pp. 103–118). Basingstoke: Palgrave Macmillan.
MacIntyre, P.D. and Serroul, A. (2015) Motivation on a per-second timescale: Examining approach-avoidance motivation during L2 task performance. In Z. Dörnyei, P.D. MacIntyre and A. Henry (eds) *Motivational Dynamics in Language Learning* (pp. 109–138). Bristol: Multilingual Matters.
MacIntyre, P.D., Dörnyei, Z. and Henry, A. (2015) Conclusion: Hot enough to be cool: The promise of dynamic systems research. In Z. Dörnyei, P.D. MacIntyre and A. Henry (eds) *Motivational Dynamics in Language Learning* (pp. 419–429). Bristol: Multilingual Matters.
Mercer, S., Ryan, S. and Williams, M. (eds) (2012) *Psychology for Language Learning: Insights from Research, Theory and Practice.* Basingstoke: Palgrave Macmillan.
Pavlenko, A. (2013) The affective turn in SLA: From 'affective factors' to 'language desire' and 'commodification of affect'. In D. Gabryś and J. Bielska (eds) *The Affective Dimension in Second Language Acquisition* (pp. 3–28). Bristol: Multilingual Matters.
Scovel, T. (1978) The effect of affect on foreign language learning: A review of the anxiety research. *Language Learning* 28, 129–142.
Skehan, P. (1989) *Individual Differences in Second-Language Learning.* London: Edward Arnold.
Williams, M., Mercer, S. and Ryan, S. (eds) (2015) *Exploring Psychology in Language Learning and Teaching.* Oxford: Oxford University Press.

Part 1
Theoretical Insights

2 An Overview of Language Anxiety Research and Trends in its Development

Peter D. MacIntyre

Introduction

It is safe to say that language anxiety has been the most widely studied emotion in second language acquisition (SLA), perhaps because it is both an intense and a frequent experience. For the purposes of this review, the research literature on language anxiety will be broken into three broad approaches, reflecting both historical trends and assumptions about the topic. The first might be called the Confounded Approach because the ideas about anxiety and their effect on language learning were adopted from a mixture of various sources without detailed consideration of the meaning of the anxiety concept for language learners. The second trend might be called the Specialised Approach, wherein anxiety experiences that were specifically associated with language were identified, defined and studied. A third, relatively recent line of research reflects a contextualised Dynamic Approach in which anxiety is studied in connection with a complex web of language experiences. Although these are fuzzy categories, they help to organise the issues as research into language anxiety has developed.

Confounded Phase

The landmark work during this period was Scovel's review of the language anxiety literature. In his introductory remarks, Scovel described the state of the art in 1978:

> The research into the relationship of anxiety to foreign language learning has provided mixed and confusing results, immediately suggesting that anxiety itself is neither a simple nor well-understood psychological construct and that it is perhaps premature to attempt to relate it to the global and comprehensive task of language acquisition. (Scovel, 1978: 132)

The issue facing researchers at the time was one of defining and measuring both anxiety and the dimensions of language acquisition to which it might be related. Scovel (1978) noted that anxiety might be measured physiologically through indicators of arousal, behaviourally by the actions people perform when anxious or through self-report using structured questionnaires to ask about anxiety experiences. All of these types of measures were available and used for various purposes at the time in psychology, the discipline from which Scovel and other language researchers were taking their lead. However, what was not clear at the time was that the measures of anxiety that were adapted from psychology for use in language studies had little to do with language itself. The issue is captured well by Horwitz (this volume), who suggested '...it seems unlikely that insect anxiety has anything to do with one's response to or ultimate success in language learning even though *entomophobia* is subsumed under the general label of anxiety'.

The essence of the confounding problem is that not all types of anxiety that can be defined and measured are likely to be related to language learning. When Scovel (1978) reviewed the literature, he employed concepts under the label of anxiety which prior research had presumed to be potentially applicable to language. Closer inspection reveals that the 'mixed and confusing' results were generated primarily by two studies – Chastain (1975) and Kleinmann (1977). To account for the inconsistent results, Scovel primarily appealed to the distinction between facilitating and debilitating anxiety. He also noted a distinction between trait and state conceptualisations of anxiety that differentiated the tendency to experience anxiety (trait) from the experience of feeling anxiety (state), based on Spielberger's (1966) well-known work. It will be argued that the facilitating/debilitating explanation has not been a particularly useful path for SLA research but the trait/state distinction has been conceptually solid.

The original distinction between facilitating and debilitating anxiety was popularised in a paper by Alpert and Haber (1960). In the English language, the word *anxiety* typically refers to a negative emotional state with feelings of unpleasant tension and a sense of pressure to remove the source of anxiety or escape the situation. In the extreme, anxiety can be associated with phobias such as fear of spiders or public speaking – items that generate an intense and possibly debilitating anxiety reaction in many people. However, English also allows a more positive frame for anxiety, one of anticipation ('I am anxious to start my summer holidays') that facilitates an approach reaction. Alpert and Haber suggested that these two types of anxiety are not opposite ends of one continuum but are best considered two different dimensions. This is a critically important distinction with conceptual and methodological implications that have been overlooked.

Whereas the facilitating–debilitating distinction has heuristic value, it is 'dangerous' for language teachers who attempt to apply it to their students (Horwitz, this volume), and has been equally dangerous for researchers. The problem lies in a misapplication of Alpert and Haber's (1960) original position. Alpert and Haber (1960: 213) themselves claimed that '(i)n fact, these two constructs of debilitating and facilitating anxiety may be uncorrelated. Thus, an individual may possess a large amount of both anxieties, or of one but not the other, or of none of either'. They used two different scales, one to measure facilitating and another to measure debilitating anxiety; the scales correlated significantly but not substantially (median $r=-0.37$). Therefore, the original and still proper use of the concepts of facilitating and debilitating anxiety lies in viewing them as two different but related dimensions of experience and measuring both concepts separately. Instead of retaining Alpert and Haber's approach, however, several SLA research projects since then have used the concept of facilitating and debilitating anxiety in a *post hoc* fashion to account for a variety of sometimes unexpected or counterintuitive correlations. The trouble is that the reasoning is circular – positive correlations are taken to indicate facilitating anxiety, negative correlations suggest debilitating anxiety and zero correlations must reflect something of a blend of the two. Chastain's (1975) study seems to have been the first to do this, though he was quite cautious in presenting the 'tenuous' results and urged replication. In discussing his results for test anxiety, Chastain said:

> Surprising as it may seem, the direction of correlation was not consistent. In one case, French audio-lingual, the correlation was negative; in German, Spanish and all languages it was positive. Perhaps some concern about a test is a plus while too much anxiety can produce negative results. Whether or not some aspect of the audio-lingual class heightened test anxiety and resulted in a negative influence is not clarified by the data. (Chastain, 1975: 160)

At the time, Chastain was struggling to account for inconsistent correlations, but the problem seems to have been that the measure of anxiety he used is not necessarily or consistently related to language. The other study cited in Scovel's (1978) review, Kleinmann (1977), showed that the use of unusual linguistic structures correlated positively with facilitating anxiety but the use of other structures was negatively correlated with debilitating anxiety. Kleinmann followed the advice of Alpert and Haber and used separate scales to measure facilitating and debilitating anxiety. Unfortunately, Chastain's study has been linked to Kleinmann's (1977) study consistently in the literature and their findings have been inappropriately conflated.

Even within the confounded phase, seeds for the next phase were buried in the groundwork of Gardner's socio-educational model of language learning motivation. For Gardner and colleagues, anxiety carried the strong possibility of interfering with motivation to learn a language. Gardner's (1985, 2010) concept of integrative motivation was tied specifically to language learning and was not drawn as a general theory of motivation or even motivation in pedagogical contexts – integrative motivation was all about bringing the social side of language into the learner's mind. The emphasis on the uniqueness of language learning extended to the anxiety variables that Gardner developed. In his studies of anglophones in Canada, Gardner chose to measure French classroom anxiety and French use anxiety. These scales were included in the Attitude Motivation Test Battery (AMTB; Gardner, 1985) even though the focus was not on anxiety *per se* and it was not consistently included in the socio-educational model of motivation (MacIntyre & Gardner, 1991).

The noteworthy point emerging from studies of the socio-educational model is that a conceptualisation of anxiety that was specific to language could be used, unlike the anxiety concepts used by studies in Scovel's review. In data sets that featured a language anxiety construct as part of the socio-educational model, a consistent pattern of results was found. A fairly comprehensive review of the literature up to the beginning of the 1990s found that

> (c)overing several measures of proficiency, in several different samples, and even in somewhat different conceptual frameworks, it has been shown that anxiety negatively effects performance in the second language. In several cases, anxiety provides some of the highest simple correlations of attitudes with achievement. (MacIntyre & Gardner, 1991: 103)

The confounding of various types of anxiety and their inconsistent applicability to language was coming to an end, as specialised concepts of language-related anxiety emerged.

The Specialised Approach

Horwitz *et al.* (1986) argued convincingly that the conceptualisation and measurement of anxiety in SLA had to be reoriented. Their research was grounded in the moderate-to-severe anxiety experiences of learners, in particular those who sought assistance in reducing anxiety from teachers and counsellors. They drew upon both the inconsistencies in prior research that were highlighted by Scovel's (1978) review and the measurement approach to French classroom anxiety that Gardner had been using in the socio-educational model (Gardner *et al.*, 1976). Gardner

(1985: 34) was suggesting that '...a construct of anxiety which is not general but instead is specific to the language acquisition context is related to second language achievement'. Horwitz et al. (1986) were influenced by Gardner's work. They undertook to develop their concept of foreign language classroom anxiety based on language students' descriptions of specific aspects of their courses that were particularly anxiety-provoking, including experiences with speaking the language aloud, frequent testing and fear of being negatively evaluated by their teachers and peers. Horwitz et al. (1986: 125) argued that these sources of anxiety coalesce into a '...conceptually distinct variable in foreign language learning', a position that received empirical support in several subsequent studies. Horwitz has argued that some authors have misunderstood the nature and unity of the language anxiety concept; it is not simply a combination of test anxiety, communication apprehension and fear of negative evaluation (Horwitz, 2010; also see Horwitz, this volume, for a discussion of the issue).

Horwitz et al. (1986) developed a 33-item scale that has been widely used in a large number of subsequent research projects (see Horwitz, 2010). In the first study published using the Foreign Language Classroom Anxiety Scale (FLCAS), Horwitz (1986) reported excellent reliability for the scale among Spanish students. Results also showed modest correlations of FLCAS with trait anxiety, communication apprehension and fear of negative evaluation, and stronger correlations with test anxiety, expected course grade and actual course grade. Horwitz (1986) offered 'preliminary evidence' that helped to cement the reliability and validity of the FLCAS and, by extension, the language anxiety construct. Further support was obtained in a study of learners of Japanese, a replication of Horwitz et al. (1986) that found similar reliability and validity results but less association with test anxiety and a slightly different factor structure that showed weak correlations between FLCAS and test anxiety (Aida, 1994).

The FLCAS includes items that refer to typical experiences in language situations, such as 'It embarrasses me to volunteer answers in my language class'. The only other scales at the time to adopt a similar approach were Gardner's (1985) French classroom anxiety and French use anxiety scales, part of the larger battery of scales focused on attitudes and motivation (the AMTB). This approach to conceptualising and measuring language anxiety has been labelled as 'situation-specific' (Horwitz et al., 1986; MacIntyre & Gardner, 1989). A situation-specific anxiety can be differentiated meaningfully from a generally anxious personality and/or a moment-to-moment experience of feeling anxious. The differentiation between anxiety-provoking situations occurs as anxiety is repeatedly experienced in a certain type of situation such as a language class; at some point learners come to associate the language class with anxiety (MacIntyre & Gardner, 1989). Using the above FLCAS item as an example, situation-specific language anxiety develops in part as a student feels embarrassed when volunteering to answer a language teacher's questions and then comes to anticipate the embarrassment happening again. Based on the research results in the literature and the consistently high reliability of the FLCAS, the student who endorses this item is more likely to report the other anxiety experiences described in FLCAS items.

Differentiating a situation-specific conceptualisation of language anxiety from the previous approach that confounded various types of anxieties clearly was a turning point in the research literature (Dewaele, 2002). The development of the situation-specific scales allowed researchers to examine the correlations between various anxiety measures. MacIntyre and Gardner (1989) used factor analysis on nine anxiety scales and found that a general anxiety dimension could be differentiated from a communicative anxiety dimension that included measures of language anxiety, a measure of native language speaking anxiety and a measure of audience sensitivity. The authors suggest that the '...dimension of general anxiety and those scales that comprise it are not related to language behavior *in a reliable manner*' (MacIntyre & Gardner, 1989: 268, emphasis added). Additional analyses, however, strongly and consistently supported the role of the second language (L2; French) language-specific measures of anxiety in the learning and recall of French vocabulary items in a computer-controlled learning environment, lending support to Horwitz et al.'s (1986) seminal arguments. Further evidence of the differentiation between types of anxiety measures was offered by MacIntyre and Gardner (1991), who employed 19 anxiety measures, including four scales related to L2 learning (French in this case). Factor analysis produced three factors reflecting general/social-evaluative anxiety, state anxiety and a distinct language anxiety factor. Additional results revealed that only the language anxiety factor was related to performance on two measures of processing linguistic material in French.

Having established language anxiety as a situation-specific concept, research in this area was able to flourish. Attention turned to the various sources of anxiety, ways in which language anxiety might affect language learning and the processes by which those effects emerge (see Table 2.1). An early study by Steinberg and Horwitz (1986) investigated the subtle effects of anxiety on language use. They found that people who were treated in a way that made them feel anxious tended to avoid using their L2 to offer novel, personal interpretations of ambiguous pictures. They argued that, over time, subtle effects of anxiety arousal can have a significant impact on the communication of students in the classroom and beyond.

Following up on the analysis of the subtle effects of anxiety, MacIntyre and Gardner (1994b) included 29 measures of second and native language performance organised across three stages of cognitive processing. They examined (1) the language input stage, (2) processing and interpreting the

Table 2.1 Effects of language anxiety

Academic effects	• Lowered grades and poor academic achievement. • Impaired performance on tests. • Affected achievement in second languages. • Decreased self-perception of second language competence. • Lower result scores on measures of actual second language competence. • 'Overstudying'– increased effort at learning resulting in lower levels of achievement than expected.
Cognitive effects	• Increased self-related cognition (thoughts of failure, performance worry, self-deprecating thoughts). • Interferes with cognitive performance at any and all three stages of learning: input, processing and output. • At the input stage, anxiety acts like a filter preventing information from getting into the cognitive processing system. • During the processing stage, speed and accuracy of learning can be influenced. • At the output stage, the quality of second language communication can be affected by disrupting the retrieval of information. • Affected time required to recognise words, ability to hold words in short-term memory, memory for grammar rules, ability to translate a paragraph, length of time studying new vocabulary items, memory for new vocabulary items, time required to complete a test of vocabulary, retrieval of vocabulary from long-term memory, ability to repeat items in native language (L1) and second language (L2), ability to speak with an L2 accent, complexity of sentences spoken and fluency of speech. • Students require more time to intake information and more time to achieve the same result as a student not experiencing language anxiety. • A nervous student risks performing more poorly than a relaxed one.
Social effects	• Reduced linguistic self-confidence, a motivating influence for the language learner. • In an environment where the second language is predominantly spoken, students experience higher apprehension in their native language. • Anxious learners do not communicate as often as more relaxed learners.

language and (3) the output stage at which knowledge of the language can be demonstrated. The authors proposed measuring both anxiety and performance at each of these three stages. They developed three new scales, reflecting language anxiety at the input, processing and output stages. Their approach was to become highly specific about measuring the types of anxiety that might be experienced. Among the various language-related measures, a series of interrelated effects was observed. On some tasks, language anxiety was associated with needing extra time and effort to compensate for problems in acquiring information from a previous stage. This was consistent with Horwitz *et al.* (1986), who identified over-studying as a potential reaction to language anxiety. On other tasks, where the time to respond was fixed, language anxiety was associated with lower-quality performance at the output stage. The authors concluded that

> (t)he potential effects of language anxiety on cognitive processing in the second language appear pervasive and may be quite subtle. Performance measures that examine only behavior at the output stage may be neglecting the influence of anxiety at earlier stages as well as ignoring the links among stages. (MacIntyre & Gardner, 1994b: 301)

Support for the notion of differentiating anxiety at the input, processing and output stages was obtained by Onwuegbuzie and colleagues (Bailey *et al.*, 2000; Onwuegbuzie *et al.*, 1999), who confirmed and extended many of the findings previously reported for the three stages of processing.

Exploring language anxiety in specific language processes has led to research into specific language skill areas. Spoken language has been strongly implicated in the measures of language anxiety discussed thus far, including the different measures developed by Horwitz and Gardner. Researchers also have defined skill-based language anxiety constructs and measures to focus on reading and writing anxiety (Hilleson, 1996). For example, Cheng *et al.* (1999) were able to differentiate the speaking and writing components of language anxiety using the FLCAS and an adapted version of a first language (L1) writing anxiety scale. Along similar lines, Saito *et al.* (1999) developed a new scale to measure L2 reading anxiety, in part because it seemed that prior research had assumed that reading was not especially anxiety-provoking. The authors were successful in identifying differences between reading anxiety and the more general FLCAS measure and establishing that reading itself has the potential to be anxiety-arousing, especially with unfamiliar cultural references and writing scripts. Finally, listening also poses difficulties as the speed of native language speech can be overwhelming for novice learners. Scarcella and Oxford (1992) note that anxiety can be exacerbated when learners believe they must understand every word or fear losing the meaning of the communication. Later, Sellers (2000: 512) reported that highly anxious readers tend to experience 'more off-task, interfering thoughts than their less anxious counterparts', thus limiting their recall of passage content. Research shows that, as anxiety increases, listening comprehension decreases (Elkhafaifi, 2005). Considering the language skills as a group, Gregersen and Horwitz (2002) suggested that anxiety may be heightened further when a learner is aware of a significant disparity in his or her abilities across the skills (e.g. a learner reads comfortably but is anxious about speaking).

Along with research that explored the communicative, linguistic and specific learning correlates of language anxiety in detail, other research examined its relationship to other broader learner factors, such as learner personality, perceived competence and willingness to communicate. Dewaele (2002) studied the correlations among three basic personality traits, extraversion (outgoing, sociable), psychoticism (cold, aloofness) and neuroticism (anxious, fearful), and language anxiety in French (L2) and English (third language [L3]) within a sample of Flemish students. The pattern of results was complex, but one of the more important results showed that there were significant differences between the way personality correlated with language anxiety in L2 and L3. This result implied that each language that a person is learning might generate a different anxiety profile. Dewaele (2002) contrasted his findings with the prior work of MacIntyre and Charos (1996) and concluded that the relationship of language anxiety to personality can differ substantially depending on social context and language use patterns. Dewaele *et al.* (2008) extended the earlier work on basic personality traits to include emotional intelligence, reporting a very strong tendency for participants low in emotional intelligence to experience higher language anxiety in their L1 and up to four languages. A later study by Dewaele (2013) provides an extensive analysis of language anxiety across a number of variables, including L1 to fifth language (L5), age of onset, acquisition context, frequency of use, socialisation, age, gender, trait emotional intelligence and other factors. The results show that most learner variables are associated with language anxiety in patterns that can be predicted from prior research on learner variables (see also Onwuegbuzie *et al.*, 1999). Other research has also shown higher language anxiety to be associated with stronger tendencies towards perfectionism (Dewaele, this volume; Gregersen & Horwitz, 2002) and hesitation to act (MacIntyre & Doucette, 2010). Studies in the present volume carry the research on these themes and more into the present day.

One of the most consistent correlates of language anxiety has been perceived communication competence. Several studies have reported significant correlations between them (e.g. MacIntyre & Charos, 1995). MacIntyre *et al.* (1997) proposed that higher anxiety might negatively bias the perception of competence. They found that learners with higher anxiety tended to systematically underestimate and relaxed students overestimate their actual ability to use the L2 as judged by an expert native speaker. These findings were supported by Dewaele *et al.* (2008) and indicate that anxiety arousal can bias cognitive processing in anxiety-sustaining ways (see Eysenck, 1979). MacIntyre *et al.* (1998) integrate this tendency into their 'pyramid' model of willingness to communicate, wherein a combination of lower anxiety, higher perceptions of competence and the desire to speak to a specific person at a specific time underlie the willingness to engage in L2 speaking.

Alongside establishing the correlates of language anxiety, research has progressed by considering the role of anxiety as described by the learners themselves. In addition to the descriptions of learner experiences initially reported by Horwitz *et al.* (1986), several qualitative studies of language anxiety pointed to a substantial list of anxiety triggers and consequences. One of the early studies used learner diaries to show that the relationships among learners and with teachers are important anxiety triggers. In particular, competitiveness and negative comparisons with other learners, along with the relationship between learner and teacher, contribute to feelings of anxiety and a negative perception of the learning experience (Bailey, 1983). Diary studies have also suggested that language and the sense of self are so closely tied together that a threat to one is a threat to the other; one student described language learning as the '... smashing of a well-developed positive self-concept' (Cohen & Norst, 1989: 68–69). Further accounts of learners' reactions implicate a wide range of issues with anxiety. Both enduring and routine/everyday embarrassments were described by the learners interviewed by Price (1991). In other studies, learners described major life events such as abandoning one's career goals after devoting two years to advanced graduate study because of a high-stakes requirement to use underdeveloped language skills (Oxford, 1999). Across the various studies, research has established that there can be an enormous toll taken on a person by language anxiety.

The orderly progression of research into the various effects of language anxiety has occasionally been interrupted by Sparks and Ganschow (1995), who challenge one of the key assumptions of the literature – that anxiety is a cause of problems with the language. Drawing upon their background in learning disabilities, Sparks and Ganschow argued that language anxiety resulted from deficits in linguistic coding that produced both anxiety and lower scores on various measures of language achievement with which anxiety has been shown to correlate. The question of whether anxiety should be considered a cause or effect of performance had been posed before (Young, 1986), but Sparks and Ganschow argued as strongly as possible that anxiety is merely a consequence of language aptitude and coding problems. This issue has become a standard point of discussion in reviews of the language anxiety literature. Considering all the writing about language anxiety that has been done over the years, it is unfortunate that the debate itself has produced little more than a self-perpetuating cycle of summarising the debate.

Detailed arguments for and against Sparks and Ganschow's position were advanced twice in *The Modern Language Journal*, first in 1995 (MacIntyre, 1995a, 1995b; Sparks & Ganschow, 1995) and again in 2000 (Ganschow & Sparks, 2000; Horwitz, 2000). The details of those position papers will not be reviewed here and interested readers are encouraged to digest the arguments for themselves. Although all of the authors involved agree that linguistic coding problems can generate anxiety, the heart of the issue is that Horwitz, MacIntyre and their collaborators have repeatedly insisted that we must go beyond the aptitude domain to understand the many sources of anxiety and the real, observable consequences to both the arousal of anxiety and the efforts to cope with it (see Table 2.2). As the literature review above demonstrates, anxiety is both a result of problems encountered in the learning process and a cause of further difficulties; Sparks and Ganschow have repeatedly disagreed with the latter half of that position.

One reason that the debate has seemed to produce more heat than light is that both sides have been inferring causality from correlational data, with the exception of the few experimental studies noted below. Correlations can be difficult to interpret. There are three basic ways to account for a correlation between two variables (X and Y – for example, anxiety and achievement): changes in X cause or contribute to changes in Y, changes in Y cause or contribute to changes in X or some third factor

Table 2.2 Causes of language anxiety

Academic causes	• Errors in pronunciation.
	• Unrealistic learner beliefs.
	• Instructors who intimidate their students with harsh and/or embarrassing error correction in front of other students.
	• Methods of testing.
Cognitive causes	• Fear of losing one's sense of identity.
	• Biased perceptions of proficiency.
	• Personality traits and/or shyness.
	• Low self-esteem.
Social causes	• Fear of being laughed at, being embarrassed and making a fool of oneself.
	• A poor-quality accent.
	• Misunderstanding communication or using incorrect words.
	• Cultural gaffes.
	• Competitiveness.
	• Frequency and quality of contact with native speakers.

produces changes in both X and Y. In terms of research results, on the one hand, many language anxiety researchers have shown that reported levels of anxiety are correlated with measures of achievement taken at a later time. But on the other hand, Sparks and Ganschow (2011) have shown that native language difficulties in early school years correlate with language anxiety and lower achievement in later years. It is worth mentioning that Sparks and Ganschow's own correlational data allow for other interpretations, including potentially offering support for the anxiety-as-a-cause position although they obviously do not favour such explanations.

To move beyond the debate over causality, a few studies of language anxiety have adopted the experimental approach, which can lead to causal interpretations. Steinberg and Horwitz (1986) used a two-group experimental procedure and measured the amount of denotative and interpretative content in participants' L2 speech when describing an ambiguous image. To arouse anxiety, one group was randomly assigned to be treated in a 'cold and official' manner by the experimenter, with emphasis on the presence of video and audio recording equipment and instructions designed to increase stress. The other group was treated in a 'warm and supportive' manner, comfortably seated, asked to do their best and encouraged to enjoy the session. Both groups were formed in a way to create an equal number of high and low proficiency participants in each group. Results show that, compared to the low-anxiety group, the experimental procedure was effective in creating both higher anxiety and lower levels of interpretive content in the speech produced by the high-anxiety group.

A second experiment investigated anxiety arousal at three stages of cognitive processing (MacIntyre & Gardner, 1994a). In this study, participants were randomly assigned to one of four groups: a control group, a group with anxiety arousal at the input stage, a group with anxiety arousal at the processing stage and a group that had anxiety aroused at the output stage. Participants were given a vocabulary learning task with English–French (L1–L2) noun pairs that was divided into three stages: an input stage where the words to be learned were viewed, a processing stage where L1 and L2 were paired and an output stage where L2 output required the use of newly learned vocabulary items. Results showed that the video camera consistently generated anxiety and that anxiety arousal was consistently associated with performance deficits. The expected anxiety effect occurred at each stage of the learning task. Additional results showed that the anxiety arousal dissipated fairly quickly as participants became accustomed to the presence of a video camera. As anxiety declined, participants were partially (but not fully) able to compensate for deficits that occurred at prior stages, for example by additional time spent studying the words.

Experimental methods are the gold standard in behavioural research that seeks to understand causality. In the literature on language anxiety, there are surprisingly few experiments, given that the issue of causality is covered so often. As Gardner *et al.* (1992) note with respect to experiments:

> because of the control that can be exercised, and the elimination of the many other factors that operate in the real world context, patterns that appear in the laboratory that are consistent with *in situ* findings help to strengthen and clarify generalizations made in those settings. (Gardner *et al.*, 1992: 212)

It must be noted that the experiments reviewed here establish that anxiety *can* cause performance problems, but they do not establish the prevalence of this pattern and are silent on the issue of anxiety-as-a-consequence. There is a pressing need for additional experiments to help clarify causal connections between language anxiety and performance.

If additional experiments are on the horizon, they seem most likely to begin from a starting point that embraces complexity and dynamic systems theory (Larsen-Freeman & Cameron, 2008). A dynamic approach adopts a different epistemology than much of the research reviewed above. For example, dynamic systems are open and multiply determined, they are affected by interacting processes that operate on multiple timescales and they produce emergent properties that can be perceived by learners as qualitatively different states (e.g. a state of anxiety, comfort or playfulness). The dynamic approach is just beginning to be explored but already is producing interesting research findings.

Dynamic Approach

The third type of research into language anxiety begins from a contextualised, dynamic perspective. This new, emerging tradition emphasises situating anxiety among the multitude of interacting factors that affect language learning and development. Anxiety is continuously interacting with a number of other learner, situational and other factors including linguistic abilities, physiological reactions, self-related appraisals, pragmatics, interpersonal relationships, specific topics being discussed, type of setting in which people are interacting and so on. Anxiety is an emotion that fluctuates over time and that might be examined on a timescale of seconds and minutes, as in the rising and falling of anxiety during communication or a timescale of days, as in fluctuations during a week of classes or a timescale of months/years or as in the trajectory of anxiety across the years of a language programme. A number of prior cross-sectional studies have examined anxiety across cohorts, including grade levels in junior high school, high school and university pre-service teaching programmes, but these studies do not address issues of longitudinal – or an individual's change in – anxiety over time. There have not yet been many studies in this dynamic tradition, but the initial results are quite promising.

A recently published study provides an example of the dynamic approach. Gregersen *et al.* (2014) studied six pre-service teachers who were making a classroom presentation in their L2 (Spanish). During the presentation, the speakers wore a heart rate monitor, but otherwise the talk was a normal part of their course. Following the presentation, all students in the course (including the six research participants) met with the instructor to review and evaluate a video recording of the presentation. The six research participants viewed the video using the idiodynamic procedure (MacIntyre, 2012) that produces a continuous set of ratings of anxiety, showing changes in anxiety in real time. Three of the participants were identified as low-anxious and three as high-anxious by the FLCAS (Horwitz *et al.*, 1986). Results showed a number of interesting fluctuations in the data that were explained partially in the interviews. For example, spikes in anxiety occurred when speakers forgot words or got confused with the flow of their presentation. Anxious students were more prone to spikes in anxiety because they tended to memorise their presentations – a strategy that makes it easy to lose one's place. However, the value of a dynamic approach was demonstrated in one interesting set of results for a participant identified as low anxious by the FLCAS. This student had an unexpected anxiety reaction during her talk. Asked why she had a spike in anxiety, she said:

> You've got me hooked up to this thing [heart rate monitor] (1) with a camera rolling (2) recording me speaking a language that is not mine (3) in front of a group of people (4) with the teacher grading me (5). Wouldn't that put you on edge a bit? (Gregersen *et al.*, 2014: 584)

The various sources of quantitative and qualitative data in the study showed that her physical, emotional, cognitive and behavioural systems converged on what was for her an atypical anxiety reaction. The results also demonstrate that even students who typically are comfortable in their L2 can experience bouts of high anxiety and that the emerging anxiety experience can be influenced by several interacting factors.

The value of a dynamic approach was also demonstrated by MacIntyre and Serroul's (2015) study of dynamic changes in motivation. The authors developed the 'four horsemen' account of the process of running into difficulty during L2 communication. The emerging model suggests that when language vocabulary and grammar processes are strained or perceived to be failing, a complex reaction takes place. An inhibition system is activated by the appraisal of a clear and present threat (e.g. 'I don't know how to say what I need to say'). Attention shifts to the interlocutor and his or her reactions to the problems to evaluate the threat to one's positive sense of self and to the interpersonal relationships involved. A speaker's expectancies (what Dörnyei [2005] calls the 'ought-to self') are evaluated against L2 learning experiences to assess whether the speaker should be able to show competent use of the L2 in the situation; mistakes of a novice speaker can be more easily forgiven in a face-saving way. If the difficulties persist and the individual feels that she or he ought to be able to say something, coping efforts are activated. If the communication difficulties continue for a few moments or more, the speaker is likely to consciously perceive the emerging anxiety reaction (as the student quoted in the preceding paragraph described so well). At this point, the irony of anxiety sets in – the anxiety reaction itself begins to exacerbate communication difficulties in a cascading, sometimes overwhelming surge of emotion. This reaction generates distracting, self-deprecating cognition (such as 'I should know this', 'What's wrong with me', 'I look like an idiot') that shifts cognition towards saving face, making the best of a bad situation or even escaping from the communication altogether. Along with these cognitive, emotional and linguistic difficulties come the familiar physical reactions associated with elevated levels of anxiety, such as perspiration, a racing heart, shaky limbs and butterflies in the stomach. Additional effects can be observed in increasing avoidance motivation, declining perceptions of competence and lower willingness to communicate. MacIntyre and Serroul (2015: 130) note that '...these moments can be enormously frustrating for the L2 speaker' and the anxiety state reflects the coalescence of a number of dynamically changing processes.

Taking a qualitative approach to describing the dynamics of learner states, Waninge (2015) used dynamic systems theory as a basis for examining 'attractor states' that occur during language learning. Attractor states are characterised by stability and a recognisable phenomenological quality that provides coherence and predictability across a wide range of phenomena (Hiver, 2015). An anxiety reaction, of the type described by MacIntyre and Serroul (2015), might be considered an unpleasant attractor state. In order to examine participants' typical attractor states, Waninge (2015) conducted a series of semi-structured interviews wherein respondents described their state of mind during language learning experiences. Four consistent attractor states were identified – interest, boredom, neutral attention and anxiety. With respect to the latter, some learner accounts described anxiety as a sort of 'default state' for themselves, but others described it as a transient experience that would wax and wane during a specific classroom lesson. Waninge concludes that

> ... an important finding arising from the analysis of learners' narratives is the almost inseparable nature of cognition, motivation, affect and context... (A) combination of factors often surfaces together in the learners' accounts, supporting or undermining a student's interest by the way they interact and reinforce one another, thereby making it difficult to separate their influence and pinpoint any straightforward causality. (Waninge, 2015: 211)

Although the emphasis in this study was on the concept of interest, it is not at all difficult to apply the above comment to the conceptualisation of anxiety wherein a sense of the dynamics of the experience comes into focus. The issue of causality shifts from a simple cause-and-effect model to one that accounts for changes over time using multiple interacting systems.

Prior research in language anxiety has tended to adopt a cross-sectional approach, with very few longitudinal studies having been published. A recent exception is Piniel and Csizér (2015), who used a variety of techniques, including latent growth curve modelling and longitudinal cluster analysis, to assess the relationship between anxiety and motivation over the length of a 14-week L2 academic writing course. Their complex data analysis showed several interesting results, including the presence of a trajectory over time among some learners associated with consistently low anxiety and high motivation and a different trajectory among other learners that paired high anxiety with high motivation in a less stable combination. The approach taken by Piniel and Csizér shows that dynamic changes in anxiety and related variables (motivation, self-efficacy) follow complex but somewhat predictable pathways. They succeeded in showing the variability of the relationship between anxiety and motivation.

There is much to recommend the recent focus on the dynamics of language anxiety. One lesson that emerges emphasises the importance of context, not only the interpersonal and social context of the surrounding environment but also the psychological context of the learner, including physiological and emotional processes. Dynamic studies emphasise the complex interactions of multiple factors that influence the anxiety reaction, including the ongoing interactions among learner variables such as anxiety, perceived competence, willingness to communicate and the features of the learning/communication situation. A second lesson emerging from the dynamic approach is the need to reconsider notions of causality as the language learning experience unfolds. Much of the prior research has, in effect, frozen a moment in time for analysis, such as when variables are measured for correlations in a cross-sectional design or when an experimental procedure assesses the effects of an anxiety-arousing manipulation on specific linguistic outcomes of a task. The dynamic perspective is both complex (influenced by multiple interactions) and more complicated because it emphasises that learners' experience of language and communication is both continuous and integrated.

Conclusion

Having reviewed the significant trends in the literature, there clearly is a progression of thought from an initial confounding of anxiety types to a clear delineation of a specific type of anxiety applicable to language situations. More recent descriptions of the dynamics of anxiety are providing additional insights. As a concluding comment, there are perhaps three issues that have arisen consistently in the literature that now can be put to bed, once and for all.

(1) Is anxiety facilitating or debilitating? Consistent with Horwitz's (this volume) position, anxiety is best conceptualised only as debilitating. Anxiety is a complex experience and has a number of sources and effects. Whereas the emotional arousal or increasing coping efforts that accompany anxiety might temporarily push learners to study more, there is virtually no reliable evidence of facilitating anxiety in the literature that cannot otherwise be explained by (1) using a measure of anxiety that is not specific to language (e.g. trait anxiety, test anxiety, etc.) or (2) misusing the original idea of facilitating anxiety as a separate dimension of experience requiring its own measurement that is not simply the low end of a scale of anxiety (Alpert & Haber, 1960).

(2) Is anxiety a cause or an effect of language performance? Most often associated with Sparks and Ganschow's assertion that only aptitude and linguistic coding differences are responsible for the negative correlation between anxiety and performance, the available evidence points to anxiety as both a consequence and a cause of language performance. Experimental evidence shows that anxiety arousal causes declines in performance. That is sufficient evidence to put to rest the notion that anxiety is only a consequence of differences and difficulties in linguistic coding. The dynamic perspective emphasises the continuous, complex interactions between anxiety and a host of other factors, thereby rejecting the notion of simple causality out of hand. Considered alongside the extensive literature on performance anxiety in music, public speaking, test-taking and other areas, this question effectively has been settled: anxiety is both a cause and a consequence of performance.

(3) Is language anxiety an internal state or socially constructed? The social turn in SLA has meant that several concepts, including language anxiety, have been reinterpreted as socially constructed. It would be counterproductive to spend research time debating whether anxiety is an internal experience or one constructed in the social context. The research into complex, dynamic systems accounts shows that anxiety is influenced

by internal physiological processes, cognition and emotional states along with the demands of the situation and the presence of other people, among other things, considered over multiple timescales. Anxiety has both internal and social dimensions.

Future research that takes into account the trends in the literature and moves forward with new and interesting research questions will help to sharpen our focus on language anxiety and what it means to be an anxious learner or to be a learner who is feeling anxious.

References

Aida, Y. (1994) Examination of Horwitz, Horwitz, & Cope's construct of foreign language anxiety: The case of students of Japanese. *Modern Language Journal* 78 (2), 155–168.
Alpert, R. and Haber, R.N. (1960) Anxiety in academic achievement situations. *Journal of Abnormal and Social Psychology* 61 (2), 207–215.
Bailey, K.M. (1983) Competitiveness and anxiety in adult second language learning: Looking at and through the diary studies. In H.W. Seliger and M.H. Long (eds) *Classroom-Oriented Research in Second Language Acquisition* (pp. 67–102). Rowley, MA: Newbury House.
Bailey, K.M., Onwuegbuzie, A.J. and Daley, C.E. (2000) Correlates of anxiety at three stages of the foreign language learning process. *Journal of Language and Social Psychology* 19, 474–490.
Chastain, K. (1975) Affective and ability factors in second language acquisition. *Language Learning* 25 (1), 153–161.
Cheng, Y.S., Horwitz, E.K. and Schallert, D.L. (1999) Language writing anxiety: Differentiating writing and speaking components. *Language Learning* 49 (3), 417–446.
Cohen, Y. and Norst, M.J. (1989) Fear, dependence and loss of self-esteem: Affective barriers in second language learning among adults. *RELC Journal* 20, 61–77.
Dewaele, J.-M. (2002) Psychological and sociodemographic correlates of communicative anxiety in L2 and L3 production. *International Journal of Bilingualism* 6 (1), 23–38.
Dewaele, J.-M. (2013) The link between foreign language classroom anxiety and psychoticism, extraversion, and neuroticism among adult bi- and multilinguals. *The Modern Language Journal* 97 (3), 670–684.
Dewaele, J.-M., Petrides, K.V. and Furnham, A. (2008) The effects of trait emotional intelligence and sociobiological variables on communicative anxiety and foreign language anxiety among adult multilinguals: A review and empirical investigation. *Language Learning* 58 (4), 911–960.
Dörnyei, Z. (2005) *The Psychology of the Language Learner: Individual Differences in Second Language Acquisition*. Mahwah, NJ: Lawrence Erlbaum Associates.
Elkhafaifi, H. (2005) Listening comprehension and anxiety in the Arabic language classroom. *The Modern Language Journal* 89 (2), 206–220.
Eysenck, M.W. (1979) Anxiety, learning and memory: A reconceptualization. *Journal of Research in Personality* 13, 363–385.
Ganschow, L. and Sparks, R.L. (2000) Reflections on foreign language study for students with language learning problems: Research, issues, and challenges. *Dyslexia* 6, 87–100.
Gardner, R.C. (1985) *Social Psychology and Second Language Learning: The Role of Attitudes and Motivation*. London: Edward Arnold.

Gardner, R.C. (2010) *Motivation and Second Language Acquisition: The Socio-Educational Model*. New York: Peter Lang Publishing.

Gardner, R.C., Smythe, P.C., Clement, R. and Gliksman, L. (1976) Second language acquisition: A social psychological perspective. *Canadian Modern Language Review* 32, 198–213.

Gardner, R.C., Day, J.B. and MacIntyre, P.D. (1992) Integrative motivation, induced anxiety and language learning in a controlled environment. *Studies in Second Language Acquisition* 14 (2), 197–214.

Gregersen, T.S. and Horwitz, E.K. (2002) Language learning and perfectionism: Anxious and non-anxious language learners' reactions to their own oral performance. *The Modern Language Journal* 86 (4), 562–570.

Gregersen, T., MacIntyre, P.D. and Meza, M.D. (2014) The motion of emotion: Idiodynamic case studies of learners' Foreign Language Anxiety. *The Modern Language Journal* 98 (2), 574–588.

Hilleson, M. (1996) 'I want to talk with them, but I don't want them to hear': An introspective study of second language anxiety in an English-medium school. In K.M. Bailey and D. Nunan (eds) *Voices from the Language Classroom* (pp. 248–277). Cambridge: Cambridge University Press.

Hiver, P. (2015) Attractor states. In Z. Dörnyei, P.D. MacIntyre and A. Henry (eds) *Motivational Dynamics in Language Learning* (pp. 20–37). Bristol: Multilingual Matters.

Horwitz, E.K. (1986) Preliminary evidence for the reliability and validity of a foreign language anxiety scale. *TESOL Quarterly* 20 (3), 559–562.

Horwitz, E.K. (2000) It ain't over 'til it's over: On foreign language anxiety, first language deficits and the confounding of variables. *The Modern Language Journal* 84 (2), 256–259.

Horwitz, E.K. (2010) Foreign and second language anxiety. *Language Teaching* 43 (2), 154–167.

Horwitz, E.K., Horwitz, M.B. and Cope, J. (1986) Foreign language classroom anxiety. *The Modern Language Journal* 70 (2), 125–132.

Kleinmann, H.H. (1977) Avoidance behaviour in adult second language acquisition. *Language Learning* 27 (1), 93–107.

Larsen-Freeman, D. and Cameron, L. (2008) *Complex Systems and Applied Linguistics*. New York: Oxford.

MacIntyre, P.D. (1995a) How does anxiety affect second language learning? A reply to Sparks and Ganschow. *The Modern Language Journal* 79 (1), 90–99.

MacIntyre, P.D. (1995b) On seeing the forest and the trees: A rejoinder to Sparks and Ganschow. *The Modern Language Journal* 79 (2), 245–248.

MacIntyre, P.D. (2012) The idiodynamic method: A closer look at the dynamics of communication traits. *Communication Research Reports* 29 (4), 361–367.

MacIntyre, P.D. and Gardner, R.C. (1989) Anxiety and second-language learning: Toward a theoretical clarification. *Language Learning* 39 (2), 251–275.

MacIntyre, P.D. and Gardner, R.C. (1991) Language anxiety: Its relationship to other anxieties and to processing in native and second languages. *Language Learning* 41 (4), 513–534.

MacIntyre, P.D. and Gardner, R.C. (1994a) The effects of induced anxiety on cognitive processing in computerised vocabulary learning. *Studies in Second Language Acquisition* 16, 1–17.

MacIntyre, P.D. and Gardner, R.C. (1994b) The subtle effects of language anxiety on cognitive processing in the second language. *Language Learning* 44 (2), 283–305.

MacIntyre, P.D. and Charos, C. (1996) Personality, attitudes, and affect as predictors of second language communication. *Journal of Language and Social Psychology* 15 (1), 3–26.

MacIntyre, P.D. and Doucette, J. (2010) Willingness to communicate and action control. *System* 38 (2), 161–171.
MacIntyre, P.D. and Serroul, A. (2015) Motivation on a per-second timescale: Examining approach-avoidance motivation during L2 task performance. In Z. Dörnyei, P.D. MacIntyre and A. Henry (eds) *Motivational Dynamics in Language Learning* (pp. 109–138). Bristol: Multilingual Matters.
MacIntyre, P.D., Noels, K.A. and Clement, R. (1997) Biases in self-ratings of second language proficiency: The role of language anxiety. *Language Learning* 47 (2), 265–287.
Onwuegbuzie, A.J., Bailey, P. and Daley, C.E. (1999) Factors associated with foreign language anxiety. *Applied Psycholinguistics* 20 (2), 217–239.
Oxford, R.L. (1999) Anxiety and the language learner: New insights. In J. Arnold (ed.) *Affect in Language Learning* (pp. 58–67). Cambridge: Cambridge University Press.
Piniel, K. and Csizér, K. (2015) Changes in motivation, anxiety and self-efficacy during the course of an academic writing seminar. In Z. Dörnyei, P.D. MacIntyre and A. Henry (eds) *Motivational Dynamics in Language Learning* (pp. 164–194). Bristol: Multilingual Matters.
Price, M.L. (1991) The subjective experience of foreign language anxiety: Interviews with highly anxious students. In E.K. Horwitz and D.J. Young (eds) *Language Anxiety: From Theory and Research to Classroom Implications* (pp. 101–108). Englewood Cliffs, NJ: Prentice-Hall.
Saito, Y., Horwitz, E.K. and Garza, T.J. (1999) Foreign language reading anxiety. *The Modern Language Journal* 83 (2), 202–218.
Scarcella, R.C. and Oxford, R.L. (1992) *The Tapestry of Language Learning: The Individual in the Communicative Classroom*. Boston, MA: Heinle and Heinle.
Scovel, T. (1978) The effect of affect on foreign language learning: A review of the anxiety research. *Language Learning* 28 (1), 129–142.
Sellers, V.D. (2000) Anxiety and reading comprehension in Spanish as a foreign language. *Foreign Language Annals* 33, 512–520.
Sparks, R.L. and Ganschow, L. (1995) A strong inference approach to causal factors in foreign language learning: A response to MacIntyre. *The Modern Language Journal* 79 (2), 235–244.
Sparks, R.L. and Ganschow, L. (2011) Anxiety about foreign language learning among high school women. *The Modern Language Journal* 80 (2), 199–212.
Spielberger, C. (1966) *Anxiety and Behaviour.* New York: Academic Press.
Spielberger, C. (1983) *Manual for the State-Trait Anxiety Inventory (Form Y).* Palo Alto, CA: Consulting Psychologists Press.
Steinberg, F.S. and Horwitz, E.K. (1986) The effect of induced anxiety on the denotative and interpretative content of second language speech. *TESOL Quarterly* 20 (1), 131–136.
Waninge, F. (2015) Motivation, emotion and cognition: Attractor states in the classroom. In Z. Dörnyei, P.D. MacIntyre and A. Henry (eds) *Motivational Dynamics in Language Learning* (pp. 195–213). Bristol: Multilingual Matters.
Young, D. (1986) The relationship between anxiety and foreign language oral proficiency ratings. *Foreign Language Annals* 19, 439–445.

3 On the Misreading of Horwitz, Horwitz and Cope (1986) and the Need to Balance Anxiety Research and the Experiences of Anxious Language Learners

Elaine K. Horwitz

Introduction

Horwitz *et al.* (1986) is often noted as one of the pioneering statements of the existence and nature of foreign language anxiety. In that article, we argued that a specific anxiety that we called Foreign Language Classroom Anxiety was primarily responsible for the debilitating effects of anxiety on second language learning and achievement. We also described three representative specific anxieties, Communication Apprehension, Test Anxiety and Fear of Negative Evaluation, that we saw as conceptually related to foreign language classroom anxiety to help readers understand the concept of a specific anxiety. Contrary to a number of subsequent interpretations, Horwitz *et al.* did not argue that Communication Apprehension plus Test Anxiety plus Fear of Negative Evaluation formed an equation that resulted in Foreign Language Classroom Anxiety. Rather, by arguing the existence of a specific anxiety called Foreign Language Anxiety or Foreign Language Classroom Anxiety, we argued that foreign language anxiety is different from those three constructs. Since the publication of the original article, a number of scholars have attempted to determine the components of Language Anxiety by using factor analytic approaches. To make clear the problematic nature of 'the three factor model of Language Anxiety', this chapter will review the literature on the components of Language Anxiety, including recent work utilising a facilitative–debilitating dichotomy. It will also describe the curvilinear relationship between anxiety and achievement and distinguish facilitative anxiety from constructs like *flow*. The chapter recommends that research on language anxiety should be guided by applied questions directed at understanding and helping anxious language learners rather than more basic psychological questions about the nature of anxieties.

A Historical Perspective on Language Anxiety

The possibility of anxiety inhibiting language learning is self-evident to many language learners and teachers. Many students report anxiety reactions in the course of their attempts to learn a new language, and many teachers report their own or their students' anxiety in language learning (Horwitz, 1996). Horwitz *et al.* (1986) is often noted as one of the pioneering statements of the existence and nature of Language Anxiety.[1] To date, according to Google Scholar, this article has been cited almost 3700 times (18 January 2017). Building on Scovel's (1978) warning that the role of anxiety in second/foreign language learning cannot be understood without specifying the type of anxiety being examined, Horwitz *et al.* argued that a specific anxiety that we called *Foreign Language Classroom Anxiety* was primarily responsible for any (or at least most) negative effects of anxiety on second language learning and achievement.

Scovel's review of the then existing literature on the relationship of anxiety to second language achievement noted that several studies had found positive relationships between anxiety and achievement, but no relationship or even negative relationships were found in other studies (Chastain, 1976; Swain & Burnaby, 1976; Tucker *et al.*, 1976). Scovel used these inconsistent findings as evidence of the need to specify the type of anxiety that is being investigated before claiming that anxiety has any impact on language learning. Interestingly, citing Stephen Krashen's (1976) then newly articulated distinction between second language *acquisition* and second language *learning*, Scovel also speculated that various aspects or kinds of language learning might be differentially influenced by anxiety.

Scovel taught us that the term anxiety is overly broad to explain a relationship with second language learning (or with any type of learning for that matter). There are many types of anxiety and some of them are more likely to impact language learning than others. To offer a frivolous example, it seems unlikely that insect anxiety has anything to do with one's response to or ultimate success in language learning even though *entomophobia* is subsumed under the general label of anxiety.

While Scovel primarily talked about anxieties in terms of their targets, anxieties can also be classified with respect to their pervasiveness. Individuals who tend to be anxious in their everyday lives are said to have Trait Anxieties, while State Anxieties refer to the onset of anxiety at particular moments; when a teacher announces a pop quiz, for example (Spielberger, 1966). Specific anxieties, Horwitz *et al.*'s classification for the construct of the (Foreign/Second) Language Anxiety that they proposed, include an individual's tendency to be anxious in specific situations; in this case, the *situation* of language learning. Thus, specific anxieties resemble Trait Anxiety but are applied only in a limited range of settings. When individuals experience Language Anxiety, we could think about them as having the *trait* of feeling *state* anxiety when participating in (or sometimes even thinking about) language learning and/or use.

Horwitz *et al.*'s (1986) article included descriptions of three specific anxieties: Communication Apprehension, Test Anxiety and Fear of Negative Evaluation, to help readers understand the concept of a specific anxiety. In describing these three anxieties, we were also taking up Scovel's challenge to define the type of anxiety that would impede language learning. Communication Apprehension is a specific anxiety directed towards (public) speaking in one's primary language, Test Anxiety is a specific anxiety experienced in testing situations or in anticipation of testing situations and Fear of Negative Evaluation is a fear that people will judge you negatively. Although we offered these related anxieties as examples of specific anxieties, we did not mean them as a statement of the components of foreign language classroom anxiety. Specifically, we did not mean to argue that Communication Apprehension plus Test Anxiety plus Fear of Negative Evaluation in various proportions formed an equation that resulted in Foreign Language Classroom Anxiety. Rather, we hoped that by considering these other specific anxieties, readers could better understand the anxiety construct we were proposing and why some people might experience a specific anxiety in response to language learning.

The theoretical argument in Horwitz *et al.*, that Language Anxiety was only analogous to – and not composed of – the three related anxieties, was supported by the study reported in Horwitz (1986). This paper described the development and validation of the Foreign Language Classroom Anxiety Scale (FLCAS). To help establish the independence of foreign language anxiety from other previously reported specific anxieties, this paper reported on the correlations between the FLCAS and other types of anxieties including Trait Anxiety, Communication Apprehension, Test Anxiety and Fear of Negative Evaluation. Thus, this study explicitly examined the degree of relationship (overlap) between foreign language anxiety and the three analogous anxieties in order to establish the construct validity of a scale designed to elicit foreign language anxiety.

Importantly, this study found clear evidence of the independence of Language Anxiety. It found non-significant correlations of $r=0.28$ ($p<0.063$) between the FLCAS and a frequently used measure of communication apprehension, the Personal Report of Communication Apprehension (PRCA) (McCroskey, 1970), and of $r=0.36$ ($p=0.007$) between the FLCAS and the Fear of Negative Evaluation Scale (FNES)

(Watson & Friend, 1969). The correlation between the FLCAS and the Test Anxiety Scale (TAS) (Sarason, 1978) was found to be significant ($r=0.53$, $p=0.001$), but even so, the shared variance of these two scales was less than 30% (0.53^2).[2] At the time, I argued that these results support the contention 'that foreign language anxiety can be discriminated from these related constructs, although it appears that foreign language classroom anxiety is moderately associated with test anxiety' (Horwitz, 1986: 561). Thus, people who experienced test anxiety were somewhat more likely to experience language anxiety and vice versa. In addition, the correlation of the FLCAS with the Trait scale of the State-Trait Anxiety Inventory (Spielberger, 1983) was $r=0.29$ ($p=0.002$), suggesting that people who are generally anxious in their lives may be slightly more likely to be anxious in language learning. This finding also means that many anxious language learners do not experience a general tendency to anxiety in their daily lives.

The relatively small amounts of shared variance between the FLCAS and the other anxiety measures examined in this study support the construct validity of the FLCAS and the existence of Language Anxiety as a specific anxiety, independent of other types of anxiety. This evidence is supportive of the discriminant validity of the FLCAS. Discriminant validity refers to the idea that two instruments (scales) that are supposed to be measuring different constructs should yield different scores. This early finding that the FLCAS does not correlate significantly with instruments measuring Communication Apprehension and Fear of Negative Evaluation supports the conclusion that these are separate types of anxiety and disputes the idea that Language Anxiety is a composite of these other anxieties.[3] And, as argued earlier, the correlations between the FLCAS and Test Anxiety and Trait Anxiety are significant but small ($r=0.29$ and $r=0.53$, respectively). Furthermore, Horwitz (1986) found a correlation of 0.77 ($p=0.001$) between the FLCAS and the straightforward item, 'Rate your anxiety-level concerning your foreign language class'. All these findings support the existence of Language Anxiety as separate from the other types of anxiety.

Is Language Anxiety a Composite of Communication Apprehension, Test Anxiety and Fear of Negative Evaluation?

Aida (1994: 157) was the first to conduct a factor analytic study 'to discover the underlying structure of the FLCAS and to examine whether or not the structure reflects the three kinds of anxiety presented earlier'. By 'the three kinds of anxiety presented earlier', Aida is, of course, referring to Communication Apprehension, Test Anxiety and Fear of Negative

Evaluation. In fact, Aida goes so far as to call this conceptualisation 'Horwitz, Horwitz, and Cope's Construct of Language Anxiety'. Importantly, Aida poses an additional question in this paper about the role of the specific target language and the specific language learning context in the nature and functioning of Language Anxiety. She wonders whether learners of Japanese might have greater levels of Language Anxiety because Japanese is both a language that is generally perceived to be difficult for American language learners and a less commonly taught language in the United States. Thus, in addition to the general question about whether Communication Apprehension, Test Anxiety and Fear of Negative Evaluation constitute the components of foreign language anxiety, Aida asks whether these components vary in kind or proportion in different groups of language learners.

Aida conducted principal components analysis with Varimax rotation on a slightly modified version of the FLCAS in which she substituted *Japanese* for *my foreign language* (class). The purpose of factor analysis is to reduce the items of a scale to a more manageable number of intercorrelating factors. Since the FLCAS has 33 items, this approach has the potential for both theoretical and practical usefulness. After orthogonal rotation, Aida concluded that four factors, which she labelled (1) Speech Anxiety and Fear of Negative Evaluation, (2) Fear of Failing the Class, (3) Comfortableness in Speaking with Japanese People and (4) Negative Attitudes towards the Japanese Class, best accounted for the variance in FLCAS items. In total, these four factors accounted for approximately 55% of the variance in the FLCAS scores.

Aida's findings differed from the three-factor model of Language Anxiety in several important ways. First of all, she found a composite factor that included both Speech Anxiety and Fear of Negative Evaluation, which would suggest that fear of speaking and fear of being negatively evaluated functioned in concert in her group of learners. In addition, Aida found three factors not mentioned by Horwitz *et al.*: Fear of Failing the Class, Comfortableness in Speaking with Japanese People and Negative Attitudes towards the Japanese Class. Fear of Failing the class and Negative Attitudes towards the Japanese Class would seem to capture feelings about Japanese as a university class. Finally, in sharp contrast to the Horwitz (1986) finding, Aida did not find Test Anxiety to be related to Language Anxiety: 'Yet the present study did not support Horwitz *et al.*'s claim (sic) that test anxiety is the third component of foreign language anxiety' (Aida, 1994: 162).

Thus, at best, Aida found only partial support for a three-factor model of Language Anxiety. There are several possible reasons for her findings. It is possible that Language Anxiety manifests itself differently in American students of Japanese than in the American students of Spanish and French who participated in the original FLCAS studies. Pragmatic issues are especially important in Japanese, and it is possible that these learners were particularly fearful about speaking with natives of Japan. In addition, there are always issues of item and factor interpretation in factor analysis, and factor labelling is necessarily subjective (Park, 2014). Finally, and most importantly, since the 33 original FLCAS items came from a number of sources including the experiences of anxious language learners and were not chosen to represent a three-factor model of Language Anxiety, it is clearly not possible to classify the FLCAS in that way.

Since Aida's study, there have been a number of other factor analytic studies that sought to determine the components of language anxiety, including the possibility of the three-factor model. Park (2012, 2014)[4] reviews this literature and reports that there is variety in both the number of factors found and the content of these factors. In addition, he notes that most of the studies 'have used only exploratory factor analysis, which could be criticized for subjective judgment in factor rotation and labeling' (Park, 2014: 264).[5] Park (2014) proposes that a two-step process using exploratory factor analysis followed by confirmatory factor analysis would be a more appropriate and accurate procedure. Exploratory factor analysis would identify 'the underlying components of the FLCAS' and confirmatory factor analysis would 'examine whether "a priori" components generated by exploratory factor analysis adequately fit the data' (Park, 2014: 264). Using this procedure, Park found two factors accounting for approximately 39% of the variance in his Korean version of the FLCAS: (1) Communication Apprehension and Understanding and (2) Communication Apprehension and Confidence. Thus, as has been often observed (Aida, 1996; Horwitz *et al.*, 1986; Saito *et al.*, 1999; Young, 1990), Park found that Language Anxiety was particularly associated with speaking the new language. Park speculates that Communication Apprehension either separately or in conjunction with other factors is the core component of the FLCAS.

At this point, I do not mean to argue that Language Anxiety as measured by the FLCAS is a single, non-divisible construct. The preponderance of the factor analytic studies have found between two and five factors of various content and focus. On the other hand, Park found evidence to support the possibility of a unitary anxiety construct centring around second language communication apprehension. Such a conceptualisation would be consistent with the strong internal consistency of the FLCAS. Horwitz (1986) reported that internal consistency for the FLCAS, as measured by Cronbach's alpha, was 0.93, and Aida and Park had similar findings as have many other studies (Park, 2014). In sum, although there is currently insufficient evidence to conclude that Language Anxiety is a unitary construct, there is little theoretical or empirical evidence at present for the three-factor model of Language Anxiety (erroneously) attributed to Horwitz *et al.* (1986).

Exploring Relationships between Language Anxiety and Other Individual Difference Variables

There is a second reason that researchers have been interested in dividing the FLCAS into factors or subscales. A number of factor analytic studies have been conducted as a step in conducting correlational studies examining the relationships between Language Anxiety and other learner variables, especially language learning strategies (Yang, 1999) and learner beliefs about language learning (Horwitz, 1988). Unlike the FLCAS, both Oxford's (1989) Strategy Inventory for Language Learning (SILL) and Horwitz's Beliefs about Language Learning Inventory (BALLI) were designed to include items addressing a wide range of student beliefs and learning practices. As such, they do not constitute a single scale in the way the FLCAS does. By attempting to be comprehensive, these scales make it impossible to speak of higher or lower total scores on the instrument. In the case of the SILL, it is possible to add up the number of strategies that a particular language learner reports using, but the sheer number of strategies used does not seem very important in understanding how a learner approaches language learning. While it may be somewhat useful to know whether a learner uses more strategies in one or more of Oxford's strategy categories or another, it is much more important to know about the specific strategies that are employed. With respect to the BALLI, even this small amount of summary is not very helpful. How does one meaningfully add scores for responses to the item *Some languages are easier to learn than others* to scores for the item *Students and teachers should only speak English during English classes?* Thus, since researchers have necessarily conducted factor analyses to make the number of SILL and BALLI items more manageable, it was natural to add the FLCAS items into the analyses in order to see which specific strategies or beliefs were associated with specific anxiety items.

Why Does it Matter if Language Anxiety is Viewed as a Composite of Communication Apprehension, Test Anxiety and Fear of Negative Evaluation or Something Else?

It probably doesn't matter much to anxious language learners whether their teachers conceive of their anxiety as a specific response to language learning or think of them as worrying about speaking in front of others, feeling like they are constantly being tested and/or worrying that their classmates or conversational partners will view them negatively when they speak the new language, or any combination of these factors. In any case, students would benefit from teachers who acknowledge their anxious feelings and attempt to offer a less anxiety-inducing environment. I believe strongly that making speaking and testing situations more comfortable and encouraging teachers (and students) to be more supportive would make important contributions to lessening students' Language Anxiety. Palacios (1998) found significant negative correlations between students' perceptions of teacher support, affiliation and involvement with their levels of foreign language anxiety. That is, lower levels of anxiety were associated with higher levels of teacher support (helpfulness and concern) as well as higher levels of student involvement with the class and with each other. Such findings suggest that levels of Language Anxiety can be attenuated to some extent by a positive environment. Gregersen and Horwitz (2002) suggested that anxious and non-anxious pre-service teachers differed in their orientation to second language communication. The more anxious teachers seemed to perceive the goal of speaking in English as not making mistakes, while the non-anxious teachers hoped to simply keep talking even if they made mistakes. Perhaps anxiety could also be lessened by helping students approach second language communication more realistically or simply to see the goal as getting past the mistake and continuing to talk.

My point here is that we don't need to thoroughly identify the components of Language Anxiety or understand the interactions among them before we can help anxious learners. An overemphasis on clarifying the components of Language Anxiety may actually keep the language teaching profession from taking the already understood straightforward steps to help anxious language learners. Although psychologists and therapists encounter individuals experiencing a wide array of anxieties, they typically choose from a small list of anxiety reduction approaches including support, desensitisation and cognitive therapy. Since language teachers are not mental health professionals, individual support within the context of a positive classroom environment would seem to be our best approaches for helping our anxious students.[6] Then, with these logical steps in place, we can continue our search to better understand the nature of Language Anxiety so that even more targeted anxiety-reduction procedures can be developed and implemented.

The starting point of this chapter must also be strongly reiterated here: Horwitz *et al.* (1986) did not argue that (Foreign) Language Anxiety is composed of Communication Apprehension, Test Anxiety and Fear of Negative Evaluation. If we want to better understand the nature of Language Anxiety, we simply cannot start with a false premise.

It is also unlikely that Language Anxiety is an invariable construct. Interviews with anxious language learners (Palacios, 1998; Price, 1999) indicate individual and cultural variation in students' anxious reactions to language learning. For example, Price found that some anxious learners had had specific unpleasant and unusual learning experiences that led them to become extremely anxious about language learning without a previous history of anxiety. Yan and Horwitz (2008) found that some anxious language learners in Shanghai worried that their rural childhoods had caused them to have poor fluency in Mandarin. Since they were embarrassed by the way they spoke Chinese, they felt that they would be at a disadvantage in developing a standard variety of English. These two examples remind us that for any model of Language Anxiety that may emerge, there will likely be substantial individual and group variation.

Why a Search for Facilitating Language Anxiety is a Huge Step Backwards

Recently, in addition to a search for the components of Language Anxiety, there has been an increasing interest in identifying its facilitating and debilitating aspects. Ohata (2005: 144) found that a number of the experienced language teachers he interviewed believed that some amount of anxiety, which some of the teachers referred to as facilitative anxiety, helped students: 'Anxiety can be either helpful or devastating, depending on the individual students. But in general, if they don't feel any pressure or anxiety, they would not do anything after all'.

The concept of facilitating and debilitating anxiety in academic contexts (Alpert & Haber, 1960) has a long history and was applied to second language learning as early as Kleinmann's (1977) study. In fact, Scovel singled out Kleinmann's study as a promising approach to understanding how different anxieties impacted language learning in different ways. In general, the argument is that some amount of anxiety called facilitative anxiety focuses language learners and causes them to have better language performance, while too much anxiety called debilitating anxiety causes performance to be diminished. Kleinmann, for example, found that English as a second language (ESL) students with facilitating anxiety attempted more complex grammatical structures than students with higher levels of anxiety.[7] Frankly, I feel that a search for facilitative Language Anxiety is a very dangerous trend.

It is beyond the scope of this chapter to review the enormous literature on the relationships and interrelations between and among anxiety, student ability, task difficulty and level of task stress. The short conclusion is that the level of anxiety that can be tolerated before it becomes debilitating is reduced by the level of stress in the task, the task difficulty and the individual's ability level. In other words, smaller amounts of anxiety can impair performance in more difficult tasks, more stressful tasks and/or in lower-ability learners. H.J. Eysenck (1982), M.W. Eysenck (1985) and M.W. Eysenck and Calvo (1992) articulate a theory of how the division of attention functions to lower task performance.

Psychologists often speak of an inverted U relationship between anxiety and task performance. With small amounts of anxiety, performance is improved to an optimal level of anxiety, but when this optimal level is passed, performance falls off sharply (see Hancock & Ganey [2003] for a discussion of this relationship). But with more difficult tasks, more stressful task situations and/or lower-ability individuals, performance falls off more quickly. Thus, if we as language teachers want to speak of facilitative Language Anxiety, we would, at best, be walking a very fine line between *helpful* and *harmful* anxiety.

Why would I call a search for facilitative anxiety a *step backwards* and even a dangerous trend? The short answer is that language learning is inherently stressful to some people. Specifically, I see the inability to present oneself authentically and the resulting threat to self-concept as inherently stressful to some people. In addition, even beyond other types of academic learning, language learning is already a high-stakes endeavour in many parts of the world, since English achievement is a gate to future educational and career possibilities for many learners. Language learning is also complicated and large, much bigger and more difficult than the tasks typically examined in anxiety and performance studies. At the same time, many learners perceive themselves to have low language learning aptitude (Horwitz, 1988). With such a confluence of factors that interact to increase anxiety and decrease learning, I cannot conceive of why teachers would want a reason to add even more anxiety. I also worry that the idea of facilitative anxiety returns us to the time before Horwitz *et al.* (1986), when it was less common for language teachers to be concerned about the experiences of anxious language learners.

I can see how the idea of facilitative anxiety would be attractive to teachers when students are perceived to be unmotivated. However, as Horwitz *et al.* noted almost three decades ago, some anxious language learners may appear unmotivated by avoiding studying or skipping class entirely. We recommended at the time that teachers consider the possibility that students who appear to be unmotivated are really anxious about language learning. Offering these students more anxiety would be truly sad and, in my opinion, unethical. But offering a higher level of *facilitative* anxiety is not a good approach for helping learners who are actually unmotivated either.[8] Language learning continues over years, if not a lifetime. What kind of anxiety could a teacher possibly offer that would have more than a temporary impact? How could the teacher be sure not to cross the boundary into debilitating anxiety? Don't tests, grades, access to higher-level educational opportunities and parental pressure offer sufficient anxiety for any normal purpose? If lack of motivation is actually the problem, then we should target students' motivation and help them develop realistic and personal goals for language learning and more effective language learning strategies.

To my mind, the recent trend to understand the pleasurable aspects of language learning is a much more promising approach for helping language learners. In the tradition of Flow Theory (Csíkszentmihályi, 1997), Takahashi (2001) and Dewaele and MacIntyre (2014) talk about language learning as an exhilarating and enjoyable experience for some learners. Looking at the pleasurable aspects of language learning could help teachers incorporate these types of experiences into language classes. Teachers could also help students identify the aspects of language learning that particularly appeal to them. I would also speculate that a move towards increased learner autonomy will generally contribute to a lessening of Language Anxiety (Hauck & Hurd, 2005). As language learners take on and have more control over their learning, anxiety emanating from measures like grades and tests should lessen.

What is the Nature of Language Anxiety?

Ultimately, I feel that the emotions evoked by Language Anxiety go much deeper than a simple combination of other anxieties. I have argued repeatedly (Horwitz, 1996, 2000, 2013a, 2013b) that some people experience anxiety in language learning because of distress at their inability to be themselves and to connect authentically with other people through the limitation of the new language. I have likened this discomfort – perhaps overly superficially – to our feelings when we have a bad haircut or must wear unfashionable or unflattering clothing.[9] In those instances when people do not feel like themselves when using the new language, some people perceive a threat to their identity. Even before the identification of a specific anxiety associated with second language learning, Alexander Guiora (1983) described language learning as *a profoundly unsettling psychological proposition* and Jennybelle Rardin (Young, 1992) speaks of people's fears of losing their true selves when learning a new language. Horwitz *et al.* describe the essential difficulty in using a second language to interact with the world:

> Authentic communication also becomes problematic in the second language because of the immature command of the second language relative to the first. Thus, adult language learners' self-perceptions of genuineness in presenting themselves to others may be threatened by the limited range of meaning and affect that can be deliberately communicated. In sum, the language learner's self-esteem is vulnerable to the awareness that the range of communicative choices and authenticity is restricted. The importance of the disparity between the 'true' self as known to the language learner and the more limited self as can be communicated at any given moment in the foreign language would seem to distinguish foreign language anxiety from

other academic anxieties such as those associated with mathematics or science. Probably no other field implicates self-concept and self-expression to the degree that language study does. (Horwitz *et al.*, 1986: 128)

I must therefore argue strenuously that to simplify the construct of Language Anxiety to a composite of Communication Apprehension, Test Anxiety and Fear of Negative Evaluation, even with the addition of individual or cultural factors, is to miss the essence of the experiences of anxious language learners. I use the phrase *authentic self-presentation* (Horwitz, 2013a) to describe what a language learner must be able to do to achieve full second language competence. I don't mean to suggest that less than full competence is not valuable or useful to learners. Rather, I believe that Language Anxiety emanates from the discomfort some language learners have when they must interact in the language but are unable to present themselves authentically when doing so.

Going Forward

It is still theoretically and practically useful to seek to better understand the components of Language Anxiety, but it is important for the language teaching profession to achieve an appropriate balance between understanding the nature of Language Anxiety in order to help learners be more comfortable and successful and understanding the nature of Language Anxiety to contribute to the basic psychological literature on human anxieties. At the same time, whatever our findings, there will be no magic treatments to help anxious language learners. In most cases, the straightforward approaches of teacher support and an encouraging classroom environment will remain the best options. I would go so far as to say that teacher support and positive classrooms should be commonplace for all students, whether anxious or not. And with respect to some of the issues raised in this chapter, interest in facilitative anxiety should not be used as a rationale for maintaining or even encouraging stress in language learning environments.

Here are some slightly more specific suggestions that I offer to new language teachers:

- Acknowledge students' discomfort. Many students are relieved to learn that they are not the only ones experiencing anxiety.
- Acknowledge students' feelings of culture shock and offer opportunities for students to talk about their experiences.
- Use the FLCAS to help identify anxious learners and to start a discussion about anxiety.
- Help students develop more realistic expectations for language learning.

- Arrange contacts with more advanced students so that students see that people like them can learn the language.
- Correct errors gently.
- Use humour and games to distract attention away from individual speakers.
- Use small-group and pair activities rather than whole-class activities.
- Have students imagine becoming anxious while speaking and overcoming that anxiety. (Horwitz, 2013a: 12)

In addition to the factor analytic studies of the components of Language Anxiety and the renewed interest in the role of facilitative and debilitating anxieties in language learning, recent research on Language Anxiety has focused on several specific language learning anxieties connected to different aspects of language learning. These include second language listening anxiety (Bekleyen, 2009; Elkhafaifi, 2007; Kim, 2000; Vandergrift, 2007), second language reading anxiety (Saito *et al.*, 1999; Sellers, 2000) and second language writing anxiety (Cheng, 2002; Cheng *et al.*, 1999). It is important to point out that some people find listening, reading or writing in a second language more anxiety-provoking than speaking. In addition, culture shock or anxieties associated with immersion in new cultures have long been recognised (Horwitz, 2008). The role of anxiety at different stages of language learning also remains relatively unexplored (Saito & Samimy, 1996).[10]

So, in order to move forward, I believe that identifying the unique anxiety profiles of individuals and members of different cultural and other demographic groups would make important contributions to understanding and alleviating Language Anxiety. It would also be helpful to think of anxiety within a larger complex of individual factors such as within the Willingness to Communicate (WTC) paradigm (MacIntyre *et al.*, 1998). How does anxiety interact with other learner factors such as motivation within specific sociocultural, social and interpersonal contexts? What do learners themselves think would help them feel more comfortable? Young (1990) found that students preferred to perform communicative activities in small groups rather than in front of the class. The WTC model would suggest that the task specifics and the group membership would impact anxiety levels. Bandura (1989) posits that people who believe that they have coping abilities and more control over a situation will perceive a lower level of stress. He argues that 'perceived coping ability operates as a cognitive mediator of anxiety' (Bandura, 1989: 1177). It would seem, therefore, that supporting learner autonomy and encouraging positive self-concepts as language learners would make worthwhile contributions to reducing Language Anxiety.

For these reasons, a balanced research agenda on Language Anxiety would include case studies of anxious language learners from a variety of cultures and language learning situations. To those, I would add case studies of individuals who have overcome Language Anxiety. Such studies could generate potential models of Language Anxiety to be examined by the two-stage factor analytic procedure advocated by Park (2014). But as we conduct these studies, it is essential to remember that research on Language Anxiety was initiated from the experiences of anxious language learners and its ultimate goal is to make language learning more comfortable for vulnerable learners. We do not have to wait for new findings to take logical steps to reduce anxiety: talk with our students, listen to their stories, share our own difficulties, let them have more control over their learning and give them opportunities for genuine communication in a safe environment.

Horwitz et al. (1986: 131) observed that 'educators have two options when dealing with anxious students: (1) they can help them learn to cope with the existing anxiety-provoking situation; or (2) they can make the learning context less stressful'. The preponderance of research findings on Language Anxiety suggest that presenting yourself to the world through an imperfectly controlled new language is inherently anxiety-provoking for some people. Since language teachers cannot change the nature of language learning or of language learners, we must change the nature of language classrooms to make the learning context as supportive as possible.

Notes

(1) Although the original Horwitz et al. article used the term Foreign Language Anxiety, I prefer the more general term Language Anxiety and will use it throughout this chapter so as not to seem to imply a difference in anxiety between foreign and second language learning.
(2) The correlations between the FLCAS and the PRCA and the FNES achieved probability values that approach significance, but even if these correlations were significant, such a finding would indicate that the measures shared less than 13% of the variance in common (0.36^2).
(3) As noted earlier, the correlation between the FLCAS and the TAS was significant but not large. Moreover, the correlation between the TAS and final grades was not significant ($r=-0.16$, $p=0.391$) while the correlation between the FLCAS and final grade was significant $r=-0.53$ ($p=0.002$), even when Test Anxiety was statistically controlled.
(4) Dr Park was my doctoral student.
(5) Park also notes that somewhat different versions of the FLCAS, including different translations, were used in the various studies, and this variation may be the source of some of the different findings.
(6) Of course, when a students' anxiety becomes a matter of serious concern, teachers should follow appropriate procedures for referrals to appropriate resources.
(7) I always hesitate to cite this study because it seems to support the idea that teachers should help students develop *facilitative anxiety*.
(8) And I am truly at a loss as to how teachers could accomplish this.

(9) I often refer to this discomfort as *pink dress anxiety* in public presentations (Horwitz, 2013b).
(10) Importantly, there is some evidence that anxiety can remain elevated even as perceived competence and WTC increase (MacIntyre *et al.*, 2002).

References

Aida, Y. (1994) Examination of Horwitz, Horwitz, and Cope's construct of foreign language anxiety: The case of students of Japanese. *The Modern Language Journal* 78, 155–168.

Alpert, R. and Haber, R. (1960) Anxiety in academic achievement situations. *Journal of Abnormal and Social Psychology* 61 (2), 207–215.

Bandura, A. (1989) Human agency in social cognitive theory. *American Psychologist* 44 (9), 1175–1184.

Bekleyen, N. (2009) Helping teachers become better English students: Causes, effects, and coping strategies for foreign language listening anxiety. *System* 37 (4), 664–675.

Chastain, K. (1975) Affective and ability factors in second language acquisition. *Language Learning* 25, 153–161.

Cheng, Y.S. (2002) Factors associated with foreign language writing anxiety. *Foreign Language Annals* 35 (6), 647–656.

Cheng, Y.S., Horwitz, E.K. and Schallert D.L. (1999) Language writing anxiety: Differentiating writing and speaking components. *Language Learning* 49, 417–446.

Csíkszentmihályi, M. (1997) *Finding Flow: The Psychology of Engagement with Everyday Life.* New York: Harper Collins.

Dewaele, J.-M. and MacIntyre, P.D. (2014) The two faces of Janus? Anxiety and enjoyment in the foreign language classroom. *Studies in Second Language Learning and Teaching* 4 (2), 237–274.

Elkhafaifi, H. (2005) Listening comprehension and anxiety in the Arabic language classroom. *The Modern Language Journal* 89 (2), 206–220.

Eysenck, H.J. (1982) Introduction. In H.J. Eysenck (ed.) *A Model for Intelligence.* (pp. 1–12) Berlin: Springer.

Eysenck, M.W. (1985) Anxiety and cognitive-task performance. *Personality and Individual Differences* 6 (5), 579–586.

Eysenck, M.W. and Calvo, M.G. (1992) Anxiety and performance: The processing efficiency theory. *Cognition & Emotion* 6 (6), 409–434.

Hancock, P.A. and Ganey, H.C. (2003) From the inverted-U to the extended-U: The evolution of a law of psychology. *Journal of Human Performance in Extreme Environments* 7 (1), 5–14.

Hauck, M. and Hurd, S. (2005) Exploring the link between language anxiety and learner self-management in open language learning contexts. *European Journal of Open, Distance and E-learning* 8 (2).

Horwitz, E.K. (1986) Preliminary evidence for the reliability and validity of a foreign language anxiety scale. *TESOL Quarterly* 20 (3), 559–562.

Horwitz, E.K. (1988) The beliefs about language learning of beginning university foreign language students. *The Modern Language Journal* 72 (3), 283–294.

Horwitz, E.K. (1996) Even teachers get the blues: Recognizing and alleviating language teachers' feelings of foreign language anxiety. *Foreign Language Annals* 29 (3), 365–372.

Horwitz, E.K. (2000) It ain't over til it's over: On foreign language anxiety, first language deficits, and the confounding of variables. *The Modern Language Journal* 84 (2), 256–259.

Horwitz, E.K. (2008) Cultural identity and language anxiety: How self-concept and cultural expectations mediate performance in a second language. In P. Cheng and J.X. Yan (eds) *Who Are We: Cultural Identity and Language Anxiety* (pp. 57–69). Hong Kong: City University of Hong Kong Press.

Horwitz, E.K. (2013a) *Becoming a Language Teacher: A Practical Guide to Second Language Learning and Teaching* (2nd edn). Upper Saddle River, NJ: Pearson.

Horwitz, E.K. (2013b) Anxiety and beliefs: On learners, teachers, and pink dresses. Invited presentation at the annual meeting of the International Association of Teachers of English to Speakers of Other Languages.

Horwitz, E.K., Horwitz, M.B. and Cope, J. (1986) Foreign language classroom anxiety. *The Modern Language Journal* 70 (2), 125–132.

Kim, J.H. (2000) Foreign language listening anxiety: A study of Korean students learning English. Unpublished PhD thesis, University of Texas at Austin.

Kleinmann, H. (1977) Avoidance behavior in adult second language acquisition. *Language Learning* 27, 93–107.

Krashen, S. (1976) Formal and informal linguistic environments in language acquisition and language learning. *TESOL Quarterly* 10, 157–168.

Kunt, N. (1997) Anxiety and beliefs about language learning: A study of Turkish speaking university students learning English in North Cyprus. Unpublished PhD thesis, University of Texas at Austin.

MacIntyre, P.D., Dörnyei, Z., Clément, R. and Noels, K.A. (1998) Conceptualizing willingness to communicate in a L2: A situational model of L2 confidence and affiliation. *The Modern Language Journal* 84 (4), 545–562.

MacIntyre, P.D., Baker, S., Clément, R. and Donovan, L. (2002) Sex and age effects on willingness to communicate, anxiety, perceived competence, and L2 motivation among junior high school French immersion students. *Language Learning* 52, 537–564.

Ohata, K. (2005) Language anxiety from the teacher's perspective: Interviews with seven experienced ESL/EFL teachers. *Journal of Language and Learning* 3 (1), 133–155.

Oxford, R.L. (1989) Use of language learning strategies: A synthesis of studies with implications for strategy training. *System* 17 (2), 235–247.

Palacios, L.M. (1998) Foreign language anxiety and classroom environment: A study of Spanish university students. Unpublished PhD thesis, University of Texas at Austin.

Park, G.P. (2012) Investigation into the constructs of the FLCAS. *English Teaching* 67, 207–220.

Park, G.P. (2014) Factor analysis of the Foreign Language Classroom Anxiety Scale in Korean learners of English as a foreign language. *Psychological Reports* 115 (1), 261–275.

Saito, Y. and Samimy, K.K. (1996) Foreign language anxiety and language performance: A study of learner anxiety in beginning, intermediate, and advanced-level college students of Japanese. *Foreign Language Annals* 29 (2), 239–249.

Saito, Y., Horwitz, E.K. and Garza, T.J. (1999) Foreign language reading anxiety. *The Modern Language Journal* 83 (2), 202–218.

Scovel, T. (1978) The effect of affect on foreign language learning: A review of the anxiety research. *Language Learning* 28 (1), 129–142.

Sellers, V.D. (2000) Anxiety and reading comprehension in Spanish as a foreign language. *Foreign Language Annals* 33 (5), 512–520.

Spielberger, C.D. (1966) Theory and research on anxiety. In C.D. Spielberger (ed.) *Anxiety and Behavior* (pp. 3–20). New York: Academic Press.

Swain, M. and Burnaby, B. (1976) Personality characteristics and second language learning in young children: A pilot study. *Working Papers in Bilingualism* 11, 115–128.

Takahashi, K. (2001) The development and implementation of a Japanese language exhilaration scale: An exploratory study. Unpublished PhD thesis, University of Texas at Austin.

Truitt, S.N. (1995) Anxiety and beliefs about language learning: A study of Korean university students learning English. Unpublished PhD thesis, University of Texas at Austin.

Tucker, R., Hamayan, E. and Genesee, F. (1976) Affective, cognitive, and social factors in second language acquisition. *Canadian Modern Language Review* 32, 214–226.

Vandergrift, L. (2007) Recent developments in second and foreign language listening comprehension research. *Language Teaching* 40 (3), 191–210.

Yan, J.X. and Horwitz, E.K. (2008) Learners' perceptions of how anxiety interacts with personal and instructional factors to influence their achievement in English: A qualitative analysis of EFL learners in China. *Language Learning* 58 (1), 151–183.

Yang, N.D. (1999) The relationship between EFL learners' beliefs and learning strategy use. *System* 27 (4), 515–535.

Young, D.J. (1990) An investigation of students' perspectives on anxiety and speaking. *Foreign Language Annals* 23 (6), 539–553.

Part 2
Empirical Investigations

4 Anxiety and L2 Self-Images: The 'Anxious Self'

Erdi Şimşek and Zoltán Dörnyei

Introduction

Anxiety is an elusive and complex phenomenon, known for inhibiting people in various activities and, in extreme cases, even potentially damaging their lives. Anxiety has also been recognised to affect foreign/second language (L2) learning and use, and the second language acquisition (SLA) literature typically distinguishes 'language anxiety' from other types of anxiety (e.g. Dörnyei & Ryan, 2015). Given the phenomenological saliency of anxiety, it may be surprising to many that there is no generally accepted definition of the construct, making it one of the most elusive concepts among individual difference characteristics (e.g. Eysenck, 1979; Horwitz et al., 1986; MacIntyre, 1995; Scovel, 1978; Spielmann & Radnofsky, 2001; Young, 1991). One reason for the prevailing ambiguity is that anxiety can be conceptualised at various levels of abstraction, as is illustrated by the following four statements:

'I am an anxious person'.
'I am anxious when at the dentist'.
'I feel anxious'.
'I avoided the party because I was anxious about meeting people'.
(Edelmann, 1992: 1)

The first example denotes a strong, personality-related characteristic of anxiety that one would define as a trait, but the second example demonstrates that anxiety can also emerge in specific situations. The third statement foregrounds the affective dimension of anxiety and the last example concerns anxiety as an antecedent of behaviour. Such variations have led scholars to view anxiety through several different lenses, from diverse perspectives. Some scholars regard it as part of personality (e.g. Gregersen & Horwitz, 2002; Simpson, 1980), others as a primary emotion (e.g. Dewaele, 2010; Gray, 1982; Spielberger, 1972), and it has also been mentioned as a key motivational component (e.g. Dörnyei & Ushioda, 2011).

52 Part 2: Empirical Investigations

Since the genesis of language anxiety research in the 1970s, there has been a consensus in the SLA community that language anxiety is an *emotional experience* evoked by certain L2 learning situations. Accordingly, most scholars in the field would probably agree with Gray's (1982: 5) statement that 'whatever else anxiety is, it is undoubtedly an emotion; sometimes, reading the work of psychologists, one is tempted to think that it is the only emotion'. However, we shall see in this chapter that other conceptualisations can also be fruitful, and we will propose a self-based approach to capture the essence of the 'anxious self'.

The Need for New Ideas in Anxiety Research

Not only has language anxiety been a highly elusive concept, but a review of the literature reveals that anxiety research has been at a relative standstill for more than a decade. To illustrate this, a search in six leading journals in applied linguistics (*Applied Linguistics, Language Learning, Language Teaching, Modern Language Journal, Studies in Second Language Acquisition* and *TESOL Quarterly*; for a justification of these forums, see Boo *et al.*, 2015) indicated that the total number of articles in these journals was fewer than 10 between the years 2005 and 2013, representing a decreasing trajectory in comparison with the previous two decades (see Figure 4.1). Interestingly, there has been a dramatic increase in this respect over the past two years, but it is fair to conclude that the recent surge presented little discussion of theoretical perspectives and developments in models of anxiety but focused primarily on practical aspects of combating anxiety. One valuable exception to this trend has been a recent paper by Dewaele and MacIntyre (2014), which highlighted the need to reflect on the *functions* of emotions rather than merely categorising them as positive or negative ones, thereby initiating a serious rethink about the conceptualisation of anxiety.

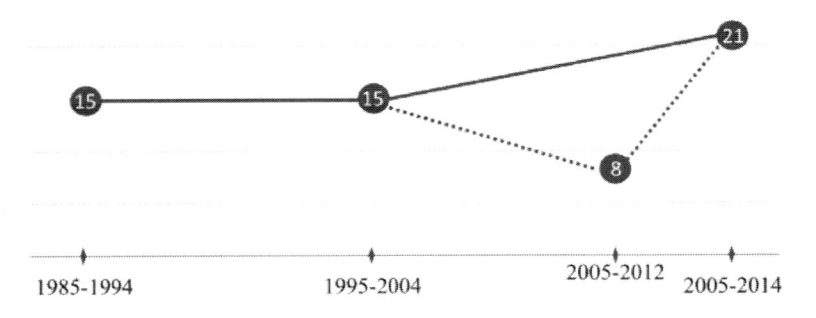

Figure 4.1 Number of articles on anxiety published in six prominent journals on applied linguistics in the last three decades

In the light of the above considerations, it is reasonable to conclude that we may need a fresh approach to re-establish the momentum of language anxiety research. Therefore, the study reported in the current chapter started out by collecting exploratory qualitative data from highly anxious learners in order to gain new insights from their vantage point as they experience the debilitating effects of the construct (although we must note here that foreign language anxiety [FLA] may also have a facilitating but rather inconsistent impact; see Horwitz, 1990; Kleinmann, 1977; Phillips, 1992). Because our proposed notion of the 'anxious self' has directly emerged from this empirical data, we start the discussion by introducing the methodology of our study before returning to some further theoretical discussion.

The Study

Phase 1

In order to obtain a broad understanding of the nature of anxiety, we decided to focus our research on learners whose experience of language anxiety was so strong that it resulted in a debilitating effect. First, we contacted two instructors of English and two assistant professors at four different universities in Turkey, who all had an awareness of language anxiety as a result of their academic studies, and asked them to refer us to students who exhibited some of the well-known symptoms of debilitating language anxiety, such as the inability to express themselves while performing language skills, freezing up during oral production, displaying physiological symptoms (e.g. blushing, shaking, sweating) when called on, avoiding eye contact with the teacher, excessively worrying about being left behind and over-studying with no gains. As a result of the teachers' help as well as of subsequent snowball sampling, we conducted qualitative interviews with 20 participants on Skype, each lasting for approximately half an hour and involving questions to elaborate on how students perceived anxiety, what made them anxious and when/whether they became aware of anxiety. All these participants were Turkish learners of English at an intermediate level and they were all interviewed in their first language (L1), Turkish.

Phase 2

In order to further clarify and build on the obtained findings, we first administered an anxiety questionnaire – comprising the Foreign Language Classroom Anxiety Scale (Horwitz *et al.*, 1986) and the general anxiety section (neuroticism) of the Big Five Inventory (John *et al.*, 1991, 2008) – to 19 male and 55 female participants (mean age 19.8 years) who were studying English at Turkish universities. For interviewing, we selected 16 of them with the highest anxiety measures on one or both scales – the distribution of the data was such that these 16 participants formed a natural cluster with a considerable gap between them and the next group of learners in terms of their anxiety scores. All the selected participants were studying English language teaching, with their English proficiency being at an upper-intermediate level. The rationale for choosing students with such a relatively high level of proficiency was to exclude cases where anxiety was caused purely by the limited language code at lower proficiency levels. Each participant was interviewed face-to-face and the data were submitted to stepwise content analysis to distill salient themes.

Data analysis

Although, as mentioned above, our study included a quantitative component, this was primarily used for the principled selection of interviewees for the subsequent, dominant qualitative phase. All the interviews were transcribed and analysed through latent content analysis to elicit general themes and patterns concerning both the symptoms of anxiety and the classroom situations that might trigger these characteristics. First, we highlighted relevant extracts in the transcripts and assigned codes for them. Then, we examined the codes and established broader themes among them based on the research aims and interview questions (e.g. anxiety-provoking situations, behaviours and thoughts while feeling anxious, describing anxiety, language anxiety vs general anxiety). Following this, in an adaption of Crabtree and Miller's (1992) template approach, we developed an analysis guide that reflected McAdams's New Big Five model and his three-level conceptual framework (see later in this chapter for details) and juxtaposed the categories of the coding themes and the template in order to identify the relevant qualitative data for our study. Each broad theme was then submitted to a more detailed analysis that enabled us to form more specific categories under each theme (e.g. stage fright, fear of negative evaluation, heightened expectations). This hierarchical pattern not only helped provide a general model but also allowed us to discover some fine links and distinctions within and between the initial broad themes and levels in the template. In addition to this, the questionnaire data were submitted to some basic statistical analyses of the two main variables (general and language anxiety) to examine their correlation with each other and their distribution across gender.

The 'Anxious Self'

One of the main themes emerging from the first round of interviews was the fact that several learners talked about the way in which they were affected by anxiety in a somewhat detached manner, referring to an anxious persona that they were not fully in control of. The following two extracts from two different participants illustrate this point well:

> I envy my classmates because they can express their ideas the way they want and I can't. When I am anxious, I am aware of myself and my behaviours yet I cannot control my movements and I often ask myself: 'What am I going to do now?' ... I cannot reflect on my inner speech while performing; I keep telling myself that I should always smile but I have an anxious side and I cannot deny it. I believe that I can control the anxious side of me more and more, yet I do not know exactly how. (Female interviewee 1, hence FInt 1)
>
> Normally I can do whatever I want but the person who presents (herself in the English class) cannot do what she wants. (FInt 6)

Thus, some learners found it conducive to describe their anxious manifestations in L2 performance as if those were the outworking of a fairly independent dimension of their overall self. This framing of the issue had obvious links to the recent emphasis in SLA on the significance of the learner's self-concept (e.g. Csizér & Magid, 2014) and, within the domain of motivation research, the L2 Motivational Self System (Dörnyei, 2005, 2009a, 2009b). This prompted us to explore whether conceptualising the 'anxious self' might be a fruitful approach to shed new light on the subject. Our search for a potential conceptual framework that might accommodate this new conceptualisation led us to an influential recent theory of individual differences by Dan McAdams, the New Big Five model (e.g. McAdams, 2006a, 2006b; McAdams & Pals, 2006), which we then adopted as the guiding theoretical paradigm for our data analysis. Therefore, before presenting a more detailed examination of our qualitative data, let us provide a brief overview of this theoretical model.

Situating Anxiety in McAdams's Theory of Personality

Personality factors have long been seen as key aspects of our understanding of variation in people's performance, and personality traits have also been registered as some of the main contributors to anxiety (e.g. Beatty & McCroskey, 2009; Eysenck & Eysenck, 1985; Gregersen & Horwitz, 2002; MacIntyre, 1999; Young, 1991). The currently dominant personality construct, McCrae and Costa's 'Big Five', includes five personality dimensions – extraversion, neuroticism, conscientiousness, agreeableness and openness to experience – and within this construct anxiety is one of the primary facets of the 'neuroticism' dimension (Costa & McCrae, 1994; Goldberg, 1993; McCrae & Costa, 2003, 2008; McCrae & John, 1992). This anxiety component is normally equated with trait anxiety (Eysenck, 1997), and Goldberg (1993) suggests that people with a high level of trait anxiety often experience nervousness or general emotional impairment across a range of situations. This, however, leaves the issue of state anxiety open, which is the point where McAdams's approach becomes relevant. In his 'New Big Five' model (McAdams, 2006a, 2006b; McAdams & Pals, 2006), he proposes a three-tiered conceptual framework consisting of *dispositional traits, characteristic adaptations* and *integrative life narratives*. Thus, the new model views the overall personality of the individual as the interaction of three different levels, with each explaining psychological individuality using its own discourse (for a recent summary, see Dörnyei & Ryan, 2015).

Dispositional traits involve personality features such as extraversion, neuroticism, friendliness, dominance, dutifulness and depressiveness, that is, attributes that tend to be relatively stable across situations and over time; essentially we are talking about the main components of the Big Five model here. These traits act as the foundation for human individuality and provide a signature that an individual expresses in a variety of circumstances over a long stretch of time.

Characteristic adaptations refer to context-dependent constructs containing 'motives, goals, plans, strivings, strategies, values, virtues, schemas, self-images, mental representations of significant others, developmental tasks, and many other aspects of human individuality' (McAdams & Pals, 2006: 208). This domain has been the primary focus of the classic individual difference paradigm. In comparison with traits, characteristic adaptations fit better into the social nature of everyday life as they are enacted in the light of, and are also moulded by, the ordinary demands of social situations. However, we should note that due to the fact that specific situations may collate with several different characteristic adaptations and thereby result in compositions of more general learner characteristics, 'the distinction between dispositional trait and characteristic adaptation may not be perfectly clear in every case' (McAdams & Pals, 2006: 208); for example, an individual's anxiety tendencies can be manifested in specific forms of anxieties, a point that we will return to below.

What makes McAdams's model genuinely integrative is the third level of the construct, *integrative life narratives*, which involves the 'narrative identity' that individuals create for themselves to help to define who they are, to connect with others and ultimately to make sense of their lives and regulate their behaviour. Narrative identity can be defined as 'a person's internalized and evolving life story, integrating the reconstructed past and imagined future to provide life with some degree of unity and purpose' (McAdams & McLean, 2013: 233). The significance of the concept lies in the assumption that individuals compose and comprehend their experiences to a large extent as narratives (e.g. excuses, explanations, myths or stories), and that these narratives then turn into the underpinnings of individuals' self-concept. Indeed, self-narratives are not just stories about what happened in a specific time and spot; they also provide both an assessment of past occasions in relation to the self and a feeling of transient progression (Bruner, 1990; Habermas & Bluck, 2000).

An *L2 narrative identity* is described by Dörnyei and Ryan (2015: 202) as 'the specific aspect of an individual's ongoing internal narrative that relates to learning and using a second/foreign language', which integrates past L2-related experiences and future goals. The unique practical importance of the third level of McAdams's model lies in the fact that this is the component that humans can control the most, because its relationship with the overall framework is bidirectional: narrative identity not only unifies the personality system but also applies a developmental impact to it. Accordingly, shaping the life narrative can lead to shaping the whole mindset.

As will be illustrated below, language anxiety is reflected seamlessly in the three levels of McAdams's model: first, it includes an initial element of inherent tendency that is biologically/genetically related; second, state anxiety can be understood as an example of characteristic adaptations; and third, our interviews confirm that people regularly produce narratives to create cohesion in their experiences and perceptions so that the unified narrative can become a kind of guide to be used to deal with the negative consequences of anxiety. Let us look at the three levels more closely in the light of our data.

Dispositional trait level

It is a well-known observation that anxious learners often experience one or more unpleasant symptoms. The most common ones are physiological, such as a high heart rate, stomach pain, feeling hot, trembling voice, blushing and shaking of hands or legs and so on. For example, our interviewees report,

> I feel my heartbeats. (FInt 1)
>
> I suddenly feel hot and my hands start shaking. I don't know if my face really turns red but I certainly feel like that. (MInt 8)
>
> My legs shake. Sometimes it is so extreme that I barely stand. (FInt 14)

Some of these symptoms were observed during the interviews themselves. Additionally, anxious students can sometimes have difficulty concentrating and can find themselves freezing up while performing; for example,

> It feels like I am paralysed. When I am on the stage, something unidentifiable happens. Last year, even though I was well-prepared for a topic, I could not even talk about it. (FInt 12)

Anxiety may also manifest in some extreme symptoms such as unexplained pain, muscle stiffness or even fainting:

> It was during an exam period. I woke up early in the morning. All I thought about was the exam that day. I felt dizzy and headed to the bathroom. Then, I fainted on the way there. (FInt 3)

The interview data elicited from our participants offers a clear indication that there is a tendency in some learners to experience symptoms of anxiety on a recurring basis, resulting in a rather resigned, settled disposition. The following three extracts are typical examples in this respect:

> It (anxiety) is somehow inside me. I can't get rid of it. I am an introvert person and I think that is all because of it. (FInt 4)
>
> I get nervous easily. I am concerned about the reactions I may be receiving upon my decisions or participations. It is not extreme but it prevents me from making decisions freely. (FInt 15)
>
> I think it is my general personality. I do not like talking to people because I do not feel comfortable. (FInt 9)

One of the most recognisable features of dispositional traits is that they are relatively consistent across different circumstances, and indeed, the qualitative data suggest that most of the participants experienced detrimental effects of anxiety in different walks of their lives. For example, one interviewee (FInt 15) stated, 'No matter what I do or which subject I study, I will become anxious as it is one of my main characteristics'. Moreover, as the following extract illustrates, some of our data also point to the heritable nature of dispositional traits (even though further research would be needed to determine exactly what and to what extent is inherited): 'My mother has always had anxiety. She often tells me that we are similar to each other in terms of anxiety' (FInt 11).

Additional quantitative analysis

As mentioned earlier, we have conducted some basic statistical analysis of the questionnaire data, which confirmed the existence of a dispositional level of anxiety. Although the literature suggests contradictory results about the relations of general anxiety and language anxiety (Dewaele, 2002, 2013; MacIntyre & Gardner, 1989), our questionnaire showed that there was a strong positive association between the neuroticism and language anxiety variables ($r=0.60$, $p<0.001$). This indicates that the stronger someone's general anxiety tendency, the more likely he/she is to realise it in the language classroom setting; in other words, emotionally stable individuals are likely to suffer less from language anxiety. This generalisable trend, however, is modified by gender differences, which is another area where opinions do not fully converge (e.g. Dewaele, 2013; Matsuda & Gobel, 2004; Woodrow, 2006). Our data set revealed that female learners scored higher on both language anxiety and neuroticism scales (mean [M]=2.7, standard deviation [SD]=0.51; M=3, SD=0.62) in comparison with male learners (M=2.42, SD=0.48; M=2.6, SD=0.65) (t [71]=−2.02, p<0.05; t [71]=−2.42, p<0.02). That females were found to be more anxious than males might be explained by sociocultural aspects of anxiety (MacIntyre, 1995; Yan & Horwitz, 2008), because in male-dominant societies, females have been reported to be more anxious than males and more reluctant to interact with others in learning a foreign language (Park & French, 2013). Therefore, one possible reason why past research has shown different results could be the diverse sociocultural contexts in which the studies were carried out, which forms a link between dispositional trait level and the characteristic adaptation level of McAdams's model.

Characteristic adaptation level

Some people experience a debilitating, fear-like emotion in certain situations, which not only reduces the productivity and the efficiency of their performance but also causes a great deal of uneasiness in them. However, unlike dispositional traits, these emotions are characteristic of only specific aspects of particular people's social life, with some well-known adaptations of this kind including *stage fright* and *test anxiety*. Stage fright is a widely known and experienced anxiety manifestation in a distinct type of communication situation; it can be understood as a 'dynamic event that revolves around fluctuations in individuals' perceptions of their own competency in public speaking settings' (MacIntyre & MacDonald, 1998: 360). Giving a speech, singing or acting before an audience are some of the most common situations in which people experience stage fright, and we also find several examples of it in our own data set; for example, 'I can easily become anxious in front of a group of people. I also feel anxious if there is an authority – you know, the feeling of being evaluated' (FInt 4). This extract also highlights the role of the presence of an authority as another factor contributing to anxiety arousal.

Test anxiety is one of the clearest demonstrations of how a specific instructional task can mediate anxiety. With the growing impact of examinations in modern society, test anxiety has become a pervasive issue (Huang & Hung, 2013; Sarason, 1986; Zeidner, 1998), as individuals increasingly come across test situations not only in classroom settings but also in other aspects of life such as job interviews or applying for educational programmes. One of our participants (FInt 5), for example, reported: 'I am anxious not only in classes in English but also in others, especially during exams. Sometimes I cannot even focus on the questions'.

Besides the above examples of adaptation to communication situations and task types, our data also highlight several other archetypical adaptation forms. A frequent anxiety type concerns the *fear of negative evaluation* – for example, 'Others might think that I am not capable enough. I might fail and others might laugh at me' (FInt 6) – which may be particularly salient within a competitive classroom goal structure: '... when I see my friends studying or participating more than I do, I feel anxious' (FInt 1). It is no coincidence that the adaptations that we have mentioned so far as emerging from our data correspond with the three well-known components – communication apprehension, fear of negative evaluation and test anxiety – that Horwitz *et al.* (1986) identified in their seminal paper as shaping FLA.

Our interviews with anxious learners suggested two more common characteristic adaptations. One of these is related to the *content* of the communication, particularly unfamiliar content. The best example of this type in our data set involved an account where a participant who normally displayed heightened language anxiety talked about a situation when this did *not* happen:

> The lesson started with what we already knew, for example with Facebook, we were familiar with the topic and were able to understand it. We started talking about this... I was very relaxed. I could answer everything. (FInt 16)

Finally, a theme that would resonate with many anxious learners concerns the perception of heightened *expectations*:

> I have to express my ideas freely and I have to answer when people ask questions. I am a second year university student. People have expectations. This is what an educated person should do. When I cannot answer I feel like an idiot. (FInt 11)

We have argued earlier that characteristic adaptations are mediators that bring to the fore general anxiety tendencies in the individuals' actual lives, and therefore we asked our interviewees *when* they first came to realise their anxiety dispositions. Many students reported that they first experienced their anxiety in adolescence, as they tried to find their position among their peers. For example, one of the students stated that she became aware of her anxiety during social interactions in her high school years when she noticed that she actually cared about the other students' opinions:

> I think I started to be anxious in high school when social relationships became more serious. I am generally comfortable in the school but

when I feel that the outcome of my task performance may be negative, then I start feeling anxious. I can't help thinking what others might think about it. (FInt 7)

However, with some other interviewees (FInt 4), the first memories of experiencing anxiety go back to a younger age ('I have always had this problem. When I was 10 years old there were classroom representative elections. I gave a speech and I started crying'), while some others first encountered it only when they attended university:

It (my anxiety) started at university because the classroom activities demanded extra effort...I remember my first presentation in English. I looked at my friends' faces and I saw that they were all looking at me... (FInt 1)

Narrative identity level

The narrative level of anxiety concerns learners' attempts to make sense of their anxious reactions, to understand why and how those occur as well as to organise and process them through explanations and rationalisations. Interviewing, as a research method, taps into this narrative mode by definition, and the analysis of our corpus foregrounded three typical approaches the participants' narratives took, representing three reaction styles: *fighter, quitter* and *safe player.*

Fighter

Some students explicitly expressed that they would like to get rid of their anxiety, adding that they had already started developing a disposition of adopting such combative behaviour. It was promising to see that, through such a conscious stance, these students – who, we should recall, had often experienced a debilitating degree of anxiety – started to deal with their anxiety in a constructive manner, as illustrated by the following two examples:

Now I am more aware of myself. I am not as anxious as I was before. Only in a few circumstances – I am going to be a teacher of English. English language will be my job. So I cannot be an anxious teacher, right? (FInt 10)

Actually, I often criticise the anxious me and find it unnecessary to be anxious. The positive side is that I have become a person who does detailed research to be well prepared before attending to a lecture, going somewhere or doing something. I have also started reading about anxiety. What I am saying is I do not give up. I am trying to improve myself. It is getting better and I feel happier. (FInt 1)

Quitter

In contrast to the fighters, some other students perceived their anxiety in an unconstructive and non-forward-pointing manner, even though the actual symptoms they experienced were no more severe than those felt by the fighters. They became resigned to failure in trying to overcome their anxiety, as is expressed clearly by the following statement: 'I do not think I can change. It is typical me. I have always been anxious and I will always be, I know' (FInt 9). As a result, the typical coping mechanisms such students adopted were characterised by *flight* rather than fight; for example, in the following example one of the interviewees reported the intention of taking another course at university instead of the L2-related subject he was studying:

> I want to talk in the classroom but I can never take the first step. It does not matter whom or where I speak... As long as I speak in English, I am always nervous. To tell you the truth, I do not struggle. I have not attended the presentation sessions this semester and I will fail for that. I consider changing my course and study educational sciences instead of English language... (MInt 8)

Safe player

Our findings show that anxious students sometimes employ 'safety-seeking behaviours', which are measures that an individual takes to circumvent a potentially negative event. In the language classroom, these students avoid or minimise the chance of being asked to perform in the L2 by not initiating speech, avoiding eye contact, sitting at the back of the class or giving monosyllabic answers (for a detailed description of this disposition, see King, 2014; Oxford, 1999). As the following example illustrates, such behaviours can turn into a cohesive avoidance type that would also affect other aspects of the individual's everyday life:

> If I noticed an item I bought from a store was damaged I would never go there to ask for a new one. It is the same in the classroom. I never take responsibility and answer a question. Most of the time I sit at the back of the classroom. (FInt 11)

Finally, we also found examples of students who simply had not produced a clarifying narrative for themselves and thus had not constructed any cohesive meaning of their experiences. This was revealed when they indicated to us that taking part in the interview – which, by definition, pushed them into a narrative mode – played a conducive role in helping them to make sense of their experiences. For example, at the end of an interview, one participant (FInt 6) said, 'Thank you! Really... I have found that the problem is within myself because I limit myself'.

One of the most remarkable findings of our interview data has been the observation that when students managed to structure painful memories into constructive narratives, this had a 'redemptive' impact on their negative thoughts or feelings. Some individuals, for example, were ready to share their personal narratives with others, and interestingly, they seemed to coincide with the ones showing a fighting disposition. On the other hand, it seems that a reluctance to share stories with others may leave students alone with their anxious thoughts, which might in turn make it more difficult to let students process their experiences. For example, one of the interviewees has defined anxiety as a difficult concept to explain and told us how she became resigned to it, even though she attended classes:

> I can't really explain it (my anxiety). I sometimes cry after my presentations then people see how sad I feel and they try to cheer me up. This is how I am and I accepted it. (FInt 4)

When we examined our data to understand how people explained such an avoidance, it appeared that a key contributing factor involved the fact that the people concerned *feared* others' negative opinions about themselves and chose therefore not to talk about their experiences because they thought others might perceive them as a weakness; for example, 'I do not want them to think bad about me or have pity on me' (FInt 13).

The 'Anxious Self' Revisited

In the interview extracts cited in the previous section, several participants described themselves as cohesive personas – or as one participant called it, 'the anxious me' – when they operated in an anxious state, and in several cases they talked about this 'anxious self' as a side of themselves that was fairly distinct from other aspects of their existence, having a life of its own. From this perspective, the three reaction styles emerging from the narratives can be viewed as manifestations of three typical anxious self types that are given shape by the narrative level of the students' self-system. Yet, we need to stress that the anxious self concerns anxiety facets at all three levels of McAdams's three-tiered model, and the following two narratives offer illustrations of how the various dimensions contribute their unique impact to the mix.

> I attended an English Language Teaching department two years ago and I had to take an exam for preparatory year exemption. When I first arrived at the university I knew no one. I did not even know where the exam would take place. I was so anxious that I could hardly breathe. As a result, I decided not to take the exam and I went back

home. That would cost me one extra year at the university and I was depressed for a while questioning my action. After one or two months, as I started to take the preparatory class, I came to realize that I actually needed it. I was going to become an English teacher but I did not feel proficient. In a way, that year was an opportunity for me to learn English well. I also met some really nice friends. We are still in the same classroom. If I had taken that exemption test probably I would not have been in a different position. I would not be self-confident. Now I am more aware of myself. I am not as anxious as I was before. Only in a few circumstances – I am going to be a teacher of English. English language will be my job. So I cannot be an anxious teacher, right? (FInt 10)

I am generally an anxious person. Homework, not being well prepared for tasks, attempting to do something – these things often make me anxious. Sometimes I can feel my heartbeat and I feel like talking to someone to tell what has happened. ... I do not think I am worse than my classmates (in terms of English language skills) but, especially in the classroom setting, when I see my friends studying or participating more than I do, I feel anxious. I start questioning my style. I can say that I feel insecure in English. ... Actually, I often criticise the anxious me and find it unnecessary to be anxious. The positive side is that I have become a person who does detailed research to be well prepared before attending to a lecture, going somewhere or doing something. I have also started reading about anxiety. What I am saying is I do not give up. I am trying to improve myself. It is getting better and I feel happier. (FInt 1)

These extracts make it evident that both students had anxiety tendencies and suffered from these by experiencing some of the well-known symptoms. Yet, they showed marked differences at the characteristic adaptations level: the first student's anxiety mostly manifested itself in test situations, whereas the second student was more affected by the competitive perspective. The narrative level, however, shows a common feature in the two students: both of them were able to develop a cohesive narrative with a positive trajectory regarding their anxiety experiences, resulting in fight rather than flight. However, by looking at a third extract below, we can also see how some students construct counterproductive narratives that lead them to give up fighting. Even though this student reported to have chosen willingly to train to be a teacher, she had developed a narrative with a negative trajectory through her course, which resulted in the idea of changing profession.

I think it is my general personality. I do not like talking to people because I do not feel comfortable. I prefer being alone. I have always been like this and I have not questioned why. I suffer from anxiety in almost all the other classes. Of course it is worse in English because presentations and in-class speeches put extra pressure on me. I do not like these and I often feel like not doing these. During presentations, I do not know how to react, I just imitate others and I do not like it. Actually even the presence of different faces looking at me when I talk is enough to make me anxious. As I said, I normally keep with a distance from other people but when I am anxious I am even more unbearable for them. I am not that kind of a person to talk to a group of people. That makes me think about my future career and I think I should be into a less formal profession (than becoming a teacher), such as running a small coffee shop. It seems risky but I think I will take the risk. Just I need to find the strength. … I do not think I can change. It is typical me. I have always been anxious and I will always be, I know. (FInt 15)

Interestingly, as this student tried to make sense of her anxious reactions, she observed features of the communicative context that heightened her anxiety and blamed the people around her. As a result, she decided that escaping anxiety meant escaping from crowds, implying that she had better choose a job that would require less exposure to formal group talk and to interaction in general.

Conclusion

This chapter described the process of investigation whereby the concept of the 'anxious self' emerged from our data and found an accommodating theoretical paradigm in McAdams's novel, three-tiered model of personality. Our guiding assumption has been that conceiving anxiety in terms of a dynamic combination of three relatively distinct facets offers a more nuanced understanding of how anxiety affects the learners' performance across various communication situations, language tasks, content areas and contextual conditions other than the traditional dichotomy of trait and state anxiety. The novel aspect of McAdams's model is the elevation of learner narratives to an identity-dimension status, that is, viewing the way learners form cohesive verbal accounts of their relevant experiences as an integral part of the overall holistic anxiety construct. We believe that recognising the importance of learner narratives has a broad significance that goes beyond the domain of anxiety research. Similar to how narrative approaches have helped to recontextualise personality psychology (McAdams, 2006b), they can be useful to develop a more dynamic portrayal of learner characteristics in general – indeed, Dörnyei and Ryan (2015) have recently proposed a reconceptualisation of individual difference factors along these lines.

The adaptation of McAdams's framework suggests that anxiety is not uniform. There are certain tendencies that are sometimes reflected in a pure form and sometimes in combination with some other factors, with further dynamism added by the fact that people often construct cohesive life narratives that accommodate but at the same time adjust these manifestations. In this way, individuals can integrate and organise feelings in a coherent way in order to achieve a sense of consistency and control over their lives, which allows them to constructively process anxiety-provoking experiences.

Adding a narrative component to our understanding of language anxiety also has practical implications. Learner stories can be *re-narrated*, which in turn can affect the whole tenor of the anxious self, and appropriate 'redemptive' strategies might be able to turn any negative trajectories into more positive ones. In other words, we believe that helping learners to produce constructive narratives about their overall anxious selves might offer a way to reprocess their anxiety-related experiences positively, thereby combating some of the harmful effects of debilitating anxiety.

Finally, reframing anxiety as the anxious self might offer a way to link anxiety research to other areas of SLA where the importance of the self-concept has been recognised. An obvious link in this respect would be relating the anxious self to future motivational self-guides such as the ideal self, and it may also be possible to employ imagery-based strategies in shaping the anxious self in a similar manner to how the role of vision has been explored in promoting the ideal self (Dörnyei & Kubanyiova, 2014). This paper admittedly took only the first steps in these directions, leaving several questions unanswered; further research could explore, for example, the key components of narrative identity that are responsible for determining a learner's overall developmental trajectory, and future investigations could also examine how these factors are related to the anxiety facets of the two other levels (dispositional traits and characteristic adaptations). It is also likely that learner narratives vary considerably across different cultures, which raises the question as to whether there are any universally effective processing strategies for learners to rely on when trying to cope with their anxious self-images.

References

Beatty, M.J. and McCroskey, J.C. (2009) A communibiological perspective on communication apprehension. In J.A. Daly, J.C. McCroskey, J. Ayres, T. Hopf, D.M. Ayres Sonandré and K. Wongprasert (eds) *Avoiding Communication: Shyness, Reticence, and Communication Apprehension* (3rd edn, pp. 53–66). Cresskill, NJ: Hampton Press.

Boo, Z., Dörnyei, Z. and Ryan, S. (2015) L2 motivation research 2005–2014: Understanding a publication surge and a changing landscape. *System* 55, 147–157.

Bruner, J.S. (1990) *Acts of Meaning*. Cambridge, MA: Harvard University Press.

Crabtree, B.F. and Miller, W.L. (1992) A template approach to text analysis: Developing and using codebooks. In B.F. Crabtree and W.L. Miller (eds) *Doing Qualitative Research* (pp. 93–109). Newbury Park, CA: Sage.

Costa, P.T. and McCrae, R.R. (1994) Set like plaster? Evidence for the stability of adult personality. In T.F. Heatherton and J.L. Weinberger (eds) *Can Personality Change?* (pp. 21–40). Washington, DC: American Psychological Association.

Csizér, K. and Magid, M. (eds) (2014) *The Impact of Self-Concept on Language Learning*. Bristol: Multilingual Matters.

Dewaele, J.-M. (2002) Psychological and sociodemographic correlates of communicative anxiety in L2 and L3 production. *The International Journal of Bilingualism* 6, 23–39.

Dewaele, J.-M. (2010) *Emotions in Multiple Languages*. Basingstoke: Palgrave Macmillan.

Dewaele, J.-M. (2013) The link between foreign language classroom anxiety and psychoticism, extraversion, and neuroticism among adult bi- and multilinguals. *The Modern Language Journal* 97 (3), 670–684.

Dewaele, J.-M. and MacIntyre, P.D. (2014) The two faces of Janus? Anxiety and enjoyment in the foreign language classroom. *Studies in Second Language Learning and Teaching* 4 (2), 237–274.

Dörnyei, Z. (2005) *The Psychology of the Language Learner: Individual Differences in Second Language Acquisition*. Mahwah, NJ: Lawrence Erlbaum.

Dörnyei, Z. (2009a) The L2 motivational self system. In Z. Dörnyei and E. Ushioda (eds) *Motivation, Language Identity and the L2 Self* (pp. 9–42). Bristol: Multilingual Matters.

Dörnyei, Z. (2009b) *The Psychology of Second Language Acquisition*. Oxford: Oxford University Press.

Dörnyei, Z. and Kubanyiova, M. (2014) *Motivating Learners, Motivating Teachers: Building Vision in the Language Classroom*. Cambridge: Cambridge University Press.

Dörnyei, Z. and Ryan, S. (2015) *The Psychology of the Language Learner Revisited*. New York: Routledge.

Dörnyei, Z. and Ushioda, E. (2011) *Teaching and Researching Motivation*. Harlow: Longman.

Edelmann, R.J. (1992) *Anxiety: Theory, Research and Intervention in Clinical and Health Psychology*. Chichester: John Wiley.

Eysenck, H.J. and Eysenck, M.W. (1985) *Personality and Individual Differences: A Natural Science Approach*. New York: Plenum Press.

Eysenck, M.W. (1979) Anxiety, learning, and memory: A reconceptualization. *Journal of Research in Personality* 13 (4), 363–385.

Eysenck, M.W. (1997) *Anxiety and Cognition: A Unified Theory*. Hove: Psychology Press.

Goldberg, L.R. (1993) The structure of phenotypic personality traits. *American Psychologist* 48 (1), 26–34.

Gray, J.A. (1982) *The Neuropsychology of Anxiety: An Enquiry into the Functions of the Septo-Hippocampal System*. Oxford: Oxford University Press.

Gregersen, T. and Horwitz, E.K. (2002) Language learning and perfectionism: Anxious and non-anxious language learners' reactions to their own oral performance. *The Modern Language Journal* 86 (4), 562–570.

Habermas, T. and Bluck, S. (2000) Getting a life: The emergence of the life story in adolescence. *Psychological Bulletin* 126 (5), 748–769.

Horwitz, E.K. (1990) Attending to the affective domain in the foreign language classroom. In S.S. Magnam (ed.) *Shifting the Instructional Focus to the Learner* (pp. 15–33). Middlebury, VT: Northeast Conference on the Teaching of Foreign Languages.

Horwitz, E.K., Horwitz, M.B. and Cope, J. (1986) Foreign language classroom anxiety. *The Modern Language Journal* 70 (2), 125–132.

Huang, H.-T.D. and Hung, S.-T.A. (2013) Comparing the effects of test anxiety on independent and integrated speaking test performance. *TESOL Quarterly* 47 (2), 244–269.

John, O.P., Donahue, E.M. and Kentle, R.L. (1991) *The Big Five Inventory – Versions 4a and 54*. Berkeley, CA: University of California, Berkeley, Institute of Personality and Social Research.

John, O.P., Naumann, L.P. and Soto, C.J. (2008) Paradigm shift to the integrative big five trait taxonomy: History, measurement, and conceptual issues. In O.P. John, R.W. Robins and L.A. Pervin (eds) *Handbook of Personality: Theory and Research* (pp. 114–158). New York: Guilford Press.

King, J. (2014) Fear of the true self: Social anxiety and the silent behaviour of Japanese learners of English. In K. Csizér and M. Magid (eds) *The Impact of Self-Concept on Language Learning* (pp. 232–249). Bristol: Multilingual Matters.

Kleinmann, H.H. (1977) Avoidance behaviour in adult second language acquisition. *Language Learning* 27, 93–107.

MacIntyre, P.D. (1995) How does anxiety affect second language learning? A reply to Sparks and Ganschow. *The Modern Language Journal* 79 (1), 90–99.

MacIntyre, P.D. (1999) Language anxiety: A review of the research for language teachers. In D.J. Young (ed.) *Affect in Foreign Language and Second Language Learning: A Practical Guide to Creating a Low-Anxiety Classroom Atmosphere* (pp. 24–45). Boston, MA: McGraw-Hill.

MacIntyre, P.D. and Gardner, R.C. (1989) Anxiety and second-language learning: Toward a theoretical clarification. *Language Learning* 39 (2), 251–275.

MacIntyre, P.D. and MacDonald, J.R. (1998) Public speaking anxiety: Perceived competence and audience congeniality. *Communication Education* 47 (4), 359–365.

Matsuda, S. and Gobel, P. (2004) Anxiety and predictors of performance in the foreign language classroom. *System* 32 (1), 21–36.

McAdams, D. (2006a) The role of narrative in personality psychology today. *Narrative Inquiry* 16 (1), 11–18.

McAdams, D.P. (2006b) *The Redemptive Self: Stories Americans Live By*. New York: Oxford University Press.

McAdams, D.P. and Pals, J.L. (2006) A new big five: Fundamental principles for an integrative science of personality. *American Psychologist* 61 (3), 204–217.

McAdams, D.P. and McLean, K.C. (2013) Narrative identity. *Current Directions in Psychological Science* 22 (3), 233–238.

McCrae, R.R. and Costa, P.T. Jr (2003) *Personality in Adulthood: A Five-Factor Theory Perspective* (2nd edn). New York: Guilford Press.

McCrae, R.R. and Costa, P.T. Jr (2008) The five-factor theory of personality. In O.P. John, R.W. Robins and L.A. Pervin (eds) *Handbook of Personality: Theory and Research* (3rd edn; pp. 159–191). New York: Guilford.

McCrae, R.R. and John O.P. (1992) An introduction to the five-factor model and its applications. *Journal of Personality* 60 (2), 175–215.

Oxford, R.L. (1999) Anxiety and the language learner: New insights. In J. Arnold (ed.) *Affect in Language Learning* (pp. 58–67). Cambridge: Cambridge University Press.

Park, G.-P. and French, B.F. (2013) Gender differences in the Foreign Language Classroom Anxiety Scale. *System* 41 (2), 462–471.

Phillips, E.M. (1992) The effects of language anxiety on students' oral test performance and attitudes. *The Modern Language Journal* 76, 14–26.

Sarason, I.G. (1986) Test anxiety, worry and cognitive interference. In R. Schwarzer (ed.) *Self-Related Cognitions in Anxiety and Motivation* (pp. 19–34). Hillsdale, NJ: Lawrence Erlbaum.

Scovel, T. (1978) The effect of affect on foreign language learning: A review of the anxiety research. *Language Learning* 28 (1), 129–142.

Simpson, M.E. (1980) Societal support and education. In I.W. Kutask and L.B. Schlesinger (eds) *Handbook on Stress and Anxiety* (pp. 451–462). San Francisco, CA: Jossey-Bass.

Spielberger, C.D. (1972) Anxiety as an emotional state. In C.D. Spielberger (ed.) *Anxiety: Current Trends in Theory and Research* (Vol. 1 , pp. 23–49). New York: Academic Press.

Spielmann, G. and Radnofsky, M.L. (2001) Learning language under tension: New directions from a qualitative study. *The Modern Language Journal* 85 (2), 259–278.

Woodrow, L. (2006) Anxiety and speaking English as a second language. *RELC Journal* 37, 308–328.

Yan, J.X. and Horwitz, E.K. (2008) Learners' perceptions of how anxiety interacts with personal and instructional factors to influence their achievement in English: A qualitative analysis of EFL learners in China. *Language Learning* 58 (1), 151–183.

Young, D.J. (1991) Creating a low-anxiety classroom environment: What does language anxiety research suggest? *The Modern Language Journal* 75 (4), 426–439.

Zeidner, M. (1998) *Test Anxiety: The State of the Art*. New York: Plenum.

5 Are Perfectionists More Anxious Foreign Language Learners and Users?

Jean-Marc Dewaele

Introduction

In the introduction to her overview of the research on FLCA, Horwitz (2010: 154) points out that 'It is intuitive that anxiety would inhibit the learning and/or production of a second language (L2)'. It is therefore not surprising that FLA/FLCA, defined as 'the worry and negative emotional reaction aroused when learning or using a second language' (MacIntyre, 1999: 27) and categorised as a situation-specific anxiety, is undoubtedly the most popular psychological variable in studies on second or foreign language acquisition.[1] Horwitz et al. (1986: 128) defined FLCA as 'a distinct complex of self-perceptions, beliefs, feelings and behaviours related to classroom learning arising from the uniqueness of the language learning process'. FLCA within a classroom environment can severely affect learners. Horwitz (2010) observes that most early work addressed the nature of FLA/FLCA, contrasting or relating it to other types of anxiety and focusing on the effects of FLA/FLCA on foreign language (FL) achievement. Later research was more interested in the 'sources of FLA and its stability or variation under different instructional or sociocultural conditions, the relationship of FLA with other learner factors (...)' (Horwitz, 2010: 154). The present study is clearly situated in this more recent field of inquiry, namely the relationship between FLA/FLCA and other psychological dimensions in FL learners and among FL users (Dewaele, 2002, 2012, 2013a; Dewaele & Al Saraj, 2015; Dewaele et al., 2008; Wang, 2010).

The main independent variable in the present study is Perfectionism. The relationship between FLA and Perfectionism has never been investigated on a large scale. The first study to date was by Gregersen and Horwitz (2002: 569), who compared the feedback from four low-anxiety FL students with that of four highly anxious students and suggested that the Perfectionism/FLA relationship should be investigated 'in a variety of learning groups at various stages of language learning'. With quantitative data collected from over 400 FL learners and users in three different continents, the present study will do just that.

Literature Review

The link between sociobiographical, psychological variables and FLA/FLCA

FLA has been linked to a large number of variables reflecting an individual's linguistic profile and linguistic history, as well as sociobiographical and psychological variables (Dewaele, 2012). Onwuegbuzie et al. (1999, 2000) found levels of FLA among American university students in FL classes to be linked to age and academic and FL achievement, previous contact with FLs, perceived scholastic competence, self-worth, intellectual ability and job competence. Participants who had had contact with FLs and who felt competent suffered less from FLA. The effect of perceived FL ability and the amount of contact with the FL on FLCA was confirmed in later research (see Liu & Chen, 2014; Thompson & Lee, 2013b).

An investigation into FLA in up to four FLs of more than 1500 adult multilinguals revealed that lower levels of FLA were linked to an earlier onset of acquisition of the FL, especially in combination with regular authentic use of the FL during the learning phase, frequent current use of the FL, strong FL socialisation and a large network of interlocutors with whom the FL is used regularly (Dewaele, 2013b). While the effects of gender were limited, higher age and education level were linked to significantly lower FLA in various FLs. A number of studies have uncovered significant gender effects, with females scoring higher on FLA/FLCA (Dewaele & MacIntyre, 2014; Park & French, 2013). Dewaele, MacIntyre, Boudreau & Dewaele (2016) carried out a detailed analysis of the data from 1746 FL learners from around the world on eight FLCAS items and found that female participants scored significantly higher on items reflecting mild forms of FLCA compared with male participants; they worried significantly more than their male peers about their mistakes and were less confident in using the FL. However, no difference emerged for items reflecting paralysing FLCA (Dewaele et al., 2016). More multilingual individuals seem to suffer less from FLA in both the first language (L1) and all FLs (Dewaele, 2007; Dewaele et al., 2008; Dewaele, 2010, 2013b; Thompson & Lee, 2013a). Levels of FLA have also been found to increase significantly, and linearly, in languages that pentalinguals had acquired later in life (Dewaele, 2013b). The typological distance between the target language and existing languages in the learner's repertoire also influences FLA, with lower FLA for target languages that belong to a familiar linguistic family (Dewaele, 2010).

One area of FLA research that is in full expansion is that of psychological dimensions linked to FLA (Wang, 2010). This makes perfect sense, as MacIntyre and colleagues (1998: 547) included 'Personality' (together with 'intergroup climate') in the first layer of their second language (L2) Willingness to Communicate (WTC) pyramid model. This layer, named 'social and individual context', represents the 'stable, enduring influences' (MacIntyre et al., 1998: 547) that might be at force when communicating in an L2. MacIntyre et al. (1998) argue that more research is needed on the precise mapping between variables of various layers, including the affective–cognitive context (Layer 5), the motivational propensities (Layer 4), situated antecedents (Layer 3), behavioural intention (Layer 2) and communication behaviour (Layer 1).

Dewaele (2002) looked at whether Extraversion (E), Psychoticism (P) and Neuroticism (N) were linked to communicative anxiety across 100 participants' L2 and third language (L3) to identify to what extent FLA is a stable personality trait in advanced language learners. No significant correlation emerged between the three personality variables and levels of FLA in students' French L2; however, students with higher levels of Extraversion and Psychoticism and lower levels of Neuroticism suffered significantly less from FLA in their English L3.

A further study (Dewaele, 2013a) revealed a significant positive relationship between Neuroticism and the L2 FLCA of 86 adult multilingual students enrolled in the French department at the University of London. A similar relationship emerged in the L3 in a subgroup of 66 students. A comparable pattern was found in a second group of 62 Spanish students. The relationship between Neuroticism and FLCA was significant in the students' L2, L3 and L4. It is likely that participants with higher scores on the Neuroticism scale were more worried about how their FL performance would be judged.

Dewaele and Al Saraj (2015) extended the investigation of the links between FLCA and personality using an Arabic version of the Multicultural Personality Questionnaire–Short Form (van der Zee et al., 2013) and the Arabic Foreign Language Anxiety Questionnaire (Dewaele & Al Saraj, 2013) with 348 Arabic learners of English. Multiple regression analyses revealed that more proficient and frequent users of English felt significantly less anxious (explaining over a third of the variance in FLCA) (see also Thompson & Lee, 2013b). Emotionally stable and more extraverted participants scored significantly lower on FLCA (explaining a further fifth of the variance in FLCA).

Emotional intelligence also turned out to be linked to FLA among 464 multilingual FL users, with participants scoring higher on Emotional Intelligence reporting significantly lower levels of FLA across their different languages (Dewaele *et al.*, 2008). A string of sociobiographical variables was also linked to FLA: participants reported higher levels of FLA for languages learnt later in life. Lower levels of FLA were linked to an early age of onset, FL instruction that also involved the extracurricular use of the language, the knowledge of more languages, a higher frequency of use, a stronger socialisation in a language, a larger network of interlocutors and a higher level of self-perceived proficiency in the FL. No clear gender or education effects emerged, but older participants' reported less FLA, possibly because of their vaster experience as multilingual speakers.

Finally, Dewaele and Shan Ip (2013) found that Second Language Tolerance of Ambiguity was a significant predictor of FLCA in English among 73 secondary school students in Hong Kong. Participants who were less tolerant of ambiguity reported significantly higher levels of FLCA. Second Language Tolerance of Ambiguity predicted 50% of the variance in FLCA. Table 5.1 presents an overview of the variables linked to FLA/FLCA.

Perfectionism

Perfectionism can be a blessing or a curse, depending on how perfectionist a person is. Some researchers have suggested that public self-consciousness is linked to social anxiety, primarily in perfectionists who are concerned about their mistakes, doubt their actions and who perceive perfectionist demands from their social environment. It is thus possible that social anxiety actually fosters Perfectionism (Saboonchi & Lundh, 1997).

Similarly, Hewitt and Flett (1991) referred to the relationship between anxiety and two aspects of Perfectionism, mainly self-orientated and socially prescribed Perfectionism. Self-orientated perfectionists' exaggerated concerns over their performance are said to stem from their desire to remedy the gap between their real self and their ideal self-image. Their low self-image and their lack of confidence are associated with anxiety. Socially prescribed perfectionists' inability to fulfil others' expectations and their inability to avoid criticism and negative evaluations are also linked to anxiety.

Perfectionism is not necessarily a negative trait, as Stoeber *et al.* (2010) demonstrated. They found that Perfectionism was linked to higher performance in a sample of 100 British university students performing a simple letter-detection task. They found positive correlations between degree of Perfectionism and both time on task and task performance. Regarding subjective effort, more perfectionist students reported focusing more on accuracy than on speed compared with students low in perfectionistic strivings.

Gregersen and Horwitz (2002) were the first researchers to look at the relationship between Perfectionism and FLCA. They noted the obvious similarities between descriptions of FLCA and Perfectionism and were

Table 5.1 Variables linked to FLA

Variable	Directionality of FLA	Studies
Second Language Tolerance of Ambiguity	Negative	Dewaele & Shan Ip, 2013
Emotional Intelligence	Negative	Dewaele et al., 2008
Extraversion	Negative	Dewaele, 2002; Dewaele & Al Saraj, 2015
Neuroticism	Positive	Dewaele, 2002, 2013a; Dewaele & Al Saraj, 2015
Psychoticism	Positive	Dewaele, 2002
Perfectionism	Positive	Dewaele (this volume); Gregersen & Horwitz, 2002; Pishghadam & Akhondpoor, 2011
Proficiency in FL	Negative	Dewaele et al., 2008; Dewaele & Al Saraj, 2015; Liu, 2006; Liu & Chen, 2014; Onwuegbuzie et al., 1999, 2000; Thompson & Lee, 2013b
Frequency of use of FL	Negative	Dewaele, 2010, 2013b; Dewaele & Al Saraj, 2015; Liu & Chen, 2014; Onwuegbuzie et al., 1999, 2000; Thompson & Lee, 2013b
Socialisation in FL	Negative	Dewaele, 2010, 2013b
Network of FL interlocutors	Negative	Dewaele, 2010, 2013b
Perceived scholastic competence	Negative	Onwuegbuzie et al., 1999, 2000
Self-worth	Negative	Onwuegbuzie et al., 1999, 2000
Intellectual ability	Negative	Onwuegbuzie et al., 1999, 2000
Job competence	Negative	Onwuegbuzie et al., 1999, 2000
Academic achievement	Negative	Onwuegbuzie et al., 1999, 2000
Age of onset in learning FL	Negative	Dewaele et al., 2008, 2013b
Number of languages known	Negative	Dewaele, 2007; 2010, 2013b; Dewaele et al., 2008; Thompson & Lee, 2013a
Late in chronology of acquisition of languages	Positive	Dewaele et al., 2008; Dewaele, 2013b
Context of acquisition including authentic use FL	Negative	Dewaele et al., 2008; 2013b
Typological distance between L1 and FL	Positive	Dewaele, 2010
Social class	Negative	Dewaele, 2002
Education level	Negative	Dewaele, 2013b
Age	Negative	Dewaele, 2013b; Onwuegbuzie et al., 1999, 2000
Gender	Females more FLA	Dewaele & MacIntyre, 2014; Dewaele et al., 2016; Park & French, 2013

compelled to explore any links, given that 'as for language learners, the success of perfectionists is often impeded because they spend their energy avoiding mistakes rather than focusing on learning' (Gregersen & Horwitz, 2002: 563). The authors described the aspects of Perfectionism that may prove debilitating in any learning situation using Brophy's (1999) account of working with perfectionist students. These include 'motivation from fear of failure than from pursuit of success', 'procrastination in getting started on work that will be judged' and 'all or nothing evaluations that label anything other than perfection as a failure' (Gregersen & Horwitz, 2002: 563). They also add other commonly observed behaviours of their own such as 'unwillingness to volunteer to respond to questions unless they are certain of the correct answer' and 'low productivity due to procrastination or excessive "start overs"' (Gregersen & Horwitz, 2002). The researchers video-recorded the four most anxious and the four least anxious second-year language students (out of a pool of 78 students in a Chilean university who had already completed the FCLAS [Horwitz *et al.*, 1986]) in order to observe their reactions as they watched themselves communicate in a previously videoed five-minute presentation. The feedback was subsequently analysed by research assistants who classified the results into a number of Perfectionism indicators based on Brophy's (1999) report, namely, 'personal performance standards', procrastination, emotional responses to evaluation and 'error-consciousness'. The authors found that the anxious learners scored significantly higher than the non-anxious learners on all of these metrics, indicating that the most anxious students were also more inclined towards perfectionist tendencies. Though the numbers involved in this study were arguably too small to establish a pattern, given that the group was homogenous and all of the participants 'felt that they had the potential to become English teachers' (Gregersen & Horwitz, 2000: 569), the finding that the anxious and non-anxious learners differed 'vastly' (Gregersen & Horwitz, 2000: 568) with respect to their responses to their own target language performance is a vital one that certainly calls for further research.

The second study looking at the link between FLA and Perfectionism used a quantitative design (Pishghadam & Akhondpoor, 2011). In this methodologically shaky paper, the authors looked for correlations between 300 Iranian Bachelor of Arts English majors' self-reported scores on four skills in English L2 (reading, listening, speaking and writing), grade point average (GPA) and Perfectionism. Students completed a locally developed scale, the Ahwaz Perfectionism Scale. The authors, who did not use any Bonferroni correction for multiple correlations, reported significant ($p<0.05$) negative correlations between Perfectionism and grades for speaking, reading and listening, as well as GPA. They also reported much stronger positive correlations between Perfectionism scores and Spielberger's trait and state anxiety scores, although they report the same significance values ($p<0.05$).

The Development of the Frost Multidimensional Perfectionism Scale

Researchers in the 1970s and 1980s still tended to regard Perfectionism as a general construct that could either be adaptive or maladaptive (Burns, 1980; Hamachek, 1978; Pacht, 1984). It was not until the 1990s that researchers recognised the need to consider Perfectionism from many different angles in order to be able to accurately represent the complex interplay of peoples' individual differences and develop instruments to test the various known theories. Initial efforts to formalise this multiplicity began with Frost *et al.* (1990), who conducted factor analyses on items from several existing scales (Burns, 1980), adding items of their own in order to prove multidimensionality. This culminated in the FMPS, which operationalised Perfectionism as being heavily loaded on Concern Over Mistakes (CM) and to a lesser extent on components reflecting Personal Standards (PS), Doubt About Actions (D), Parental Expectations (PE), Parental Criticism (PC) and Organization (O).

The FMPS has six subscales, measured by 35 items: five items for parental expectations (e.g. 'My parents set very high standards for me'), six items for organisation (e.g. 'Organisation is very important to me'), four items for parental criticism (e.g. 'As a child, I was punished for doing things less than perfect'), seven items for personal standards (e.g. 'I set higher goals than most people'), four items for doubts about actions (e.g. 'I usually have doubts about the simple everyday things I do') and nine items for concern over mistakes (e.g. 'I should be upset if I make a mistake').

Perfectionism is perceived as a continuous construct and the FMPS's aim is to measure the degree, rather than the type, of Perfectionism (Broman-Fulks *et al.*, 2008).

The instrument is multidimensional because it includes both positive and negative aspects. It hence acknowledges that, in its maladaptive form, Perfectionism drives people to chase an unattainable ideal (which can happen with people scoring high on Neuroticism), while in its adaptive form it can encourage people to reach a distant goal.

Grzegorek *et al.* (2004) found that maladaptive perfectionist scores were strongly correlated with self-critical depression while adaptive perfectionist scores were correlated with higher self-esteem and greater satisfaction with GPA.

Personal standards

Hamachek (1978) distinguishes between the 'normal' and the 'neurotic' perfectionist, which is important given that it is necessary to acknowledge the methodological difficulty of separating out psychopathologically perfectionist people from those who are highly accomplished and effective.

In order to illustrate his view of how the two types might differ, he compares the emotions typically involved in achieving a goal, claiming that 'normal' perfectionists 'derive a very real sense of pleasure from the labors of a painstaking effort and [....] feel free to be less precise as the situation permits', whereas 'neurotic' perfectionists are 'unable to feel satisfaction because in their own eyes, they never seem to do things good enough to warrant that feeling' (Hamachek, 1978: 27). This idea of setting excessive or unattainable personal standards is central to Hamachek's paper and he discusses how the perception of not meeting these can have serious consequences for the 'neurotic' perfectionist, such as lowered self-esteem, heightened anxiety around performing tasks and even a vulnerability to suicide. This notion of a tendency to be too harsh in self-evaluation also emerged in Burns (1980). Burns (1980: 34) observed that 'perfectionist individuals are likely to respond to the perception of failure or inadequacy with a precipitous loss in self-esteem that can trigger episodes of severe depression and anxiety'. Burns labelled this concept as 'all-or-nothing thinking' (Burns, 1980: 38). Pacht (1984: 387) also referred to this rigidity in terms of the standards that perfectionists set themselves, naming it the 'God/scum phenomenon' whereby '[perfectionists] are unable to recognise that there is a middle ground'. Both Burns (1980) and Pacht (1984) agreed that achieving flawlessness is so linked with a perfectionist's self-worth that the impact can be devastating when success is not realised, even extending to issues in their personal relationships because 'they tend to react defensively to criticism', which in turn 'usually frustrates and alienates others' (Burns, 1980: 37). This is a kind of self-fulfilling prophesy according to Pacht (1984: 387), because 'constantly frustrated by their need to achieve and their failure to do so', perfectionists ultimately 'see themselves as unlovable and lonely'.

Concern over mistakes

Further commonality between Hamachek (1978) and Burns (1980) is the recognition of the avoidance techniques employed by perfectionists to circumvent achieving less than perfection in activities. According to Hamachek (1978: 27), perfectionists 'commonly report feeling anxious, confused and emotionally drained before a new task has begun', which may indeed explain the delay in onset of tasks. Burns (1980: 37) also noted an extreme manifestation of procrastination, which he labels 'the dropout phenomenon'. He witnessed how some first-year university law students 'react with frustration, anger, depression and panic' when they have to face the reality that they may suddenly have to play an 'average' role' in their year group (Burns, 1980). Dewaele and Thirtle (2009: 636) found a similar pattern among 14- and 15-year-old FL learners for whom FLCA was a precursor to the 'abandonment of FL learning'. Educationally speaking, it seems Perfectionism is a threat for individuals who are unable to adjust to a new situation or ranking by being realistic about their personal limitations.

Gregersen and Horwitz (2002) based their descriptions of Perfectionism on Brophy's (1999) concept of this trait, which was based on Pacht's (1984: 386) conceptualisation, which is intuitive rather than systematic. Pacht himself admitted as much: 'This article is not based on data but rather represents my personal reflections on the subject, it would be labelled in most psychological circles, as unscientific'. This may have suited Gregersen's and Horwitz's purpose, which was to produce a qualitative account of the potential relationships between Perfectionism and FLCA in order to provide some pedagogical insights. However, it seems unsatisfactory for a larger, systematic, empirical, quantitative study, which is the reason why the FMPS and the Japanese version, the *Multidimensional Self-oriented Perfectionism Scale* (MSPS) (Sakurai & Ohtani, 1997), were chosen.

The FMPS operationalises Perfectionism as being heavily loaded on Concern Over Mistakes (CM) and to a lesser extent on components reflecting Personal Standards (PS), Doubt About Actions (D), Parental Expectations (PE), Parental Criticism (PC) and Organization (O). The FMPS has been generally adopted by researchers and clinicians.

Stoeber and Joormann (2001) looked at the correlations between Perfectionism, procrastination and worry. Using the FMPS, they found that worry, which they believed had a 'substantial overlap' with anxiety (Stoeber & Joormann, 2001: 50), strongly correlated with both procrastination and two dimensions of Perfectionism in particular, namely, 'perfectionist concern over mistakes and doubts' (Stoeber & Joormann, 2001: 49). The authors believed that this combination could in some way be responsible for the maintenance of the phenomenon, in other words, the individual's inability to face up to or deal with issues resulting in these becoming magnified or piling up. This can have a negative impact on learning as the fear of making mistakes may lead to a continuous deferral of tasks. In Frost *et al.* (1990), four out of six of their proposed subscales of Perfectionism in the FMPS, including 'Concern over Mistakes', correlated significantly with either frequency or severity of procrastination.

Aside from the actual extent of concern about making mistakes, another manifestation of perfectionist tendencies appears to be reporting 'a vague sense of doubt about the quality of one's performance' (Frost *et al.*, 1990: 451). Frost *et al.* (1990: 451) described perfectionists' seeming 'reluctance to complete a task'. Gregersen and Horwitz (2002) also recognised this phenomenon with respect to their (university) language students, citing Brophy (1999) and referring to perfectionists' long delays in completing assignments and their repeated starting over of assignments. Perfectionists are seen as 'compulsives' who, due to their obsession with being 'flawless', have 'trouble sensing when the point of diminishing returns has been reached and when a task has been considered complete' (Burns, 1980: 38). This is the behaviour that Frost *et al.* (1990: 453) refer to as Doubting of Actions in their FMPS.

Saboonchi and Lundh (1997) investigated the nature of the relationship between Perfectionism and anxiety. They looked at the links between various subscales of Perfectionism and different types of anxiety. They found that Concern over Mistakes, Doubts about Actions and socially prescribed Perfectionism correlated with Social Anxiety. The most significant correlation was found between Concern over Mistakes and Social Anxiety.

Organisation

Frost *et al.* (1990) included the notion of orderliness as one of six components of their model. However, there is only a very short discussion around any maladaptive practice of organisation, that is, 'an overemphasis on neatness' (Frost *et al.*, 1990: 451). 'Organization' was a preliminary step 'to test whether Perfectionism was related to a broad range of symptoms of psychopathology among normal individuals' (Frost *et al.*, 1990: 458).

Parental expectations and parental criticism

No model of Perfectionism is complete without a discussion of its possible causes. Parental beliefs and behaviours are generally thought to have a substantial influence on a child's likelihood to acquire perfectionist tendencies. Frost *et al.* (1990: 451) described them as 'integral and perhaps central components of Perfectionism'. Quite how important they are is evident from the weightings given to these constructs in the eventual FMPS (9 of a total of 35 items). Burns (1980: 41) saw this aspect as fundamental and described a child's notion 'that mistakes will lead to a loss of acceptance' when a parent withholds comfort and affection whenever that child is less than 100% successful. Pacht (1984) similarly observed that many adults are still striving for perfection in order to be rewarded with parental love. Interestingly, parental influences on Perfectionism are not included in the Gregersen and Horwitz (2002) study.

Methodology

Data were collected from three distinct groups of FL learners and users of English: an international group of adult FL users, a group of university students from Saudi Arabia learning English and a group of high school pupils from Japan learning English. Similar instruments were used, which were adapted to the local situation.

Study 1: The international group

A total of 58 adult multilingual, FL users of English (15 males and 43 females) participated in Study 1. They completed an online questionnaire after being contacted in targeted emails to multilingual colleagues who were asked to pass it onto their multilingual adult families, friends and associates in a snowball fashion. The age range of the participants was between 18 and 54 years with an average age of 30.6 years (standard deviation [SD]=9.5). The 58 participants spoke a very diverse set of L1s: the most frequent L1 was Chinese (n=9), followed by Spanish (n=7), French (n=6), Japanese (n=5), German (n=4), Basque (n=3), Polish (n=3) and Portuguese (n=3); other L1s included Arabic, Catalan, Croatian, Hindi, Hungarian, Italian, Malayalam, Mauritian Creole, Persian, Romanian, Russian, Serbian, Swedish and Thai. The participants shared 25 distinct nationalities, with Spanish (n=9) and Chinese (n=8) making up the largest groups. They also reported 17 countries of residence, with a third of participants residing in the United Kingdom. Of the 58 participants, 8 reported they were bilingual, 20 trilingual, 19 quadrilingual, 8 pentalingual and a further 3 reported knowledge of at least one further language.

Most participants (45 out of 58) had English as their L2, with the remaining 13 participants having English as their L3. They had studied English for an average of 13.2 years and were living in London at the time of the survey. Participants were quite highly educated: 7 had A-level equivalent education, 16 had a BA degree, 24 had an MA and 11 a PhD.

Perfectionism was measured using the FMPS (Frost *et al.*, 1990). Responses to the 35 statements were invited using a five-point Likert-scale format: 'strongly disagree (1); agree (2); neutral (3); agree (4) or strongly agree (5)'. Scores on this dimension ranged from 58 to 155, with a mean of 101.7 (SD=21.2). A one-sample Kolmogorov–Smirnov (KS) test showed that the distribution was normal (KS Z=0.78, p=non-significant [*ns*]).

Participants' self-reported levels of FLA outside the classroom context were determined using six items that were adapted from Taguchi *et al.*'s (2009) instrument. Internal consistency of the items was high (Cronbach's alpha=0.88). Example items from the scale are: 'I am worried that other speakers of English would find my English strange' and 'I get tense when addressed in English'. Responses to these scale items were measured on a six-point Likert rating scale with possible responses ranging from Never (1) to Always (6). Scores on this dimension ranged from 6 to 29, with a mean of 13.9 (SD=6.1). A one-sample Kolmogorov–Smirnov test confirmed that the distribution was normal (KS Z=0.26, p=*ns*).

Study 2: The Saudi group

A total of 69 undergraduate English majors (49 females, 20 males) at the Imam Mohammad Bin Saud University in Riyadh, Saudi Arabia participated in the study.

Their ages ranged from 21 to 32, with an average of 23.2 years ($SD=2$). All students spoke English besides L1 Arabic. They had studied English for at least six years as a compulsory subject in their intermediate and secondary education, where English was taught for at least three hours a week.

Five students spoke three languages and one spoke four. Other languages included Korean, French, Spanish and Japanese. Six students reported having lived abroad in an English-speaking country. The length of their stay ranged from four months to two years. In order to ensure that students understood the questions, Arabic versions of the scales were distributed. Back translation was used to ensure accurate and reliable translation of the FMPS (Frost *et al.*, 1990).

Data from the FLCAS came in the form of values on five-point Likert scales: Strongly agree=5, Agree=4, Neither agree nor disagree=3, Disagree=2 and Strongly disagree=1. The values were reversed for nine negatively worded items. Scores on this dimension ranged from 42 to 137, with a mean of 96.2 ($SD=19.7$). A one-sample Kolmogorov–Smirnov test showed that the distribution of FLCA scores was normal (KS $Z=1.1$, $p=ns$).

The Cronbach alpha value for the whole scale was 0.90. Scores ranged from 56 to 154, with a mean of 116 ($SD=20.7$). A one-sample Kolmogorov–Smirnov test showed that the distribution of the Perfectionism scores was normal (KS $Z=1.2$, $p=ns$).

Study 3: The Japanese group

A total of 323 Japanese participants (228 males and 95 females) completed an online questionnaire. The mean age was 16.3 years ($SD=0.5$), ranging from 16 to 18 years old. All were high school students with Japanese as an L1 and were studying English as an L2 at school.

Data were collected through an open-access web-based questionnaire and through a pen-and-paper-based version of the questionnaire that was distributed among adolescents at two private high schools in Japan; 258 responses were collected. This data collection process was conducted due to ease of access and to maximise the response rate. It was more efficient to ask high school students to fill out the questionnaire face-to-face in the classroom than to devise a way to conduct internet-based research with them.

Because some participants' English proficiency could have been too low to answer the questions in English, all the material – except the MSPS, which is in Japanese – was translated into Japanese. A doctoral student of educational psychology at the University of Tokyo used the back translation method in order to check the validity of the translation. The Cronbach's alpha value for the whole scale was 0.86. Scores ranged from 32 to 115, with a mean of 76.1 ($SD=12.8$). A one-sample Kolmogorov–Smirnov test showed that the distribution of the Perfectionism scores was normal (KS $Z=1.1$, $p=ns$).

Five items were extracted from FLCAS (Horwitz et al., 1986) and translated into Japanese: 'I can feel my heart pounding when I'm going to be called on in language class'; 'It embarrasses me to volunteer answers in my language class'; 'I worry about mistakes in language class'; 'I'm afraid the other students will laugh at me when I speak the foreign language'; and 'I get nervous when the language teacher asks questions which I haven't prepared in advance'. Students were asked to express their agreement or disagreement with these statements using a five-point Likert scale. The Cronbach's alpha value for the five items was 0.83, which is high. The sum of the five items constitutes the FLCA measure. The mean score was 16.6 ($SD=5.0$), with scores ranging from 5 to 28. A one-sample Kolmogorov–Smirnov test showed that the distribution of the FLCA scores was normal (KS $Z=1.3$, $p=0.051$).

Perfectionism was assessed using the MSPS, which is based on the FMPS but focuses on the self-oriented dimension of Perfectionism (Sakurai & Oya, 1997). It is a 20-item scale that measures both positive and negative dimensions of Perfectionism and is composed of four subscales. The positive dimension comprises Personal Standards (e.g. 'I always set higher goals than other people') whereas the negative dimension is captured by Concern over Mistakes (e.g. 'Even a small mistake equals complete failure for me') and Doubting of Actions (e.g. 'I sometimes worry that I might have left something undone'). The final subscale is Desire for Perfection (e.g. 'My motto is to achieve perfectly no matter what I do'). Participants responded to all items on a six-point Likert scale ranging from (1) Strongly Disagree, (2) Disagree, (3) Slightly Disagree, (4) Slightly Agree, (5) Agree and (6) Strongly Agree. With respect to its psychometric properties, the MSPS has strong internal consistency and concurrent validity with other scales (Sakurai & Oya, 1997). This scale was chosen for Study 3 because it was originally developed in Japanese, using Japanese samples.

Parametric statistics were used in the three studies, including Pearson correlation analyses, t-tests and one-way analysis of variance (ANOVA). Bonferroni corrections were applied when performing multiple analyses.

Research Questions and Hypotheses

(1) What is the link between Perfectionism and FLA/FLCA in the three groups? Based on the previous literature, a positive relationship between them is expected.

(2) Which subscales from Perfectionism are most closely linked to FLA/FLCA in the three groups? A positive link is hypothesised between Concern over Mistakes, Doubting over Action and FLA/FLCA.

(3) Are sociobiographical variables (age, gender, education level, number of languages known) linked to Perfectionism and FLA/FLCA in the three groups? No clear hypothesis can be formulated as the findings in the literature are quite divergent.

Results

Study 1: The international group

Overall Perfectionism and FLA are significantly and positively correlated ($r=0.380$, $p<0.001$, $n=58$). This result suggests that both dimensions share 14.4% of the variance, which can be described as a small effect size (Cohen, 1992).[2] It suggests that the more perfectionist respondents reported being, the higher their anxiety levels when using English FL (see Figure 5.1).

Further analysis of the link between sub-dimensions of Perfectionism and FLA showed that only two of the six sub-dimensions of Perfectionism correlated significantly ($p<0.008$ with Bonferroni correction) with FLA, namely, Concern over Mistakes ($r=0.456$, $p<0.0001$, $n=58$) and Doubts about Action ($r=0.637$, $p<0.0001$, $n=58$). In other words, the greater an individual's reported propensity for these particular perfectionist behaviours, the higher his/her reported levels of English FLA.

An analysis of the relationships between Perfectionism, FLA and sociobiographical variables revealed a significant negative correlation between age and FLA ($r=-0.44$, $p<0.001$, $n=58$), but no relationship existed between age and Perfectionism ($r=-0.24$, $p=ns$, $n=58$).

No relationship existed either between the degree of multilingualism and Perfectionism or FLA ($r=0.17$, $p=ns$; and $r=-0.24$, $p=ns$, $n=58$, respectively).

An independent t-test revealed no gender differences on both dimensions (Perfectionism: degrees of freedom $[df]=56$, $t=-1.1$, $p=ns$; FLA: $df=56$,

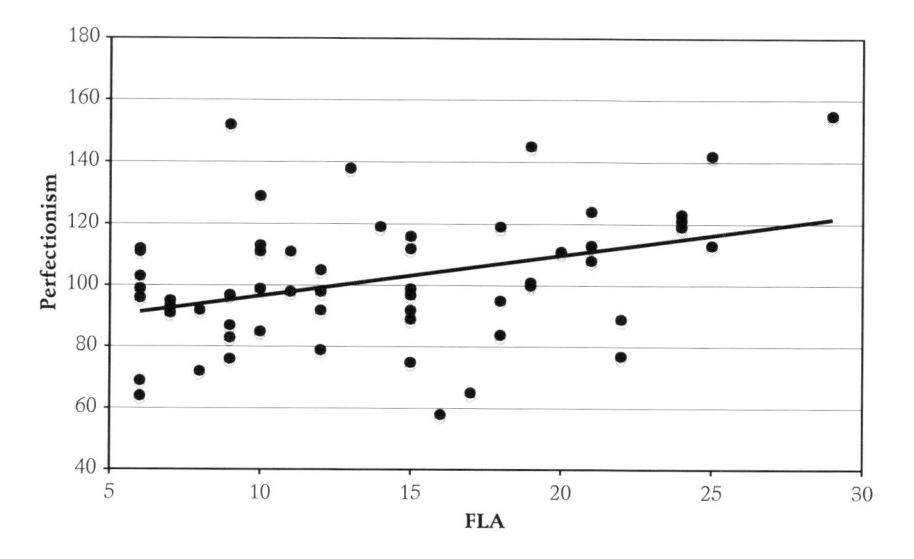

Figure 5.1 Correlation between FLA and Perfectionism in Study 1 (international)

$t=-1.5$, $p=ns$). An ANOVA with level of education as independent variable showed no effect on Perfectionism or on FLA ($df=2, 55$; $F=0.17$; $p=ns$ and $df=2, 55$, $F=0.19$, $p=ns$, respectively).

Study 2: The Saudi group

A significant relationship emerged between FLCA and Perfectionism ($r=0.29$, $p<0.018$, $n=69$). This result suggests that both dimensions share 8.4% of variance, which can be described as a small effect size. In other words, students with high levels of FLCA are also more likely to be perfectionists (see Figure 5.2).

Further analyses of six sub-dimensions of Perfectionism and FLCA showed that two sub-dimensions of Perfectionism correlated significantly ($p<0.008$ with Bonferroni correction) and one correlated marginally with FLCA. A significant relationship existed between FLA and Concern over Mistakes ($r=0.362$, $p<0.002$, $n=69$) and Parental Criticism ($r=0.320$, $p<0.007$, $n=69$); a marginally significant relationship emerged between FLCA and Doubts about Action ($r=0.301$, $p<0.012$, $n=69$). No significant relationship emerged between FLCA and Parental Expectations ($r=0.11$, $p=ns$, $n=69$), Organisation ($r=0.20$, $p=0.10$, $n=69$) and Personal Standards ($r=-0.029$, $p=ns$, $n=69$).

An analysis of the relationships between Perfectionism, FLA and sociobiographical variables showed no relationship between age and FLA

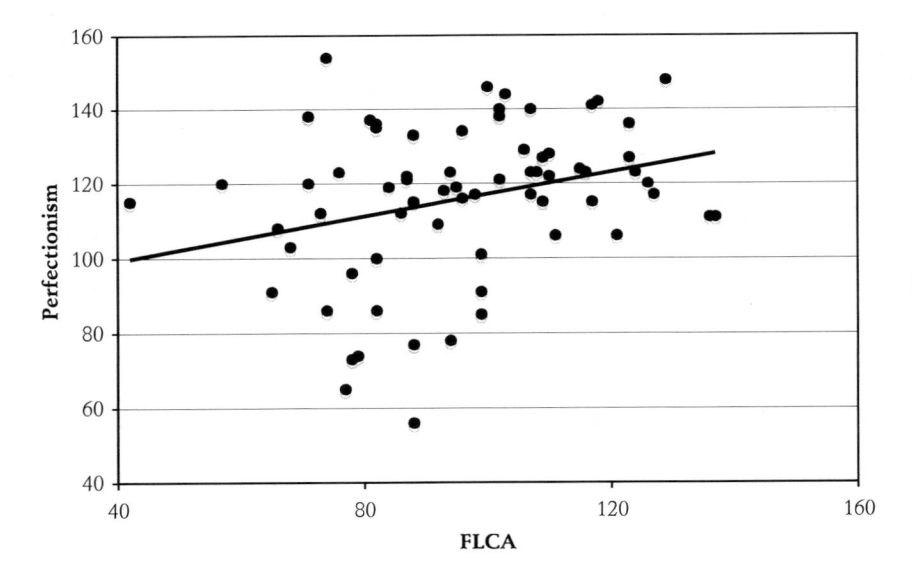

Figure 5.2 Correlation between FLCA and Perfectionism in Study 2 (Saudi)

($r=-0.08$, $p=ns$, $n=69$) or between age and Perfectionism ($r=0.06$, $p=ns$, $n=69$). A significant negative relationship was found between the degree of multilingualism and FLA ($r=-0.33$, $p<0.006$, $n=69$), but no relationship existed between the degree of multilingualism and Perfectionism ($r=-0.02$, $p=ns$, $n=69$).

An independent t-test revealed no gender difference on either dimension (Perfectionism: $df=67$, $t=-1.1$, $p=ns$; FLA: $df=56$, $t=-0.3$, $p=ns$).

Study 3: The Japanese group

Perfectionism and FLCA were found to be significantly and positively correlated ($r=0.222$, $p<0.0001$, $n=323$). This result suggests that both dimensions share 5% of variance, which can be described as a small effect size. More perfectionist participants thus reported higher levels of FLCA in English (see Figure 5.3).

Further correlation analyses of between four sub-dimensions of Perfectionism and FLCA showed that two sub-dimensions of Perfectionism correlated significantly ($p<0.012$ with Bonferroni correction) with FLCA, namely, Concern over Mistakes ($r=0.229$, $p<0.0001$, $n=323$) and Doubts about Action ($r=0.292$, $p<0.0001$, $n=323$). No significant relationship emerged between FLCA and the dimensions Desire for Perfection ($r=0.083$, $p=ns$, $n=323$) and Personal Standards ($r=0.068$, $p=ns$, $n=323$).

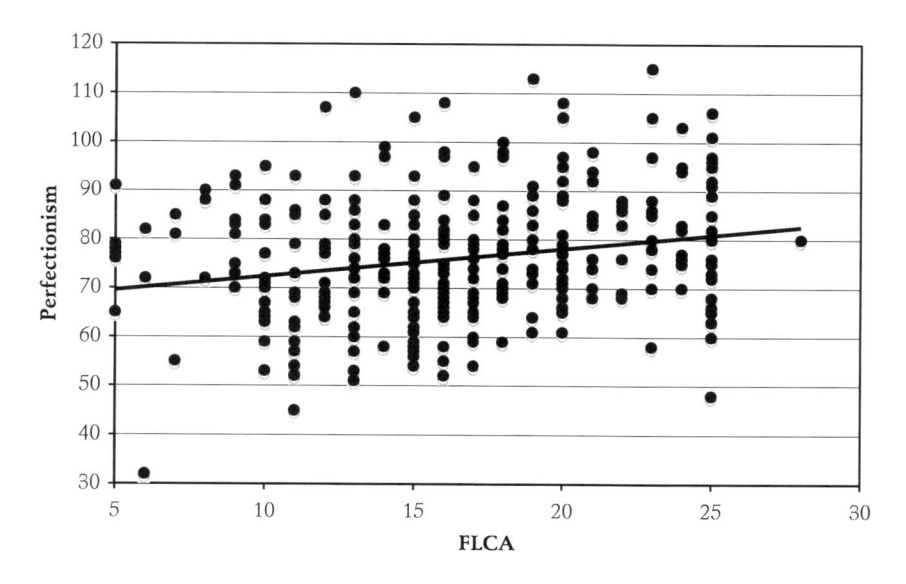

Figure 5.3 Correlation between FLA and Perfectionism in Study 3 (Japan)

An analysis of the relationships between Perfectionism, FLA and sociobiographical variables showed no relationship between age and FLA ($r=-0.005$, $p=ns$, $n=323$) or between age and Perfectionism ($r=-0.01$, $p=ns$, $n=323$).

An independent t-test revealed no gender difference on either dimension (Perfectionism: $df=321$, $t=-0.2$, $p=ns$; FLA: $df=321$, $t=-0.7$, $p=ns$).

Discussion

The findings confirm the first hypothesis: a significant positive relationship was found between Perfectionism and FLA/FLCA in three different groups, namely an international sample of adult English FL users, a sample of Saudi university students and a sample of Japanese high school pupils studying English as an FL (see Table 5.1).

The second hypothesis was also confirmed. FLA/FLCA scores correlated significantly across studies with participants' scores on the subscales Concern over Mistakes and Doubting over Action (see Table 5.1). The subscale Parental Criticism was not included in the Japanese instrument. It did correlate significantly with the levels of FLCA of Saudi university students, but not with the levels of FLA of the older, international group of FL users.

The third hypothesis was rejected, as no clear pattern emerged between sociobiographical variables (age, gender, education level, number of languages known), Perfectionism and FLA/FLCA in the three studies (see Table 5.2). The absence of clear patterns could also be linked to the nature of the samples: The students in Studies 2 and 3 were within a narrower, younger age range, and had similar levels of education and of multilingualism.

The findings confirmed the hypothesis that FLA/FLCA and Perfectionism are positively linked, and that FLA/FLCA is linked more specifically to some subscales of Perfectionism, mainly Concern over

Table 5.2 Overview of the main results

FLA/FLCA	Study 1	Study 2	Study 3
Perfectionism	**	*	***
Concern over Mistakes	***	**	***
Doubts about Action	***	*	***
Parental Criticism	ns	**	NA
Age	**	ns	ns
Gender	ns	ns	ns
Education level	ns	NA	NA
Number of languages	ns	*	NA

*$p<0.05$, **$p<0.01$, ***$p<0.0001$; ns: non-significant, NA: not applicable.

Mistakes, Doubts about Actions and, in one study, Parental Criticism. The higher the scores on these subscales, the more anxious participants are when using English. These findings suggest that the more concern over mistakes and the more doubts that participants have, the higher levels of FLA/FLCA they reported. These results are consistent with Grzegorek *et al.* (2004) and Gregersen and Horwitz (2002), who indicated that anxious FL learners share common characteristics with perfectionists. Using the FL is anxiety-provoking for perfectionist learners and users. Perfectionists who fail to achieve their own high standards in the FL react excessively to the realisation of their perceived shortcoming. It is also possible that when students/users feel unwilling to complete a task and doubt their performance to ever be satisfactory, their social anxiety increases. Using a correlational design, it is impossible to pinpoint causality. However, it is likely that Perfectionism as a personality trait can influence FLA/FLCA. It could be argued that the reverse is more difficult, as a Perfectionism trait is genetic and thus hard to fundamentally change while FLA/FLCA is situation-specific and hence more likely to change through teacher intervention. However, it is not hard to see the relationship from another angle. FLA/FLCA can arguably influence Perfectionism. Anxiety gives rise to high self-criticism, which means highly anxious students overreact to mistakes and are less satisfied with their FL achievements.

The effect of sociobiographical variables on FLA/FLCA was more scattered. Gender had no effect in any of the studies. An age effect appeared in Study 1, which had the widest age range, while no such effect emerged in Studies 2 and 3 with their respective student populations. Education level had no effect in Study 1 and was kept constant in Studies 2 and 3. The effect of number of languages known had a significant effect in Study 2 but not in Study 1 (this variable was held constant in Study 3). This result offers partial support for the finding that multilingualism seems to be linked to lower levels of FLA/FLCA (Dewaele 2007, 2013b; Dewaele *et al.*, 2008; Thompson & Lee, 2013). However, considering the fact that only a handful of students in Study 2 reported knowing more than two languages, no firm conclusion can be reached.

Conclusion

The findings of the present study confirm Gregersen and Horwitz's (2002) findings on the links between Perfectionism and FLA/FLCA in English. Gregersen and Horwitz's operationalisation of Perfectionism depended on a small number of participants (selected from a larger group on the basis of their FLCA score) and made more comments reflecting their specific perfectionist categories. The present research confirms and expands on these findings using a quantitative approach. The analysis of three different population samples, diverse in terms of age, educational level, L1 and cultural background, revealed a positive relationship between Perfectionism and FLA/FLCA. More specifically, the subscales Concern over Mistakes and Doubts about Action correlated most strongly with FLA/FLCA.

Acknowledgements

I would like to thank three bright, former MA students, Renée Finney, Tomohiro Kubota and Sana Almutlaq, who collected data for their dissertations, carried out a first analysis of their data and explored the existing literature on Perfectionism. The present study is based on some variables in the data collected by Finney *et al.*, which were extracted from the original data files and reanalysed. A previous version of the present chapter was presented as Dewaele *et al.* at the European Second Language Association conference in York in September 2014. I would like to thank the reviewers of this chapter for their excellent comments and suggestions.

Notes

(1) A search on Google Scholar reveals 429,000 hits for FLA.
(2) Cohen (1992) suggests that a 'small' effect size is 0.20, a 'medium' effect size is 0.50, and a 'large' effect size is 0.80.

References

Broman-Fulks, J.J., Hill, R.W. and Green, B.A. (2008) Is perfectionism categorical or dimensional? A taxometric analysis. *Journal of Personality Assessment* 90 (5), 481–490.
Brophy, J. (1999) *Working with Perfectionist Students* (Report No. 4). Urbana, IL: ERIC Clearinghouse on Elementary and Early Childhood Education (ERIC Document Reproduction Service No. ED 400124).
Burns, D.D. (1980) The perfectionist's script for self-defeat. *Psychology Today* 14 (11), 34–51.
Cohen, J. (1992) *Statistical Power Analysis for the Behavioral Sciences*. New York: John Wiley.
Dewaele, J.-M. (2002) Psychological and sociodemographic correlates of communicative anxiety in L2 and L3 production. *The International Journal of Bilingualism* 6, 23–39.
Dewaele, J.-M. (2007) The effect of multilingualism, sociobiographical, and situational factors on communicative anxiety and foreign language anxiety of mature language learners. *The International Journal of Bilingualism* 11, 391–409.
Dewaele, J.-M. (2010) Multilingualism and affordances: Variation in self-perceived communicative competence and communicative anxiety in French L1, L2, L3 and L4. *International Review of Applied Linguistics* 48, 105–129.
Dewaele, J.-M. (2012) Personality. Personality traits as independent and dependent variables. In S. Mercer, S. Ryan and M. Williams (eds) *Psychology for Language Learning: Insights from Research, Theory and Practice* (pp. 42–58). Basingstoke: Palgrave Macmillan.

Dewaele, J.-M. (2013a) The link between Foreign Language Classroom Anxiety and Psychoticism, Extraversion, and Neuroticism among adult bi- and multilinguals. *The Modern Language Journal* 97 (3), 670–684.

Dewaele, J.-M. (2013b) *Emotions in Multiple Languages* (2nd edn). Basingstoke: Palgrave Macmillan.

Dewaele, J.-M. and Al Saraj, T. (2013) Foreign Language Anxiety: Some conceptual and methodological issues. *Impulse. Journal of Psychology* 68 (3), 71–78.

Dewaele, J.-M. and Al Saraj, T. (2015) Foreign Language Classroom Anxiety of Arab learners of English: The effect of personality, linguistic and sociobiographical variables. *Studies in Second Language Learning and Teaching* 5 (2), 205–230.

Dewaele, J.-M. and Shan Ip, T. (2013) The link between Foreign Language Classroom Anxiety, Second Language Tolerance of Ambiguity and self-rated English proficiency among Chinese learners. *Studies in Second Language Learning and Teaching* 3 (1), 47–66.

Dewaele, J.-M. and Thirtle, H. (2009) Why do some young learners drop foreign languages? A focus on learner-internal variables. *International Journal of Bilingual Education and Bilingualism* 12 (6), 635–649.

Dewaele, J.-M. and MacIntyre, P.D. (2014) The two faces of Janus? Anxiety and enjoyment in the foreign language classroom. *Studies in Second Language Learning and Teaching* 4 (2), 237–274.

Dewaele, J.-M., MacIntyre, P.D., Boudreau, C. and Dewaele, L. (2016) Do girls have all the fun? Anxiety and enjoyment in the foreign language classroom. *Theory and Practice of Second Language Acquisition* 2 (1), 41–63.

Dewaele, J.-M., Petrides, K.V. and Furnham, A. (2008) Effects of trait emotional intelligence and sociobiographical variables on communicative anxiety and foreign language anxiety among adult multilinguals: A review and empirical investigation. *Language Learning* 58 (4), 911–960.

Frost, R.O., Marten, P., Lahart, C. and Rosenblate, R. (1990) The dimensions of perfectionism. *Cognitive Therapy and Research* 14, 449–468.

Gregersen, T. and Horwitz, E.K. (2002) Language learning and perfectionism: Anxious and non-anxious language learners' reactions to their own oral performance. *The Modern Language Journal* 86 (4), 562–570.

Grzegorek, J.L., Slaney, R.B., Franze, S. and Rice, K.G. (2004) Self-criticism, dependency, self-esteem, and grade point average satisfaction among clusters of perfectionists and nonperfectionists. *Journal of Counseling Psychology* 51 (2), 192–200.

Hamachek, D. (1978) Psychodynamics of normal and neurotic perfectionism. *Psychology* 15, 27–33.

Hewitt, P.L. and Flett, G.L. (1991) Perfectionism in the self and social contexts: Conceptualization, assessment, and association with psychopathology. *Journal of Personality and Social Psychology* 60 (3), 456–470.

Horwitz, E.K. (1986) Preliminary evidence for the reliability and validity of a foreign language anxiety scale. *TESOL Quarterly* 20 (3), 559–562.

Horwitz, E.K. (2001) Language anxiety and achievement. *Annual Review of Applied Linguistics* 21, 112–126.

Horwitz, E.K. (2010) Foreign and second language anxiety. *Language Teaching* 43 (2), 154–167.

Horwitz, E.K., Horwitz, M.B. and Cope, J. (1986) Foreign language classroom anxiety. *The Modern Language Journal* 70 (2), 125–132.

Liu, H.-J. and Chen, T.-H. (2014) Learner differences among children learning a foreign language: Language anxiety, strategy use, and multiple intelligences. *English Language Teaching* 7 (6), 1–13.

Liu, M. (2006) Anxiety in Chinese EFL students at different proficiency levels. *System* 34 (3), 301–316.

Onwuegbuzie, A., Bailey, P. and Daley, C.E. (1999) Factors associated with foreign language anxiety. *Applied Psycholinguistics* 20, 217–239.

Onwuegbuzie, A., Bailey, P. and Daley, C.E. (2000) Cognitive, affective, personality, and demographic predictors of foreign-language achievement. *The Journal of Educational Research* 94, 3–15.

Pacht, A.R. (1984) Reflections on perfectionism. *American Psychologist* 39, 386–390.

Park, G.P. and French, B.F. (2013) Gender differences in the foreign language classroom anxiety scale. *System* 41 (2), 462–471.

Pishghadam, R. and Akhondpoor, F. (2011) Learner perfectionism and its role in foreign language learning success, academic achievement, and learner anxiety. *Journal of Language Teaching and Research* 2 (2), 432–440.

Saboonchi, F. and Lundh, L.G. (1997) Perfectionism, self-consciousness and anxiety. *Personality and Individual Differences* 22 (6), 921–928.

Sakurai, S. and Ohtani, Y. (1997) Relations of 'self-oriented perfectionism' to depression and hopelessness. *Shinrigaku kenkyu: The Japanese Journal of Psychology* 68, 179–186.

Stöber, J. and Joormann, J. (2001) Worry, procrastination, and perfectionism: Differentiating amount of worry, pathological worry, anxiety, and depression. *Cognitive Therapy and Research* 25 (1), 49–60.

Stoeber, J., Chesterman, D. and Tarn, T.-A. (2010) Perfectionism and task performance: Time on task mediates the perfectionistic strivings–performance relationship. *Personality and Individual Differences* 48 (4), 458–462.

Taguchi, T., Magid, M. and Papi, M. (2009) The Motivational Self System among Japanese, Chinese and Iranian learners of English: A comparative study. In Z. Dörnyei and E. Ushioda (eds) *Motivation, Language Identity and the L2 Self* (pp. 66–97). Bristol: Multilingual Matters.

Thompson, A.S. and Lee, J. (2013a) Anxiety and EFL: Does multilingualism matter? *International Journal of Bilingual Education and Bilingualism* 16, 730–749.

Thompson, A.S. and Lee, J. (2013b) The impact of experience abroad and language proficiency on Language Learning Anxiety. *TESOL Quarterly* 48 (2), 252–274.

Van der Zee, K.I., Van Oudenhoven, J.P., Ponterotto, J.G. and Fietzer, A.W. (2013) Multicultural Personality Questionnaire: Development of a Short Form. *Journal of Personality Assessment* 95 (1), 118–124.

Wang, T. (2010) Speaking anxiety: More of a function of personality than language achievement. *Chinese Journal of Applied Linguistics* 33, 95–109.

6 Social Anxiety and Silence in Japan's Tertiary Foreign Language Classrooms

Jim King and Lesley Smith

Introduction

This chapter considers the intriguing relationship that exists between social anxiety and the silences of second language (L2) learners within a Japanese English as a Foreign Language (EFL) classroom context. Although in recent years, extensive attention has been focused on the impact anxiety has on L2 oral performance (e.g. Liu & Jackson, 2008; Woodrow, 2006), to date little consideration has been given to this issue when placing silence itself at the heart of the investigation. Rather than signifying a meaningless blank occurring during the course of a lesson, the reality of L2 classroom silence is that it has various forms and functions and emerges through complex multiple and concurrent routes (King, 2013a, 2013b). Within the Japanese context, some of the most salient of these routes connect to psychological and emotional factors that see a complex interplay of learner-internal and environmental issues interacting to support the silent behaviour of socially inhibited students.

In line with the American Psychiatric Association (2000), we define social anxiety as being a marked or persistent fear of social interactions in which one can be observed by others. Sufferers tend to have a negatively skewed self-concept and this plays into fears that their social performance will lead to embarrassment and humiliation. It is important to note from the outset that we do not consider social anxiety to be an entirely separate phenomenon to foreign language anxiety (FLA); rather it represents a deep seam running through the latter construct. In light of this, and in order to provide the most comprehensive overview of anxiety-related research conducted within Japan-related language learning contexts, our review of the literature examines anxiety in relation to the four language skills. This approach, which acknowledges that such skills do not operate in isolation of each other, enables us to provide an extensive and richly contextualised account of anxiety research through which to view the focal study of the chapter. We then go on to outline this study, conducted by the lead author

(King, 2014), which employed Clark and Wells' (1995) seminal model of social anxiety to better understand the silences produced by learners displaying an acute hypersensitivity to peers and a dread of negative evaluation within the public arena of the language classroom. The chapter concludes by offering some suggestions on how to reduce social anxiety levels within L2 classrooms and help educators comprehend and deal with silent episodes when they emerge.

An In-Depth Review of Anxiety Research in Japanese-Related L2 Contexts

To date, and in contrast to the dearth of empirical studies on the social anxiety of learners, a great deal of research has examined FLA within Japanese contexts, commonly finding that it hinders students performatively and psychologically and is often linked to poorer grades, lower self-confidence and negative attitudes towards the target language (see e.g. Aida, 1994; Matsuda & Gobel, 2004). In order to provide a comprehensive overview of anxiety-related L2 research in Japan, our review of the literature is structured primarily around the four skills of reading, writing, listening and speaking. This is in line with the assertion that a skills-based approach is a useful way of conceiving anxiety in foreign language learning because each skill bears related – but distinct – anxiety factors and should therefore be examined within its own specific context (Piniel, 2014).

Reading anxiety

Of the four main skill areas, reading might seem to cause the least anxiety for students of a foreign language. Reading is often a private activity, requiring one person rather than two or more to form meaning (Saito *et al.*, 1999), and it cannot be easily evaluated by outward means. However, Saito *et al.* (1999) propose two aspects of reading that have the potential to cause anxiety: unfamiliar orthography and unfamiliar cultural context. Foreign language reading anxiety (FLRA) arises from the inability to create a 'sound-symbol' correspondence with an unfamiliar writing system (Saito *et al.*, 1999: 203) or the inability to fully grasp the contextual meaning of a translation despite knowledge of a text's individual words. In a study of native English speakers learning a foreign language, Saito *et al.* (1999) found that while general language anxiety existed across all three languages present in their study (Japanese, French and Russian), reading anxiety was dependent on the target language and, more specifically, the orthographic system. Levels of reading anxiety increased according to the perceived difficulty of reading in the target language, where students of Japanese had the highest anxiety levels, followed by French and, finally, Russian. Similarly, differences between the English and Japanese writing systems can cause anxiety for Japanese students learning English. Matsuda and Gobel (2001) became curious about FLRA when students spoke of apprehension towards reading English. Often, their anxiety led to trouble focusing on the text, even to the extent of rereading the same phrase multiple times without comprehension. In this case, while anxiety can stem from a lack of proper knowledge, a gap in cultural knowledge might leave students nervous that, even with grammatical and lexical knowledge, they will never reach a proficient status in the target language. Unlike Saito *et al.* (1999), Matsuda and Gobel (2001) found no significant correlation between the FLA and FLRA scales, which shows that FLRA may occur independently of general FLA. Self-confidence, or the general belief in one's ability to successfully and effectively communicate in the target language (MacIntyre *et al.*, 1998), was the only significant component found in both. Here, low self-confidence correlated with higher levels of anxiety. Interestingly, unfamiliarity with English only caused significant results for first-year students, in line with Saito *et al.*'s (1999) notion that beginners tend to focus on the unknown minutiae of the target language instead of the broader contextual narrative.

In a similar study in 2004, Matsuda and Gobel investigated general FLA and FLRA in relation to gender, classroom performance and first-hand experience in the target culture. Gender had no substantial effect on general and reading anxiety but was a strong predictor of performance in first-year students, with female students tending to perform better than males. However, Kitano's (2001) study of speaking anxiety in American learners of Japanese found relevant gender differences: male students felt more anxiety when they were less confident about speaking, but this was not the case for female students. Overall, studies linking FLA and gender have produced varying results (Kimura, 2008; MacIntyre *et al.*, 2002), suggesting that gender can be, but is not always, one of the several mitigating factors in FLA. In both Matsuda and Gobel's (2001, 2004) studies, low self-confidence was found to be an important factor in both FLA and FLRA. LeBlanc (2015) points to reading circles as a way for Japanese learners of English to increase self-efficacy (i.e. positive perceptions about one's ability to perform), which can decrease reading anxiety overall. In group discussions of texts, students were able to understand difficult constructions by checking evaluations with other students and by watching colleagues perform the task successfully. One student even directly reported that she 'understood better because there were various opinions and the story could be seen from different angles' (LeBlanc, 2015: 18).

Listening anxiety

Foreign language listening anxiety (FLLA) stems from an overload of information in which students are unable to control the speed or delivery of input, potentially resulting in embarrassing misunderstandings (Kimura,

2008). This apprehension manifests in less effective information processing, compromised information retrieval and lowered concentration in students studying a foreign language (Elkhafaifi, 2005; Kimura, 2008; Vogley, 1998). Within a Japanese EFL context, research on listening apprehension as distinct from FLA remains scant, perhaps because, like reading, listening is a receptive skill not directly assessed by teachers or students. Thus, Kimura (2008) draws from Kim's (2000) doctoral dissertation on EFL classes in South Korea, adapting her Foreign Language Listening Anxiety Scale (FLLAS) for her own EFL students in Japan. Using factor analysis, Kimura proposed three subcomponents related to FLLA: emotionality, worry and anticipatory fear. She analysed university major and gender as independent variables to assess the subcomponents' distribution across groups. Her study consisted of 309 males and 143 females, all of whom were either social science or maths majors. Interestingly, the maths students were significantly different in terms of emotionality or emotional reactions to listening in English, displaying not only a lack of self-confidence but also other negative emotions such as intimidation, annoyance and discomfort. Kimura (2008) is only able to hypothesise as to the reasons for these reactions and suggests that there may be a link to the distinct learning orientation of these students. Similarly, in a descriptive study of affective variables on Japanese EFL students, Tani-Fukuchi (2005) found that only a small number of students described their English classes with positive emotions such as *enjoyment* or *happiness*, and over one-third of students reported no positive experiences at all in learning English. In Kimura's (2008: 183) study, maths and social science students did not differ in their 'cognitive perception[s] of anxiety' related to either anxiety-provoking situations or apprehension of negative consequences in these situations. Interestingly, she found that *anticipatory fear*, the factor providing the highest loadings in the data for both student groups, had not previously been discussed in similar studies of language anxiety. Since evaluation of listening skills necessarily occurs after listening has taken place, students with FLLA might interpret their fear of negative evaluation as anticipation about future events. She concludes that FLLA is a separate but related phenomenon to FLA, to which certain learner groups can be predisposed. Elkhafaifi's (2005) study of Arabic EFL learners similarly finds FLLA to be an independent but related construct of FLA, which negatively correlates with listening comprehension and final test grades. He also found intriguing group differences, namely that second-year students had the highest levels of listening anxiety. Saito and Samimy (1996) presented similar findings in their study of performance and FLA in American learners of Japanese, namely that anxiety was a higher predictor of performance in second- and third-year students than in first-year learners.

Yamauchi (2014) examined the use of challenging materials in mitigating listening anxiety in 25 low-proficiency learners of English. Students' listening anxiety stemmed from their perceived difficulty of the course materials. Perceptions of material and language difficulty can play powerful roles in FLA, affecting confidence in the ability to adequately perform in the target language (MacInytre *et al.*, 1998; Saito *et al.*, 1999). Results from the questionnaire study showed that after a 15-week course using the challenging materials, FLLA significantly decreased and students began to use top-down processes when listening, starting with general ideas about the materials and growing more specific. Her findings suggest that pre-emptively introducing students to difficult materials may mitigate listening anxiety.

Writing anxiety

Research in foreign language writing anxiety (FLWA) borrows greatly from L1 writing apprehension studies. In fact, relatively little research into writing apprehension in L2 contexts has been undertaken. Anxiety in writing can result in students choosing majors that require less writing and have low expectations in writing performance (Daly & Miller, 1975). Cornwell and McKay (1998, 2000) contribute to the scant literature in this area by providing us with two interesting studies into the factors involved in foreign language writing apprehension and its relationship to FLA and have developed a scale that accurately measures Japanese college students' L2 writing anxiety. They incorporate writing anxiety research conducted in other contexts, most notably that of Cheng *et al.* (1999), to find comparable writing anxiety subcomponents. Cheng and her colleagues compared L2 classroom anxiety to writing anxiety and writing achievement in Taiwanese English majors. They discovered three main factors specific to writing anxiety: low-self confidence in writing, adverse attitudes towards writing in English and writing evaluation apprehension. Likewise, Cornwell and McKay (2000) found similar subcomponents of FLWA for Japanese students of English such as fear of negative criticism (fear of evaluation, showing writing to others) and students' attitudes and views about their writing aptitude (enjoyment of writing, negative perceptions about writing ability). Using a modified version of Daly and Miller's (1975) Second Language Writing Apprehension Scale, they found four factors influencing L2 writing apprehension as opposed to Daly and Miller's single factor, fear of writing evaluation. Contextual differences, including L2 versus L1 contexts, could explain differences in anxiety subcomponents, as many FLA studies find multiple factors in skill-specific foreign language anxieties (Aida, 1994; Kimura, 2008; Kitano, 2001).

Takahashi (2010) examined possible correlations between L2 writing anxiety, motivation, self-perceptions of ability, proficiency and performance in English classes at a private Japanese university. Like Cornwell and McKay (1997, 2000), she used a translated and modified version of Daly and Miller's (1975) scale, along with Kitano's (2001) Can-do scale for perceived language ability and Ely's (1986) motivational scale. All four factors were negatively correlated with FLWA and, interestingly, to a greater degree than Takahashi's (2004) previous study of the same four factors and general FLA. The cause of this strong correlation, she proposes, is the weakness of English writing skills in Japanese classrooms, leading to its status as 'one of the most unpopular, disliked activities in the classroom' (Takahashi, 2010: 97). Other reasons for this relationship could be classroom context (non-English majors in a lower-level English class), an entirely different orthographic system and sound/symbol correspondences between Japanese and English.

Speaking anxiety

FLA is most commonly tied with speaking because, out of the four skills areas, it entails the most public evaluation and is the primary form of communication in the classroom. As such, researchers have found speaking anxiety to be a main component of FLA as well as a distinct skill-specific anxiety that can affect learners independently of general FLA (Aida, 1994; Horwitz et al., 1986; Matsuda & Gobel, 2004). While examining relationships between general language anxiety and FLRA, Matsuda and Gobel (2004) also found a strong correlation between experience overseas and lowered anxiety in speaking English. They proposed that the heightened self-confidence that comes with overseas experience could lead to better achievement (i.e. higher grades) by students. Aida (1994) similarly found that exposure to the target culture lowered anxiety in her study of American university learners of Japanese. Her research supports Horwitz's claim that communication anxiety and fear of negative social evaluation are the main components of general FLA and found that most students' anxieties about learning Japanese came directly from discomfort or apprehension about speaking. As we shall see later, social evaluation concerns play a powerful role in supporting language learner silence. We should reiterate the point here that social anxiety is by no means an entirely separate construct to FLA, but rather it overlaps with and feeds into the 'distinct complex of self-perceptions, beliefs, feelings and behaviours' of FLA, as characterised Horwitz et al. (1986: 128).

Interestingly, some studies have found that L2 speaking anxiety manifests both within and outside of the language classroom, supporting a 'dual conceptualization' of foreign language speaking anxiety (FLSA) (Woodrow, 2006) in situations where the target language is also the language of everyday use. Ohata (2005) interviewed five Japanese students in a US college setting to investigate their emotional struggles when studying in America, especially those related to communication anxiety. Among all students, the fear of negative evaluation or 'losing face' in front of the teacher or other students was the highest anxiety-provoking factor (see the 'Feared predictions' section). Students often avoided eye contact with the teacher, even if they were confident about the topic, so as to avoid being selected and potentially criticised or corrected by the instructor. Students in Ohata's study reported discomfort from the competitive atmosphere when speaking English in front of Japanese friends, which from the students' perception was provoked by speaking in front of native speakers. Feeling in opposition to her friends made one student in the study feel isolated and disconnected from her Japanese student group, causing great stress. Like Ohata, Woodrow (2006) found that 85% of students experienced some form of L2 speaking anxiety and that students were most anxious when communicating with native speakers, including teachers, and when performing in front of other students. The students participating in the study were non-native speakers of various ethnicities. Woodrow, distinguishing between learners from Confucian Heritage cultures (CHC), such as Japan and China, and non-CHC learners, reported that the former tended to be more anxious.

The Mixed-Methods Study into L2 Classroom Silence

The lead author conducted a large-scale, multisite investigation into the prevalence of silent behaviour among 924 learners studying English within university L2 classes in Japan. Using a low inference, structured observation instrument called the Classroom Oral Participation Scheme (COPS) (King, 2013a, 2013b), quantitative data produced by minute-by-minute, real-time coding built up a picture of students' oral participation within 30 classes located at nine institutions across Japan. This data uncovered surprisingly low levels of oral production by students. Over the course of 48 hours of minute-by-minute observation, there were a mere seven coded instances of student-initiated talk, with this type of discourse taking up less than 0.25% of total lesson time. In comparison, there were 1297 instances of teacher-initiated talk, accounting for slightly over 45% of the total observed time. Due to their power to shape oral exchanges and control the floor, prior to the commencement of the study it had been expected that teachers would dominate classroom discourse to some extent, but the disparity between the levels of student-initiated talk and teacher-initiated talk that was uncovered was remarkable. In addition to this, coded instances of no oral participation at all by any participants (i.e. neither staff nor students spoke) accounted for just over one-quarter of the study's observed lesson time. This compelling evidence suggests that there exists a robust trend towards student silence in Japan's L2 university classrooms, which displays little variation across diverse learning contexts.

While a structured observation approach proved to be highly effective in establishing the existence of silence within classrooms, it was less suited to investigating salient causes of learner reticence and, indeed, how students perceived the act of remaining silent during L2 instruction.

Therefore, in order to gain a deeper, individual-level analysis of learner silence, a qualitative phase of research was embarked upon. It was during this part of the project that data emerged suggesting that there is an intriguing and significant connection between social anxiety and the avoidance of talk by some language learners in Japan. Eleven participants, each of whom was interviewed twice in sessions lasting up to one hour, consented to take part in this phase of the study. The follow-up interviews were conducted once transcription and a preliminary analysis of each encounter had been completed. The interviewee sample reflected the diverse nature of English language education within Japan's university system and consisted of both language and non-language majors whose L2 proficiency varied considerably. In light of this variation, the participants were able to choose whether their interviews were conducted in English, Japanese, or a mixture of both languages. It was important to provide an opportunity for interviewees to discuss their ideas about classroom silence in their mother tongue as silence was a topic most had never even considered before, and to provide an illuminating account of their beliefs and experiences required a fair amount of self-reflection and the externalisation of implicit assumptions about classroom behaviour and discourse. All interview sessions were audio-recorded and transcribed in full. A systematic process of back-translation (Brislin, 1970) ensured that Japanese language data were reliably translated into English. Transcription and data analysis were performed concurrently so that findings could feed into subsequent interviews. This iterative process of content analysis saw the major theme of social anxiety and silence emerge, and it became clear after repeated coding that much of what interviewees said about refraining from talk in the L2 classroom was highly relevant to Clark and Wells' (1995) seminal model of social anxiety. It should be noted here that although the study uncovered multiple, interconnected sources of classroom silence – for example, the silence of student apathy and disengagement from the learning process that is strongly connected to teacher-centred instructional methods or the silence of non-verbal learning activities that do not require speech in order to be performed successfully – it was students' avoidance of talk because of a fear of negative evaluation by their peers that stood out as *the* recurring theme in the interview data.

Social Anxiety and Language Learner Silence

Clark and Wells' (1995) cognitive model

In this section, we discuss how the interview study's findings map onto Clark and Wells' (1995) model of social anxiety and consider how facets of the study's sociocultural context appear to interplay with learner-internal factors to support students' avoidance of classroom talk. Positing that social anxiety stems from problematic beliefs about oneself and one's social world and that these erroneous beliefs cause individuals to interpret specific social situations in an excessively negative manner, Clark and Wells' framework represents one of the best known, experimentally supported explanations of social anxiety (McManus & Hirsch, 2007). Four dynamically interacting elements are present in the model (feared predictions, self-focused attention, safety behaviours and somatic/cognitive symptoms), and these processes all work together to maintain a person's anxiety during social encounters (see Figure 6.1). Of course, it is worth pointing out here that the language classroom represents a highly public social performance situation in which one's behaviour and utterances are open to the scrutiny of others, and it appears that Japanese learners in particular tend to regard such settings as requiring what is known as a *soto* (meaning public or outside one's group) mode of communication that involves the avoidance of self-disclosure and reduced levels of verbal

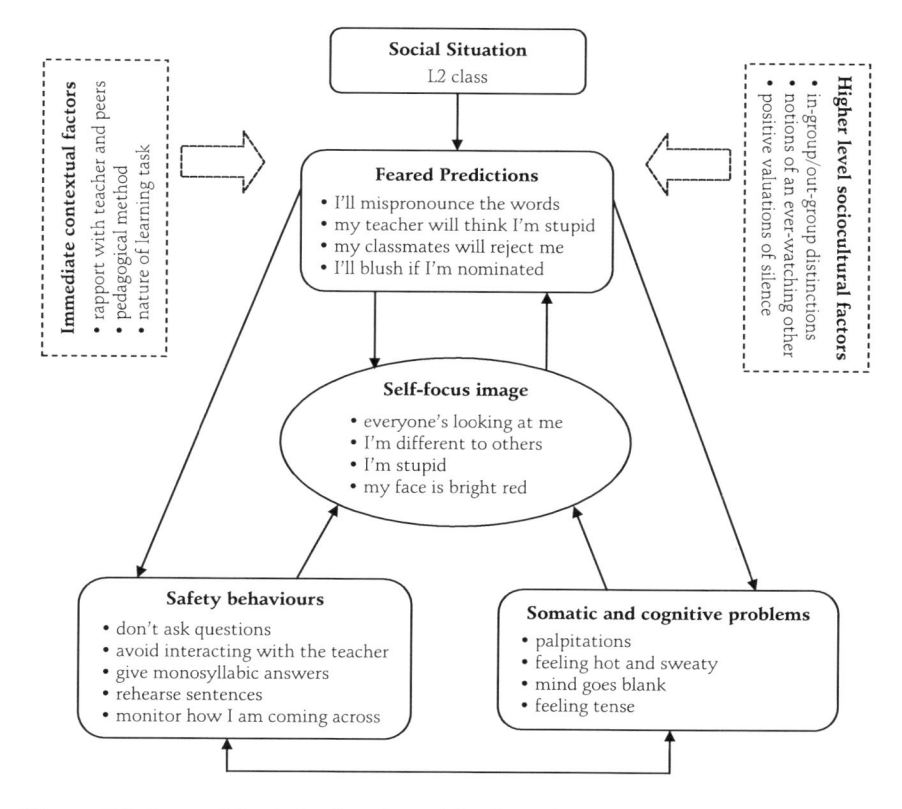

Figure 6.1 A cognitive-behavioural model of a silent L2 learner's social anxiety (Adapted from King [2014] and based on Clark and Wells' 1995 original model)

interaction (for more on how the notions of *soto* and its opposing concept of *uchi* relate to communicative behaviour in Japan, see Gudykunst & Nishida, 1993; King, 2013a; Lebra, 1993; Nakane, 2007).

Feared predictions: The 'eyes' that silence

Also known as social fear beliefs, feared predictions relate to a socially anxious individual's belief that his or her social performance is not of an acceptable standard and will likely be judged harshly by others, with any perceived deficiencies being seen as an indication of the individual's weakness. Clark and Wells (1995) point out that these dysfunctional self-concept and social action beliefs can be distinguished into three categories: (1) excessively high standards for social performance, (2) conditional beliefs concerning social evaluation and (3) unconditional beliefs about the self. Reflecting the first category, a strong theme to emerge in the data was the unrealistic perfectionism of the language learners in the sample (see Dewaele, this volume, and Gregersen & Horwitz, 2002). Interviewees repeatedly talked about their fear of making mistakes when called on to speak in the target language and related how they were concerned not only about the lexico-grammatical accuracy of their speech and whether their pronunciation was comprehensible, but also whether the content of their utterances was relevant and interesting to others. It seems such high standards of L2 conduct are only likely to feed into a learner's already existing anxiety levels, as Clark and Wells (1995) point out that setting exceptionally high standards for one's social performance tends to generate anxiety because the standards are so difficult to achieve.

Regarding the social evaluation element of feared predictions, participants spoke about feeling scrutinised and judged by peers while lessons were in progress, and a number of learners made references to the 'eyes' they felt were always around them. The sociocultural backdrop to this belief is the enculturated notion that there exists an ever-present, ever-watching 'other' within Japanese society that constantly monitors and inhibits people's behaviour with its disapproving gaze (see Clancy, 1990; Greer, 2000; Lebra, 1993; McVeigh, 2002). Under such circumstances, classrooms become emotional danger zones where speaking up brings with it the risk of negative evaluation, the potential to cause shame and embarrassment and, ultimately, the possibility of rejection by peers. Indeed, when asked to describe how they felt about being required to communicate in L2 during lessons, the term most frequently used by the interviewees was the word *hazukashii*, meaning 'it's embarrassing'. If we also consider the great importance placed on maintaining face during public social interactions in Japan (see Cocroft & Ting-Toomey, 1994), an ever-more fertile environment for the avoidance of talk becomes apparent. Franks

(2000) sums up well this notion that silence provides the ideal strategy for saving face and avoiding social penalty when he states:

> Face-saving is crucial to the Japanese way of life, and through the culture's tremendous value of face-saving (or saving the dignity of both the speaker and the listener) silence is encouraged. During communication interactions, therefore, silence together with indirect language is used to save embarrassment, to ease tension, and to respect the feelings of the speaker. The rationale here is that what you don't say cannot hurt anyone. (Franks, 2000: 6)

Self-focused attention: Distracted into silence

The social fear beliefs of socially anxious language learners appear to be maintained in part through an increase in self-focused attention during classroom situations. Clark and Wells (1995) contend that when the socially anxious enter a situation that holds the potential for negative evaluation by others, their attention is shifted inwards towards monitoring and observing their own self-generated image and how they believe their image is coming across to others. This heightened processing of the self as a social object is problematic because it directs attention towards feared anxiety responses (overemphasising them) and interferes with objective processing of feedback from the social environment. Thus, a socially anxious learner will typically overestimate the extent to which his/her anxiety symptoms are visible to others (Purdon et al., 2001). Fuelled by negatively skewed social-evaluative thoughts, the learner's hypersensitivity to peer reactions leads to an attention-draining preoccupation with impression management (Leary, 1995) and reluctance to draw further unwanted attention from peers by orally participating in the lesson. One interviewee, a second-year languages major, recounted how she feared being called on to speak during whole-class discussions because she was concerned her opinion might be rejected by the other students and that she would be perceived as 'different'. She described how her classmates were always at the forefront of her mind while lessons were in progress and that she constantly worried about how she was coming across to them, preferring to keep silent rather than take an active role in discussions. Of course, attention is a finite resource and by focusing too much on internal information (i.e. feelings of anxiety and projection of self-image), this learner would have had less attention available for linguistic processing and formulating target language utterances. By diverting concentration away from lesson content as it actually arises, this attentional shift towards self-focused attention and the heightened processing of the social self makes active oral participation all the more difficult to achieve. It is interesting to note, therefore, that rather than signifying mental passivity, silences that occur during episodes of self-focused attention may in fact represent periods of intense cognitive activity for socially anxious learners.

Safety behaviours: Maintaining anxiety through silent behaviour

The student interviewees provided rich testimony concerning the strategies they used in the classroom to try and prevent their social fears from being realised. Clark and Wells (1995) term these strategies 'safety behaviours', and explain that the socially anxious will engage in a range of different safety behaviours in order to try and avoid negative evaluation during feared situations. Participants who described their social evaluation fears spoke openly about the ways in which they either minimised, or more preferably avoided altogether, speaking (in L1 or L2) during language classes. For example, asking questions to the teacher and initiating discourse were meticulously avoided, and this pattern of behaviour is borne out unambiguously in the study's observation data. Another popular tactic for minimising verbalisation was to provide only the shortest, one-word responses when called on to speak by the instructor. Such silence-seeking behaviour is strongly supported at a learning situation level by teachers' use of pedagogical techniques employing a rigid Initiation Response Feedback (IRF) pattern of classroom discourse (Sinclair & Coulthard, 1975). This teacher-centred pattern of classroom interaction was commonly encountered during the observation phase of the study.

For some socially anxious learners, seating position appears to play a major role in their safety-seeking behaviour. As Falout (2014) rightly points out, the seating layout can majorly impact on the interpersonal dynamics of a language classroom, with rank-and-file arrangements representing essentially anti-social learning environments in which peer-to-peer communication is stymied. One fourth-year non-languages major, whose weekly English class conformed to this rank-and-file arrangement, described her reluctance to speak publicly during lessons and an almost neurotic fear of being ridiculed by her peers. She related how each week she would make for a seating position right at the back of the classroom, and would attempt to locate someone of a larger build to sit directly behind. Once ensconced in such a position, her strategy was to crouch down and keep her gaze lowered for the duration of the lesson (cf. Ohata, 2005). Through the use of these safety behaviours, it was hoped that the instructor would fail to notice the student and that she would be able to escape the daunting prospect of being nominated to speak publicly in the target language. This participant's testimony provides a good illustration of how a dynamic interplay between immediate contextual factors and learner-internal processes exists that helps shape students' classroom behaviours and discourse patterns.

In addition to physical avoidance strategies, the safety behaviours of socially anxious individuals may also comprise internal mental processes

(Clark, 1999; Clark & Wells, 1995). In the case of language learners anxious to avoid mistakes and the ensuing (imagined) negative evaluation that goes with them, this might involve mentally rehearsing something over and over again before saying it aloud or meticulously translating an utterance word-for-word in one's head before a verbal response is made. The danger with such an approach is that extended silent pausing for linguistic processing can lead to a breakdown in communication, as unnatural periods of silence do have the potential to constrain interactions. (We should note here, however, that the notion of a 'natural' turn-taking pause length is a culturally relative phenomenon [see Enninger, 1991; Scollon & Scollon, 1990], and a number of scholars [e.g. Tanaka, 1999; Yamada, 1997] assert that the Japanese do appear to have a relatively high tolerance for extended silences occurring at turn-taking junctures.) Safety behaviours, then, have the potential to make social interactions less successful and, rather than reducing an individual's anxiety, they actually contribute to it by increasing self-monitoring and self-consciousness, thus increasing the likelihood of feared predictions coming true (Clark, 1999; Clark & Wells, 1995; McManus & Hirsch, 2007; Salkovskis, 1991).

Somatic and cognitive symptoms: Discomfort in the classroom

A range of somatic and cognitive symptoms are associated with social anxiety (for an extensive list of symptoms, see Purdon *et al.*'s [2001] Social Anxiety Symptoms Scale). Interviewees in the current study spoke about experiencing a number of symptoms during their English classes. For example, one English language major, who despite being relatively proficient in the target language, described her fears surrounding being called on to speak English in front of peers and explained how she would regularly experience palpitations during lessons, with her heart rate seeming to rise as her self-perceived image plummeted. This disagreeable cocktail of phenomena was, unfortunately but perhaps unsurprisingly, accompanied by a strong desire to flee the situation. Other interviewees discussing feelings of embarrassment during L2 classes reported experiencing clammy hands, weak voices, blushing, feelings of confusion, mental blanks and a sense of panic. In a heightened state of arousal during feared situations, the socially anxious are hyper vigilant for anxiety symptoms and when these arise, they are interpreted as impending signs of failure to meet desired social performance expectations (Clark, 2001). Exacerbated by safety behaviours and unrealistically magnified by self-focused attention, it is clear that symptoms like those described above play an important role in socially anxious language learners' silences as they are intimately and dynamically linked to the other cognitive elements within Clark and Wells' (1995) model, which help to produce and maintain social anxiety.

Some Suggestions for Reducing Social Anxiety and Increasing Oral Production

In this section, we briefly discuss some ideas on how to reduce social anxiety levels within L2 classrooms, thus encouraging more oral interaction among students. But before doing this, we would like to make the point that it is not our belief that social anxiety can or should be totally eradicated from language classrooms, even if this were possible. Social anxiety exists on a continuum (McManus & Hirsch, 2007) and it is perfectly natural for students to feel some level of anxiety during demanding social performance situations, such as when giving a presentation to classmates or taking part in a speech contest. Indeed, various authors (e.g. Brown et al., 2001; Daubney, 2007) have speculated on the facilitative properties that anxiety may possess in some learning situations. However, when social anxiety acts to inhibit learners to such an extent that they are no longer able to function effectively in the classroom, retreating into the supposed safety of silence and thus missing important opportunities for L2 development through oral production and interaction, then we believe it is time for educators to act. It should be noted that the study on learner silence described in this chapter did not set out to measure the effectiveness of anxiety-reducing strategies and so our suggestions are offered only in a tentative manner.

With regard to group-orientated strategies, we believe careful consideration by language educators of how the group dynamics of their classrooms (see Dörnyei & Murphey, 2003) can best be manipulated holds the greatest potential for successfully reducing students' social anxiety levels. As social anxiety is dependent on a fear of negative social evaluation, anything instructors can do at the start of courses to promote *acceptance* (a term from Humanistic Psychology, meaning non-judgmental, positive regard) among class members will be of benefit in reducing the likelihood of negative evaluations occurring within the group. Interpersonal relationships based on acceptance acknowledge that human beings are complex and flawed but that they can still be regarded in a non-evaluative, positive manner. Classrooms characterised by a general feeling of acceptance represent learning contexts in which social fear beliefs are downplayed, and the benefits of this for socially anxious silent learners are obvious. As Schmuck and Schmuck (cited in Ehrman & Dörnyei, 1998: 116) point out, 'Students do not directly express their own ideas and opinions publicly until they have learned that their peers and the teacher will not reject them'.

Dörnyei and Murphey (2003) list various ways in which teachers can consciously promote acceptance, but one of the most important factors is that students have the opportunity to learn genuine information about each other through low-risk self-disclosure activities. Proximity and contact also play vital roles here and so it is essential that small-group membership is changed regularly within the class in order for the silencing effects of in-group/out-group distinctions to be nullified and that, if possible, seating arrangements are manipulated in such a manner so as to encourage communication and good interpersonal dynamics (see Falout, 2014). Teachers can contribute to a supportive and collaborative classroom atmosphere by providing opportunities for meaningful target language communication to take place via non-public activities (i.e. within pairs or small groups) and by reducing levels of error correction so that there is an emphasis on the fluency rather than the accuracy of students' L2 utterances.

Regarding individual-level strategies, we believe that cognitive-behavioural approaches have good potential for enabling learners to challenge and adjust their negatively skewed beliefs concerning social performance and social evaluation in the L2 classroom. Currently, research in this area is decidedly scant, but a recent study by Curry (2014) focusing on a small sample of Japanese undergraduate learners of English does seem to suggest that cognitive behavioural techniques can indeed provide students with the tools to overcome debilitating anxiety in their L2 learning. Within the Japanese tertiary context, there has been a growth of self-access centres where learning advisors provide one-to-one language advice for students, and these centres appear to be the ideal setting for implementing such techniques.

As socially anxious individuals have an unrealistically negative impression of their social performance and how they are coming across to others, generating self-images of themselves performing badly in feared situations, one idea is to use video feedback as a means of restructuring cognitive processes to achieve belief change (Clark, 2001; Hirsch & MacManus, 2007). After drawing anxious learners' attention to the role of self-focused attention and safety behaviours in maintaining anxiety, video feedback could help individuals to gain a more realistic understanding of how they appear to others rather than basing their assumptions purely on interoceptive information. Asking a learner to rate how anxious she looked during a series of L2 learning situation role plays in which she practiced focusing externally and avoided her usual in-class safety behaviours (such as not responding to teacher elicits or only providing monosyllabic answers) would help the individual to see the benefits of eschewing hypervigilant self-monitoring during lessons, helping her to gain a more objective impression of how she comes across to others. Unfortunately, space limitations mean that we are only able to touch on the use of video feedback here as a means for combating social anxiety among silent language learners, and so we direct readers to Hirsch and MacManus (2007) for a more comprehensive account of how this technique has been used as part of a systematic cognitive-based treatment within clinical contexts.

Conclusion

There are currently epidemic levels of learner disengagement within Japan's L2 university classrooms, and student silence is a trend that holds true there across a diverse range of classroom contexts. The reasons behind this silence are complex and defy simplistic generalisations. Learners may be unable or unwilling to speak up in their language classes for any number of reasons, and these reasons are shaped by interconnected variables that dynamically interplay with each other at individual and environmental levels. However, the mixed-methods study described in this chapter uncovered social anxiety as a prime factor in learners' avoidance of talk, and this silence of social inhibition appears to be well supported by unhelpful pedagogical practices on the one hand and higher-level sociocultural themes relating to the value of discretion and caution in public encounters on the other. Following a comprehensive overview of Japanese-related L2 anxiety research, this chapter has illustrated how Clark and Wells' (1995) model of social anxiety provides us with a useful framework through which we can better understand the cognitive processes and in-class safety behaviours of silently anxious learners of English in Japan. It would be interesting to replicate the mixed-methods study described here within the non-L2, general content classes of Japanese universities to see whether students' patterns of silent behaviour hold true when foreign languages are taken out of the equation. Were this true, the implications for the construct of FLA would be intriguing. One thing for certain though is that language learners in Japan can in no way claim to have a monopoly on reticent classroom behaviour and so we end our chapter with a call for more classroom-based, student-orientated research to be undertaken within a wider range of national contexts, putting silence at the very heart of the investigation.

References

Aida, Y. (1994) Examination of Horwitz, Horwitz, and Cope's construct of foreign language anxiety: The case of students of Japanese. *Modern Language Journal* 78 (2), 155–168.

American Psychiatric Association (2000) *Diagnostic and Statistical Manual of Mental Disorders* (4th edn). Washington, DC: Author.

Brislin, R.W. (1970) Back-translation for cross-cultural research. *Journal of Cross-Cultural Psychology* 1 (3), 185–216.

Brown, J.D., Robson, G. and Rosenkjar, P.R. (2001) Personality, motivation, anxiety, strategies and language proficiency of Japanese students. *Motivation and Second Language Acquisition* 23, 361–398.

Cheng, Y., Horwitz, E.K. and Schallert, D.L. (1999) Language anxiety: Differentiating writing and speaking components. *Language Learning* 49 (3), 417–446.

Clancy, P. (1990) Acquiring communicative style in Japanese. In R.C. Scarcella, E.S. Anderson and S.D. Krashen (eds) *Developing Communicative Competence in a Second Language* (pp. 27–35). New York: Newbury House.

Clark, D.M. (1999) Anxiety disorders: Why they persist and how to treat them. *Behavior Research and Therapy* 37, S5–S37.

Clark, D.M. (2001) A cognitive perspective on social phobia. In W.R. Crozier and L.E. Alden (eds) *International Handbook of Social Anxiety* (pp. 405–430). Chichester: Wiley.

Clark, D.M. and Wells, A. (1995) A cognitive model of social phobia. In R.G. Heimberg, M.R. Liebowitz, D.A. Hope and F.R. Schneier (eds) *Social Phobia: Diagnosis, Assessment and Treatment* (pp. 69–93). New York: Guilford Press.

Cocroft, B.-A.K. and Ting-Toomey, S. (1994) Facework in Japan and the United States. *International Journal of Intercultural Relations* 18 (4), 469–506.

Cornwell, S. and McKay, T. (1998) Group membership and writing apprehension: Do they affect academic writing? *Osaka Jogakuin Junior College Kiyo* 28, 193–204.

Cornwell, S. and McKay, T. (2000) Establishing a valid, reliable measure of writing apprehension for Japanese students. *JALT Journal* 22 (1), 114–139.

Curry, N. (2014) Using CBT with anxious language learners: The potential role of the learning advisor. *Studies in Self-Access Learning Journal* 5 (1), 29–41.

Daly, J.A. and Miller, M.D. (1975) The empirical development of an instrument to measure writing apprehension. *Research in the Teaching of English* 9 (3), 242–249.

Daubney, M. (2007) Language anxiety: Creative or negative force in the language classroom? *Humanising Language Teaching* 9 (5). See http://www.hltmag.co.uk/sep07/sart03.htm (accessed 7 January 2015).

Dörnyei, Z. and Murphey, T. (2003) *Group Dynamics in the Language Classroom*. Cambridge: Cambridge University Press.

Ehrman, M.E. and Dörnyei, Z. (1998) *Interpersonal Dynamics in Second Language Learning: The Visible and Invisible Classroom*. Thousand Oaks, CA: Sage.

Elkhafaifi, H. (2005) Listening comprehension and anxiety in the Arabic language classroom. *Modern Language Journal* 89 (2), 206–220.

Ely, C.M. (1986) Language learning motivation: A descriptive and causal analysis. *Modern Language Journal* 70 (1), 28–35.

Enninger, W. (1991) Focus on silence across cultures. *Intercultural Communication Studies* 1 (1), 1–37.

Falout, J. (2014) Circular seating arrangements: Approaching the social crux in language classrooms. *Studies in Second Language Acquisition* 4 (2), 275–300.

Franks, P.H. (2000) Silence/Listening and Intercultural Differences. Paper presented at the 21st Annual Meeting of the International Listening Association, Virginia Beach, VI.

Greer, D.L. (2000) 'The eyes of *hito*': A Japanese cultural monitor of behavior in the communicative language classroom. *JALT Journal* 22 (1), 183–195.

Gregersen, T. and Horwitz, E.K. (2002) Language learning and perfectionism: Anxious and non-anxious language learners' responses to their oral performance. *Modern Language Journal* 86 (4), 562–570.

Gudykunst, W.B. and Nishida, T. (1993) Interpersonal and intergroup communication in Japan and the United States. In W.B. Gudykunst (ed.) *Communication in Japan and the United States* (pp. 149–214). New York: State University of New York Press.

Hirsch, C. and McManus, F. (2007) Social phobia: Treatment. In S. Lindsay and G. Powell (eds) *The Handbook of Clinical Adult Psychology* (3rd edn, pp. 227–244). Hove: Routledge.

Horwitz, E.K., Horwitz, M.B. and Cope, J. (1986) Foreign language classroom anxiety. *Modern Language Journal* 70 (2), 125–132.

Kim, J.-H. (2000) Foreign language listening anxiety: A study of Korean students learning English. Unpublished PhD thesis, University of Texas.

Kimura, H. (2008) Foreign language listening anxiety: Its dimensionality and group differences. *JALT Journal* 30 (2), 173–196.

King, J. (2013a) *Silence in the Second Language Classroom*. Basingstoke: Palgrave Macmillan.

King, J. (2013b) Silence in the second language classrooms of Japanese universities. *Applied Linguistics* 34 (3), 325–343.

King, J. (2014) Fear of the true self: Social anxiety and the silent behaviour of Japanese learners of English. In K. Csizér and M. Magid (eds) *The Impact of Self-Concept on Language Learning* (pp. 232–249). Bristol: Multilingual Matters.

Kitano, K. (2001) Anxiety in the college Japanese language classroom. *Modern Language Journal* 85 (4), 549–566.

Leary, M.R. (1995) *Self-Presentation: Impression Management and Interpersonal Behavior*. Milwaukee, WI: Brown and Benchmark.

LeBlanc, C. (2015) Investigating high school students' self-efficacy in reading circles. *The Language Teacher* 39 (1), 15–21.

Lebra, T.S. (1987) The cultural significance of silence in Japanese communication. *Multilingua* 6 (4), 343–357.

Lebra, T.S. (1993) Culture, self, and communication in Japan and the United States. In W.B. Gudykunst (ed.) *Communication in Japan and the United States* (pp. 51–87). New York: State University of New York Press.

Liu, M. and Jackson, J. (2008) An exploration of Chinese EFL learners' unwillingness to communicate and foreign language anxiety. *The Modern Language Journal* 92 (1), 71–86.

MacIntyre, P.D., Clément, R. and Dörnyei, Z. (1998) Conceptualizing willingness to communicate in a L2: A situational model of L2 confidence and affiliation. *Modern Language Journal* 82 (4), 545–562.

MacIntyre, P.D., Baker, S.C., Clément, R. and Donovan, L.A. (2002) Sex and age effects on willingness to communicate, anxiety, perceived competence, and L2 motivation among junior high school French immersion students. *Language Learning* 52 (3), 537–564.

Matsuda, S. and Gobel, P. (2001) Quiet apprehension: Reading and classroom anxieties. *JALT Journal* 23 (2), 227–247.

Matsuda, S. and Gobel, P. (2004) Anxiety and predictors of performance in the foreign language classroom. *System* 32 (1), 21–36.

McManus, F. and Hirsch, C. (2007) Social phobia: Investigation. In S. Lindsay and G. Powell (eds) *The Handbook of Clinical Adult Psychology* (3rd edn, pp. 206–226). Hove: Routledge.

McVeigh, B.J. (2002) *Japanese Higher Education as Myth*. New York: M.E. Sharpe.

Nakane, I. (2007) *Silence in Intercultural Communication*. Amsterdam: John Benjamins.

Ohata, K. (2005) Potential sources of anxiety for Japanese learners of English: Preliminary case interviews with five Japanese college students in the US. *TESL-EJ* 9 (3), 1–21.

Piniel, K. (2014) Language Anxiety and the Four Skills. Paper presented at the Matters of the mind: Psychology and Language Learning Conference, Graz, Austria.

Purdon, C., Antony, M., Monteiro, S. and Swinson, R.P. (2001) Social anxiety in college students. *Anxiety Disorders* 15 (3), 203–215.

Saito, Y. and Samimy, K.K. (1996) Foreign language anxiety and language performance: A study of learner anxiety in beginning, intermediate, and advanced-level college students of Japanese. *Foreign Language Annals* 29 (2), 239–249.

Saito, Y., Horwitz, E.K. and Garza, T.J. (1999) Foreign language reading anxiety. *Modern Language Journal* 83 (2), 202–218.

Salkovskis, P.M. (1991) The importance of behaviour in the maintenance of anxiety and panic: A cognitive account. *Behavioural Psychotherapy* 19 (1), 6–19.

Scollon, R. and Scollon, S.W. (1990) Athabaskan-English interethnic communication. In D. Carbaugh (ed.) *Cultural Communication and Intercultural Contact* (pp. 259–286). Hillsdale, NJ: Lawrence Erlbaum Associates.

Sinclair, J. and Coulthard, M. (1975) *Towards an Analysis of Discourse*. Oxford: Oxford University Press.

Takahashi, A. (2004) Anxiety in the Japanese university EFL classroom. Unpublished PhD thesis, University of Birmingham.

Takahashi, A. (2010) Foreign language writing apprehension: Its relationships with motivation, self-perceived target language ability, and actual language ability. *Niigata Studies in Foreign Languages and Cultures* 15, 89–100.

Tanaka, H. (1999) *Turn-Taking in Japanese Conversation: A Study in Grammar and Interaction.* Amsterdam: John Benjamins.

Tani-Fukuchi, N. (2005) Japanese learner psychology and assessment of affect in foreign language study. *The Language Teacher* 29 (4), 3–9.

Vogley, A.J. (1998) Listening comprehension anxiety: Students' reported sources and solutions. *Foreign Language Annals* 31 (1), 67–80.

Woodrow, L. (2006) Anxiety and speaking English as a second language. *RELC Journal* 37 (3), 308–328.

Yamada, H. (1997) *Different Games, Different Rules: Why Americans and Japanese Misunderstand Each Other.* New York: Oxford University Press.

Yamauchi, Y. (2014) Changes in learners' English listening anxiety with use of difficult materials. *Hiroshima University Graduate School of Education Bulletin* 63 (2), 175–182.

7 Do You See What I Feel? An Idiodynamic Assessment of Expert and Peer's Reading of Nonverbal Language Anxiety Cues

Tammy Gregersen, Peter D. MacIntyre and Tucker Olson

Late one evening, an elderly member of the Cherokee Nation told his grandson about a struggle that is fought inside everyone.

He said, 'My son, the battle is between two "wolves" that reside in all of us. One is malevolent and promotes negativity. It is characterized by fear, worry, anxiety, jealousy, self-pity, resentment and superiority. The other is benevolent and nurtures positivity. It is joy, peace, love, hope, serenity, humility, kindness, empathy, generosity, and compassion'.

The enthralled grandson reflected for a moment and then asked, 'Which wolf wins?'

'The one we feed', simply replied the elderly man. (http://www.firstpeople.us/FP-Html-Legends/TwoWolves-Cherokee.html)

Introduction

Nowhere is this metaphorical struggle between wolves more evident than within anxious language learners, with teachers and classmates playing their part in the feeding of the wolves. Do we feed the benevolent wolf and receive the positive effects of well-being or are we complicit in nourishing the malevolent wolf whose existence is characterised by the negativity engendered by anxiety, fear and worry? One thing the elderly grandfather fails to mention, however, is that these inner wolves are continually vying for attention; their host's affective state is seldom stable. In an hour in a language classroom, one might find a learner feeding his/her low-anxiety wolf with self-talk reflecting enjoyment and pride at the accomplishments of a second language (L2) activity with a partner. Soon after, the teacher feeds the anxiety wolf by insensitive error correction. Friends help to feed the low-anxiety wolf with encouraging comments but also feed the anxious wolf as they express their worries about upcoming testing and the consequences of failure. Back and forth it goes. Ongoing fluctuations in anxiety beg the questions: How do we know which wolf language learners are feeding at any given moment? Can teachers tell whether the wolves are acting up?

Discerning the Presence of Anxiety

Language anxiety is 'the feeling of tension and apprehension specifically associated with second language contexts' (MacIntyre & Gardner, 1994: 284). It is one of the best predictors of language learning achievement (Gardner, 1985) and its negative tendencies restrict language learners' thought-action repertoires (MacIntyre & Gregersen, 2014). Anxious learners respond with limited efficacy to their own errors (Gregersen, 2003), are often absorbed in negative self-talk and ruminate over substandard performance that impedes their cognitive-processing capabilities (MacIntyre & Gardner, 1991). Furthermore, anxious individuals display avoidance behaviours by skipping class and/or procrastinating on tasks while retaining unattainably high personal performance standards (Gregersen & Horwitz, 2002). Classroom exchanges incite anxious learners to freeze up in role plays and to fail in their recall attempts of learned material. Anxious students tend to avoid volunteering for activities in the classroom and participate less often than their non-anxious classmates (Ely, 1986; Horwitz et al., 1986). Taken together, the repercussions of anxiety over time can reduce course grades (Gardner, 1985) and ultimately foreign language (FL) proficiency.

Mitigating the Negative Impact of Anxiety

Previous investigations using retrospective techniques have suggested a myriad of measures to mitigate the consequences of language anxiety. Anxiety reduction techniques in the literature include the transformation of students' negative self-related cognitions by focusing on positive experiences (MacIntyre & Gardner, 1991); using affectively sensitive error correction techniques (Gregersen, 2003); participating in relaxation exercises, behavioural contracting and journal-keeping (Gregersen & MacIntyre, 2014; Horwitz et al., 1986); developing realistic expectations for the language learning process (Price, 1991); increasing feelings of self-efficacy (Pappamihiel, 2002); incorporating group dynamic activities into the syllabus (Clément et al., 1994); creating student support systems

(Horwitz et al., 1986); giving more positive reinforcement (Price, 1991); and making the classroom as relaxing and friendly as possible through pair and small-group work, games, simulations and structured exercises that alter the communication pattern of the classroom (Crookall & Oxford, 1991).

Gregersen and MacIntyre (2014) dedicate an entire chapter to research on language anxiety and activities to alleviate its negative effects in their book, *Capitalizing on Language Learners' Individuality: From Premise to Practice*. To deal with anxiety, they advocate reflection, exploration and cognisance:

> As teachers reflect upon issues of language anxiety through the exploration of the following activities, they must remain cognizant that anxiety can manifest in physical, emotional, linguistic and social behaviors. Teachers, individual language learners, and the class as a whole can pull together to create a network of support and collaboration. (Gregersen & MacIntyre, 2014: 13)

Their intention in designing their activities was to create a 'classroom comfort zone' where teachers, individual learners and the group as a whole mutually encourage each other:

> Teachers will have the opportunity to review their instructional choices, classroom procedures, and language testing practices; individuals will reflect on their choices to focus on previous achievement and progress or past failures and perfection; and the group will build community and social networks that are fundamental to positive interaction. (Gregersen & MacIntyre, 2014: 13)

Identifying the Nonverbal Signs of Anxiety

But successful application of anxiety-reducing techniques with specific individuals depends on identifying anxiety as an issue. It bears emphasising that, before one can deal with the anxiety wolves, teachers and learners must recognise that they are at the door. Previous applied linguistics investigations suggest that there are nonverbal cues that indicate the presence of anxiety. Nonverbal communication includes a variety of 'codes' that capture different types of nonverbal cues; among these are kinesic cues such as gesture and posture, facial expression that includes smiling and eye behaviour and vocalics, which consists of the ways that individuals use their voices to create meaning through intonation, pitch and other prosodic features. Gregersen (2005) gathered evidence through an observation study that demonstrated that the nonverbal behaviour of anxious and non-anxious language learners differs when they participate in high-anxiety-provoking situations such as an oral language exam. She discovered variances in their facial expressiveness, eye behaviour, posture and body movements. For example, anxious learners showed limited facial activity, including brow behaviour and smiling; maintained less eye contact with the teacher and were more rigid and closed with their posture. Furthermore, with respect to gestures, anxious learners used their hands more than the non-anxious did for purposes unrelated to communication, such as self-touching and object manipulation. The less anxious learners used gesture to enhance communication by adding more illustrative and regulatory gestures to manage interaction. This finding is significant because the anxious learners tied up their hands in nonproductive ways – unlike the non-anxious who used gesture for communicative purposes.

Similar to Gregersen's (2005) nonverbal language anxiety study, Burgoon and Koper (1984) found that reticent individuals exhibited more negative arousal in the form of anxiety, tension and unpleasant affect than non-reticent participants; and fewer forms of positive arousal as demonstrated through enthusiasm, expressiveness and animation. Reticent nonverbal patterns conveyed low levels of immediacy, intimacy, assertiveness, composure and receptivity while also demonstrating high dissimilarity and submissiveness. In short, their study found that trained observers were able to see patterns of reticent nonverbal behaviour: bodily tension, self-touching, postural rigidity, protective behaviours such as closed body positions, leaning away, gaze aversion and indirect head orientation, less facial pleasantness, nodding and animation. The behavioural patterns were more pronounced as stress increased.

Preparing Teachers to Decode Anxious Behaviours

Gregersen (2007) examined teachers' accuracy in decoding the nonverbal behaviour indicative of language anxiety and found that, to a point, nonverbal decoding can be taught. She took measures of decoding ability before and after a training intervention. Results demonstrated that there was variability in the ability of trained and untrained observers to decode the nonverbal cues evidential of anxiety. Also, the teachers and trainees were more accurate in assessing the nonverbal behaviour of learners who were on the high and low ends of the anxiety scale than those whose scores fell in the middle. Because observers were more accurate once they were introduced to explicit anxiety-indicating cues, Gregersen (2007) proposed nonverbal awareness training as a means of identifying those learners who struggle with language anxiety.

Finally, Gregersen (2009) examined observers' accuracy in decoding language anxiety under three different conditions: auditory-only, visual-only and a combination of the two channels. Although her quantitative data did not confirm which channel provided a more accurate means of detection, her qualitative data revealed indicators in both visual and auditory modes that resulted in more effective judgments. By comparing what accurate decoders were seeing with what was seen by those who were not as effective in judging emotion, she concluded that one of the most problematic visual cues that led to incorrect determinations was smiling:

> Whereas the accurate decoders of anxious learners cited behavior like 'fake smile' and 'smiled too much' as an indicator of language anxious behavior, the inaccurate decoders also used 'smiled a lot' to justify identifying the same learners as non-anxious. Thus decoding accuracy did not necessarily depend on noting whether the learner smiled or not, but on making an authenticity judgment about whether the smile was genuine. (Gregersen, 2009: 57)

In terms of indicators in the auditory channel that provided confounding messages, Gregersen (2009) cited pauses as being the most problematic for nonverbal observers. Specifically, observers were not able to separate pauses that were produced due to limited language proficiency from the stuttering and non-fluencies indicative of negative affective arousal.

Nonverbal behaviour is the primary mechanism through which individuals communicate emotion in the language learning and teaching process, both in sending out behavioural cues and in decoding or recognising behavioural cues in other people (Richmond & McCroskey, 2012). Teachers who can read these cues accurately are better able to react to the changing emotional tenor in the classroom that can disrupt even the most carefully prepared lesson. Being sensitive to nonverbal emotional cues can keep the anxiety wolves at bay, avoiding some of the harmful consequences of emotional arousal that tend to narrow students' focus to dealing with the source of anxiety (MacIntyre & Gregersen, 2012).

Understanding Anxious Learners' Illusion of Transparency

Anxiety has been called a 'self-exacerbating syndrome' (Jussim & Eccles, 1995; Snyder, 1984). This means that the experience of anxiety tends to generate more anxiety, as when a student feels anxiety rising and begins to worry that others will notice it, giving rise to even more anxiety. This issue has been discussed in the literature on public speaking anxiety where it has been linked to the illusion of transparency that arises when one believes that his/her '...thoughts, feelings, and emotions are more apparent to others than is actually the case' (Gilovich et al., 1998: 618). L2 learners/speakers sometimes believe their anxious emotional state is transparent to listeners and embarrassing to themselves. The illusion of transparency is conceptually related to the spotlight effect, whereby people overestimate the extent to which their actions are noticed by others (Gilovich et al., 2000, 2002) and the anchoring and adjustment heuristic that people use to estimate how others see them. Savitsky and Gilovich (2003) argue that people have difficulty stepping back from their own experience when contemplating how others see them. How might a target language learner/speaker know whether he/she appears anxious to others? Ironically, many of the facial nonverbal cues that drive the ongoing assessment of anxiety are unavailable to learners/speakers (unless they have a mirror during their speaking or are watching themselves on video). Instead, they anchor their perceptions in their own internal state and then assume that observers will make a similar assessment, possibly with some adjustment to account for the present situation.

When an internal emotional state is particularly strong, as it is with high anxiety, perhaps it is not surprising that the learner/speaker is more aware of his/her anxiety than an external observer might be (Gilovich et al., 1998; Savitsky & Gilovich, 2003). In a study of the illusion of transparency, Savitsky and Gilovich (2003) asked participants to deliver impromptu speeches in pairs, rating their own anxiety and how visible their anxiety was to their partner. Results showed that participants tended to overestimate the extent to which their nervousness leaked out and was visible to observers. Supporting the idea of a self-exacerbating syndrome, the effects of the illusion of transparency were reduced simply by reassuring speakers that the audience could not see anxiety as clearly as the speaker believed.

Heeding the Call for Dynamic Research Techniques

Unfortunately, there have been relatively few studies that have investigated fluctuations in either ongoing anxiety among L2 speakers or observer's ratings of a speaker's anxiety. In the applied linguistics arena, emotions such as language anxiety have traditionally been measured retrospectively with instruments that have examined summative assessments of learners' anxiety over long timescales. For example, the widely used Foreign Language Classroom Anxiety Scale (FLCAS) is a 33-item measure of experiences in the classroom that reflects general tendencies (Horwitz, 2010). Measures such as the FLCAS do not capture in-the-moment reactions on shorter timescales. Interview and diary studies tend to focus on learners' typical behaviour or unusually memorable episodes (see MacIntyre, 1999; this volume). A retrospective account is always subject to the deleterious effects of time on memory, as details of events fade and the inevitable reconstruction of events takes place in memory.

This study takes a different approach. We examine emotion as part of a dynamic system that is in constant flux and is interacting with other influencing variables at any given moment; we examine fluctuations in language anxiety operating in real time. This is the second phase of a two-part study. In the first phase, the 'idiodynamic' method, a novel data-gathering means using specialised software (MacIntyre, 2012), was used to collect language learner participants' self-ratings of moment-to-moment changes in their levels of language anxiety (Gregersen et al., 2014). The term 'idiodynamic' refers to our interest in the moment-to-moment fluctuations in emotion within the individual. In this present phase, the ratings by two nonverbal observers (one 'peer' and one 'expert') were added into the mix and compared with the self-ratings of learners.

Emotions as experienced are dynamic – in constant flux and interacting with a number of influencing variables, including thoughts, physical state, the interpersonal situation, recent events and other factors at any given moment (Gregersen & MacIntyre, 2014). Learners and teachers are continuously involved in a process of 'reading' each other and reacting to each other's cues. Although previous research has recognised and catalogued the nonverbal cues indicative of language anxiety (Gregersen, 2005) and has demonstrated the efficacy of training teachers in nonverbal decoding (Gregersen, 2007), relatively little is known about the ability to recognise and respond to the dynamic, constantly changing nature of language learners' emotions – and in particular, their anxiety.

Two different external observers were used to assess whether experienced teachers or peers might show stronger convergence or divergence with the learners' self-ratings. On the one hand, previous research suggests that training in nonverbal awareness would give the expert practitioner an edge (Gregersen, 2007); yet on the other hand, 'near peer role modeling' research suggests that 'people who might be "near" to us in several ways: age, ethnicity, gender, interests, past or present experiences, and also in proximity and in frequency of social contact' understand and motivate each other (Murphey, 2001). This notion might give the peer observer an advantage in accuracy. In our data, the junctures where the expert practitioner observer was more consistent with the learners' self-ratings than the peer observer may indicate those nonverbal cues whose decoding may be more susceptible to greater experience and training. However, those points in the idiodynamic data where the peer observer was more accurate in rating the anxiety of the learner than the expert practitioner may indicate those nonverbal cues that are best understood by near peers who have greater social access and share a variety of demographic and emotional features.

To facilitate observers' sensitivity to various types of nonverbal cues, both the expert practitioner and peer observers used the same idiodynamic method to review participants' videos under three conditions: audio only, visual only and a combination of the two channels. Observers each made three sets of idiodynamic ratings that provided evidence concerning the most recognisable nonverbal manifestations of language anxiety. The relative efficacy of expert practitioners versus peers in interpreting nonverbal cues indicative of negative affect also will be considered.

Taking these previous investigations into account, we explored answers to the following questions:

(1) How do the dynamic patterns of ratings of anxiety for an L2 classroom presentation made by the speaker himself/herself compare with ratings of anxiety made by expert and peer external observers?
(2) Are there auditory and visual nonverbal indicators of language anxiety that are consistently encoded by learners, which observers can accurately idiodynamically decode? If so, what are they?
(3) How does the idiodynamic observation data drawn from an expert practitioner compare with those of a language learning peer when considering the self-ratings of anxious and non-anxious public speakers? (i.e. Is one observer more accurate than the other?)

Method

Overview of Phase One

Participants

In the previous phase of this study (Gregersen *et al.*, 2014), 6 participants were selected from a larger group of 18 adult volunteers who were enrolled in an intermediate Spanish-as-a-foreign-language class at a university in the Midwestern United States. The scores on the FLCAS, a 33-item, self-report, Likert-type measure of anxiety specific to the language learning context (Horwitz *et al.*, 1986), established the three most highly anxious (HAPs) and the three least anxious participants (LAPs) from the group of 18. These six English speakers (five female and one male), who had all completed at least one previous semester of university Spanish, were invited and consented to participate. All were of typical university age (19–23 years) and were studying a variety of different social sciences majors (social work, communications, education and psychology).

Procedures

The six participants were video recorded on the same day while giving an oral presentation in their Spanish class. Topics were self-selected by the students and the presentations were limited to three to five minutes. It should be noted that the presenters were wearing wrist and chest heart monitors to collect physiological heart rate data, which might have affected their emotions; physiological data are reported elsewhere, in Gregersen *et al.* (2014). Immediately after the class, the video files were loaded from the camera onto a computer and participants individually watched the presentations of their speeches on the computer screen. Using software designed for studies such as this (MacIntyre, 2012; MacIntyre & Legatto, 2011), participants' 'idiodynamically' self-rated the moment-to-moment fluctuations in their language anxiety levels. They signalled rising anxiety by right-clicking the computer mouse (up to '+5') or reductions in anxiety by left-clicking the mouse (down to '−5'). This procedure generated a bitmap graph and Excel spreadsheet that reflected the vacillations in each participant's self-rated anxiety.

The current study: Phase Two

Participants

Several days after collecting the participants' self-ratings of their classroom language anxiety, we asked one expert language practitioner and one peer language learner to observe the videotapes of the six presenters using the same idiodynamic data-gathering process outlined above to assess the nonverbal anxiety cues from a third-person objective perspective. That is to say, neither were involved in the Spanish class from which the participants were drawn, nor did they play any role in the data collection of Phase One.

The 'expert language practitioner' was a bilingual female Spanish-as-a-foreign-language teacher educator with over 20 years of post-secondary classroom experience who had also published peer-reviewed articles on the topic of nonverbal behaviour and emotional intelligence. The 'peer' was a 22-year-old Spanish/teacher of English to speakers of other languages (TESOL) double major who was studying to become a teacher and who did not have any teaching experience outside the simulations and observations required in her undergraduate classes. Although she was a Spanish major at the university, her proficiency did not come close to the 'balanced bilingualism' of the expert practitioner observer. Furthermore, the peer observer had not been exposed to research on nonverbal communication.

Procedures

In Phase One of this study, as reported in Gregersen *et al.* (2014), data were collected for six presenters using the idiodynamic software. In the present study, Phase Two, both the expert practitioner and peer observer watched the six videos from Phase One and followed the same 'idiodynamic' instructions as did the presenters. That is to say, a video of each speaker was played on a computer screen while the observer right- and left-clicked the computer mouse to indicate perceived increasing or decreasing anxiety in the presenter. Observers reviewed each of the six participants' videos three times under three different conditions: visual only, audio only and a combined channel of video and audio together.

The observations under each condition produced separate bitmap graphs and Excel spreadsheets, similar to those generated in Phase One for the six presenters.

It is important to note that the spreadsheet numerical data and bitmap graphs were directly linked to the video data in the case of all observers – both self and external. This means that it was possible for us to go back into the video data and discover what the presenter was doing or saying at any moment in his/her video-recorded presentation by looking for changes in facial expression, gesture, gaze behaviour and posture, and by listening for changes in vocal behaviour like false starts, prolonged vowels and fluency, among others.

Results

Research question one: Comparing expert, peer and self-ratings of anxiety

Data analysis began by comparing idiodynamic ratings of anxiety provided by the presenters themselves, the peer ratings and the expert ratings. Figures 7.1 to 7.6 show that for all six presenters, the patterns of self-ratings are considerably more variable than either the peer or expert ratings.

Table 7.1 presents the mean and standard deviations for each presenter's self-ratings and the expert practitioner and peer ratings based on the combination of audio and video channels. Although the HAPs show higher mean self-ratings during the study (as reported in Phase One; Gregersen et al., 2014), the most notable result is that for every presenter, the standard deviation of the self-ratings is dramatically larger than the

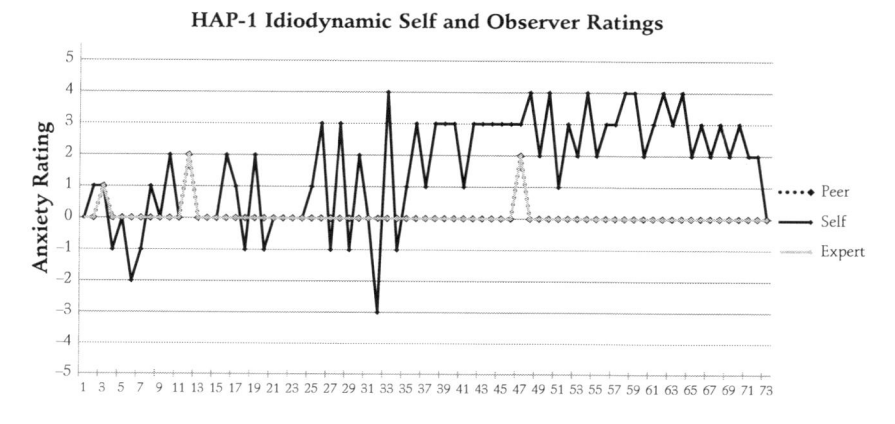

Figure 7.1

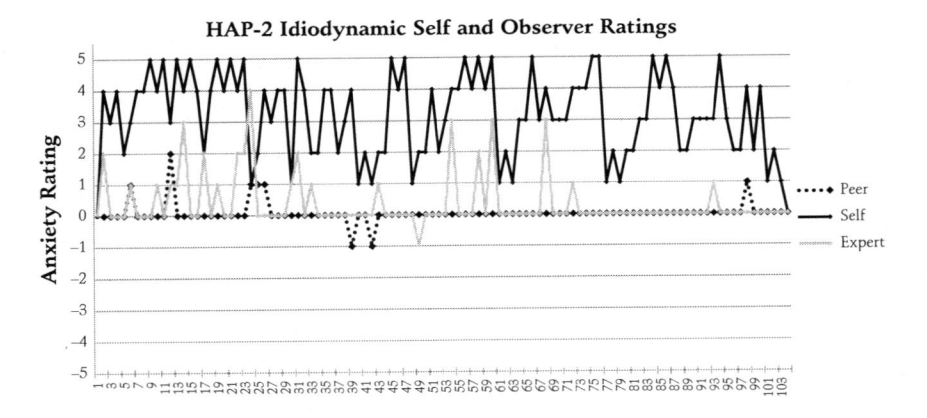

Figure 7.2

standard deviation of the expert practitioner and peer observer ratings. This suggests that there is more dynamic internal emotional activity than is perceived by external observers. Nevertheless, observers did show variability in their ratings of the presenter's anxiety. Our attention turns now to the cues that were used by observers to detect anxiety.

Research question two: Exploring auditory and visual nonverbal indicators of anxiety

The next phase of data analysis assessed where the three data sets converge. In order to identify the points of convergence, we analysed the data in a way similar to Phase One (Gregersen *et al.*, 2014), using a 'moving window' of five seconds to identify segments of time in which the

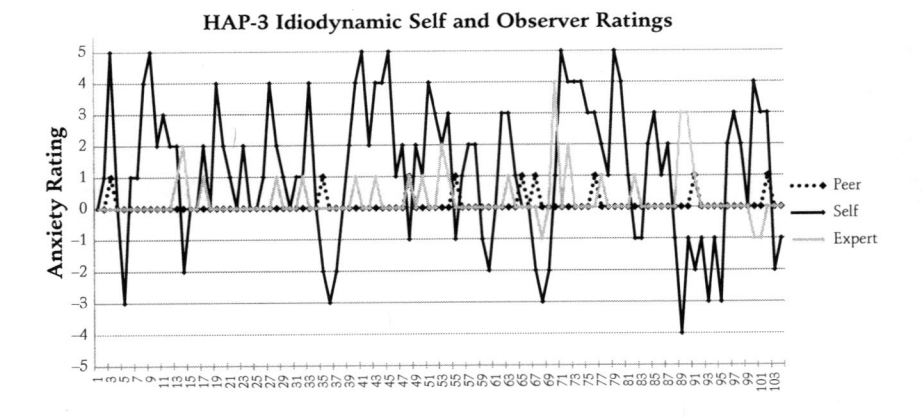

Figure 7.3

LAP-1 Idiodynamic Self and Observer Ratings

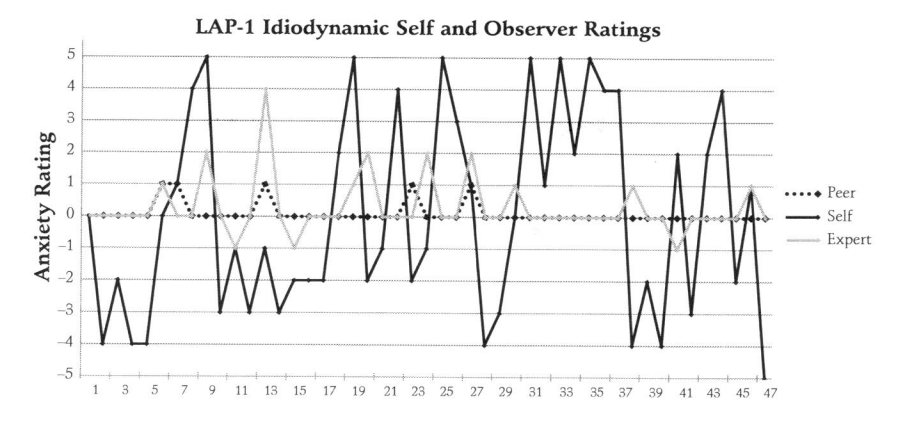

Figure 7.4

idiodynamic data shifted. The change, or slope, between each five-second window was then calculated in order to focus on the direction of change in reported anxiety rather than the degree of change, to capture movement in the ratings. These slopes reflected the dips and spikes of reported anxiety by the presenters and the anxiety detected by the observers.

In order to identify points of convergence, we calculated the difference between the self-reported anxiety slopes and those of the observer. We then selected the longest time segments with the smallest difference (±0.4) during dips and spikes. In other words, the convergence could not simply identify points in which anxiety remained constant. Table 7.2 shows the results when we calculated Pearson correlation coefficients in order to measure the strength of each convergence segment.

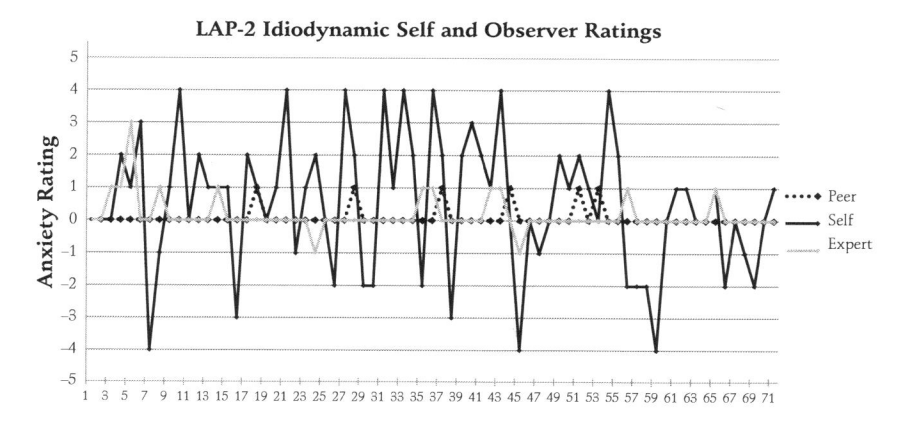

LAP-2 Idiodynamic Self and Observer Ratings

Figure 7.5

LAP-3 Idiodynamic Self and Observer Ratings

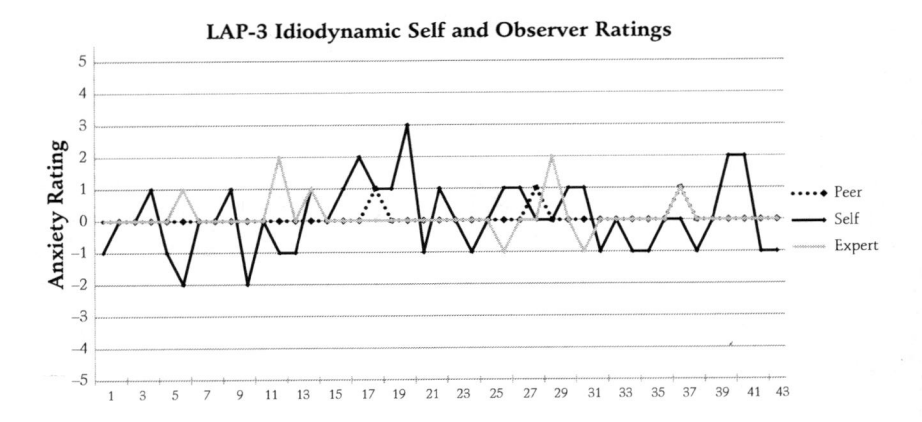

(chart showing Anxiety Rating over items 1–43 for Peer, Self, and Expert)

Figure 7.6

It should be emphasised that the correlations shown in Table 7.2 are used as a descriptive statistic in order to verify that there is a linear trend in the data from the participant and an observer. We are looking for pairs of anxiety ratings that rise and fall together during a delimited segment of communication. These correlations are not tested for significance in the usual way because we are not looking at inferring a population parameter from the sample. To be more specific, we use the correlations to focus attention on segments of communication within which a linear trend can be observed. In other research, correlations are used to estimate the strength of the relationship between the anxiety ratings of participants and observers. But in the present study, the correlations are used to identify segments of communication in which a qualitative analysis of behaviours occurs. In effect, we are asking a different type of research question here (see MacIntyre *et al.*, in press). We are asking '*when* is there a correlation between anxiety ratings made by participants and observers?' rather than a more traditional question, phrased as '*what* is the correlation between anxiety ratings of participants and observers?'

Table 7.1 Idiodynamic ratings of anxiety for self, peer observer and expert observer

	Mean			*Standard deviation*		
	Self	Peer	Expert	Self	Peer	Expert
LAP-1	0.02	0.11	0.30	3.13	0.31	0.87
LAP-2	0.54	0.08	0.15	2.04	0.28	0.52
LAP-3	0.09	0.07	0.12	1.10	0.25	0.54
HAP-1	1.60	0.07	0.07	1.68	0.34	0.34
HAP-2	3.18	0.05	0.36	1.34	0.32	0.84
HAP-3	1.19	0.09	0.25	2.20	0.28	0.73

Table 7.2 Points of convergence in different segment lengths among peer and expert observers and low and high anxious participants

Participant	HAP1	HAP2	HAP3	LAP1	LAP2	LAP3
FLACS score	125	117	106	60	51	48
Segment length (seconds)	15	20	15	20	25	15
Pearson: Participant+expert	1.0	0.43	0.87	0.91	0.54	0.50
Pearson: Participant+peer	1.0	0.85	0.87	0.96	0.54	0.50

We reviewed the video recordings of the presentations in order to identify the nonverbal behaviours present in the time segments where all three data sets converged. The categories for nonverbal behaviour included the codes we mentioned previously: facial movement, gestures, gaze, vocalics and posture. Rather than the number of occurrences, the number of presenters who exhibited a behaviour was recorded. Each behaviour must have occurred in at least two presenters to be included.

Table 7.3 illustrates the nonverbal behaviours of the presenters that were present when the slope of the presenter's self-ratings converged with those of both the peer and expert practitioner observer. There were a variety of behaviours observed across the various nonverbal codes, but none of the observed behaviours were observed in all presenters.

Research question three: Comparing data from expert and peer observers

Next, we investigated cues that were used differentially by the expert practitioner and peer observers. First, we identified points at which the peer observer ratings and the expert practitioner ratings diverged, defined by showing opposite directions in the slopes of the ratings. These windows of divergence identified between the observers lasted only 5 or 10 seconds. Therefore, we did not calculate correlations for each of these windows beyond identifying each as divergent between observers. We counted each behaviour as unique in its five-second window; therefore, the same behaviour may have been present in a given presenter's performance multiple times. In each case, the slope of the presenter's self-ratings was moving in the same direction as that of one or the other observer. The repetition of each behaviour, whether present in one presenter's performance or in several, strengthens the assumption that the observer who is converging with the presenter's slope is able to identify anxiety through nonverbal cues better than the other observer.

Together, Tables 7.4 and 7.5 display an extensive list of cues that were observed when the expert practitioner's ratings had a slope moving in the same direction as the presenter's self-ratings but the peer observer's ratings were moving in the opposite direction. In Table 7.4, the ratings are moving towards higher anxiety and in Table 7.5 towards lower anxiety.

124 Part 2: Empirical Investigations

Table 7.3 Behaviours for which both observers converged most strongly with the participant

	Face	Gesture	Gaze	Vocalics	Posture
Raising anxiety reported	Furrow brows (2)	Hands stationary at naval height (2)	Rapid alternation between screen and audience (3)	False start (2)	Rock forward into hip (2)
	Raise brows (2)	Knead hands (2)		Prolonged conjunction (2)	Arms folded (2)
Lowering anxiety reported		Unfold hands (2)	Strongly at screen (3)		Become more direct (3)
		Downward gesture, palms down (2)			Shift weight to other foot (3)

Table 7.4 Nonverbal cues present during increasing anxiety for both self-ratings and expert practitioner ratings but not peer ratings

Face	Gesture	Gaze	Vocalics	Posture
Raise brows (8)	Palms turn up (6)	Strongly at audience (8)	Frequent 'um' (7)	Indirect to audience, at screen (9)
Swallow (4)	One-handed gesture (6)	Strongly at screen (8)	Self-correction (6)	Cross legs (5)
Tilt head with inflect (3)	Hands stationary at naval height (4)	Rapid alternation between screen and audience (5)	Long pause (5)	Rock forward into hip (5)
Pucker lips (2)	Hands at side (4)	Mainly at audience, briefly to screen (5)	Pause to find word (4)	Twist at torso (4)
Furrow brows (2)	Gesture imitate words (3)	Upward to recall vocabulary (5)	Pattern alternating a word and pause (4)	Direct to audience (3)

(Continued)

Table 7.4 (Continued)

Face	Gesture	Gaze	Vocalics	Posture
Smile (2)	Hands pick at fingers (3)	Strongly down (3)	Fluid speech (3)	Shift weight to other foot (3)
Frown (2)	Bring hands together (3)	Mainly at screen, briefly to audience (3)	Repeat self (2)	Uncross legs (3)
Nod with each word (2)	Gesture to screen (3)	Briefly down (2)		Widen stance, separate feet (3)
Long blink (2)	Palms turn down (3)			Lean onto desk (2)
	Hands on desk (2)			
	Kneads hands (2)			
	Bounce hands on each word (2)			

Table 7.5 Nonverbal cues present during lowering anxiety for both self-ratings and expert practitioner ratings but not peer ratings

Face	Gesture	Gaze	Vocalics	Posture
Smile (2)				Cross legs (2)

Table 7.6 Behaviours during which rising anxiety was reported and converged between the peer observer and the presenter, but the expert practitioner observer failed to converge

Face	Gesture	Gaze	Vocalics	Posture
Raise brows (4)	Knead hands (5)	Strongly at screen (4)	Long pause (3)	Indirect to audience, at screen (2)
Smile (2)	Gestures imitate words (2)	Shift to strongly at audience (2)	Stumble on words (2)	Direct to audience (2)
Smack lips (2)	Palms turned up (2)	Briefly to audience (2)	Immediate repetition (2)	Both feet forward (2)
		Briefly down (2)		Twist body repeatedly at torso (2)

Combining Tables 7.4 and 7.5, there were many upward and downward trends in nonverbal behaviour that the expert practitioner observer noticed but that did not generate a reaction for the peer observer (see Table 7.6); that is, Tables 7.4 and 7.5 have many more elements in them than Table 7.6. Interestingly, both of the nonverbal behaviours noted in Table 7.5 (declining anxiety) were also present in Table 7.4 (increasing anxiety ratings), though both smiling and crossing the legs were more prevalent as indicators of increasing anxiety.

There were occasions when the peer observer converged with the presenter, but the expert practitioner observer did not. Table 7.6 shows nonverbal cues during the segments wherein the peer observer converged with the presenter.

Unexpectedly, there were no nonverbal cues identified during declining anxiety; therefore, there is no table showing convergence between self- and peer ratings as anxiety was falling.

Discussion

If language anxiety is like a wolf that can be fed by the reactions of observers, then this study has both good news and bad news for language learners and those who have wolves howling at their heels. First, learners might think it is bad news that anxiety can be observed accurately by examining nonverbal cues, at least some of the time. The expert practitioner in this study appears to have an advantage over a peer observer in detecting those cues. Whether a teacher's decoding ability is good news or bad news for the learner depends on her/his relationship with the teacher. Horwitz (this volume) strongly cautions teachers against deliberately promoting language anxiety because of its many negative effects; we agree with Horwitz that a wise teacher will not deliberately increase learners' anxiety. Instead, teachers' greater sensitivity to language anxiety cues can be used to find ways of reducing language anxiety for the learner/speakers (for specific suggestions, see Gregersen & MacIntyre, 2014).

There is a second source of good news for anxious learners in this data set: nonverbal anxiety cues are not necessarily easy to detect. If language anxiety in the classroom is like public speaking anxiety, then it can be considered a self-exacerbating syndrome. A nervous learner might be afraid of appearing nervous to others, especially when giving a formal presentation to an audience of teachers and peers as in the present study. Anxiety-arousal might also be called a sort of self-fulfilling prophecy or a vicious cycle where the learner is feeling strong emotion and is afraid that others can detect it and evaluate him/her more negatively. The idiodynamic ratings made by the presenters in the current study do show considerable variability, showing upward and downward slopes throughout the speaking event. However, the idiodynamic ratings made by the two observers showed far less variability, indicating that both the expert practitioner and peer observer had some difficulty identifying the emotional rollercoaster that the presenter felt. If the results of Savitsky and Gilovich (2003) are also applicable to language anxiety, then showing anxious learners their own idiodynamic ratings paired with ratings by an observer (as in Figures 7.1 to 7.6) might have an anxiety-reducing effect; this hypothesis might be tested in future research. In general, based on the present results and studies of the illusion of transparency, learners can be reassured that an audience of expert practitioners and peers does not detect all of the anxious cues that an individual might experience within himself/herself.

The observers, however, can accurately detect *some* anxiety-related cues. In this study, both expert practitioner and peer observers were more consistent in identifying cues when anxiety was rising than when anxiety was declining. The nonverbal codes that were used by both observers to accurately identify anxiety included furrowed and/or raised brows, hands either completely stationary at navel level or kneading together, rapidly alternating gaze between the screen and audience, false starts and prolonged conjunctions (e.g. aaaaaand, buuuuuut), and rocking-forward hip movements and/or arms folded. The consistency of the decoding accuracy suggests that these may be the most reliable nonverbal indicators of language anxiety.

Using the same nonverbal codes and looking for indications of lowered anxiety produced much less convergence. There were, however, a few indicators through which declining anxiety could be assessed accurately, including unfolded hands, downward gestures (palms down), an unwavering gaze, shifting weight between feet and a posture directly facing the audience.

These findings provide evidence for the notion that anxiety cues are more clearly and easily interpreted than cues associated with lowering anxiety. Perhaps it is not surprising to note that it is easier to see indicators of an emotion when it is present, but not necessarily when it is dissolving. Anxiety is a ubiquitous experience and the cues associated with rising anxiety seem to be fairly unambiguous compared with those of lowering anxiety. The arousal of anxiety has been associated with a number of processes, including physiological arousal, distracting cognition and concern about being negatively evaluated by other people (Horwitz *et al.*, 1986). Some nonverbal cues, such as swallowing, kneading the hands, twisting the torso, crossing the legs and so on, seem to be related to reducing physical discomfort associated with the physiology of anxiety. Other cues, such as long pauses, vocal fillers (such as 'ummm') and limited gestures can be produced by cognitive distraction (see Eysenck, 1979; MacIntyre & Gardner, 1994).

Finally, several nonverbal behaviours, such as frequent nodding of the head and extended gaze at the audience, are consistent with looking for reassurance or approval from the audience. Other cues, such as averted gaze and staring at the screen, can be associated with avoiding potentially negative feedback from the audience. Communications experts agree that 'we cannot not communicate'. Sigmund Freud said, in his *Introductory Lectures in Psychoanalysis*, 'He that has eyes to see and ears to hear may convince himself that no mortal can keep a secret. If his lips are silent, he chatters with his fingertips; betrayal oozes out of him at every pore'. The presenters in our study who wished to keep their anxiety private were betrayed somewhat by their hands, faces, eyes, bodies and voices.

The third research question deals with the contrast between the accuracy of an expert practitioner versus a peer observer. We need to preface the consideration of this question by mentioning that there were several notable nonverbal cues that converged among the self-ratings and the ratings of both observers. When comparing the frequency of these shared nonverbal cues, the expert practitioner observer more often produced instances of correct decoding of the nonverbal cue (defined by converging slopes with the learner/speaker's ratings) where the peer observer did not. It is important to note that the expert practitioner observer clicked during the idiodynamic evaluations of anxiety more frequently than the peer observer. Therefore, there are many more dips and spikes in the expert observer's data than in the peer observer's data. This might have produced more points of convergence or points of divergence, depending on the connection to the presenter's self-ratings. In effect, the expert practitioner observer was taking more risks by clicking more often.

It could be that the expert practitioner observer was indeed correctly identifying nonverbal cues at a rate much higher than the peer observer. It is clear that more distinct nonverbal behaviours were present in the expert observer's segments of convergence with the presenter. There were very few behaviours that the peer observer accurately decoded but the expert practitioner observer did not. The expert practitioner observer noticed cues in almost all the categories: face, gesture, eye behaviour, vocalics and posture. Previous investigations into nonverbal behaviour suggest that, although the expression of emotion is primarily displayed through facial expression, feelings can also be conveyed through posture, the manner in which a learner walks or limb movements, among other kinesic actions. Gestures that display affect convey learners' emotional reactions to what is going on, too – and the strength of those reactions. In other words, while the face is actually a more accurate determiner of the *kind* of emotion being experienced, bodily cues are better at gauging the *intensity* of the emotion being experienced. Furthermore, as far as bodily cues are concerned, posture tends to be more central in communicating emotion than gestures (Leather & Eaves, 2008). The rate with which learners move their bodies tends to be a more consistent manifestation of general emotional arousal (or lack thereof) than an indicator of a specific emotion (Collier, 1985). In reference to previous investigations of vocalics in the determination of another's emotion, Pittam and Scherer (1993) found that the ability to recognise emotion from the voice is four to five times higher than what would be expected if respondents were simply guessing. The ability to read nonverbal emotion cues can be developed through experience.

It would be too simplistic to declare that expert observers are more accurate at detecting anxiety cues than peer observers, or even that our specific expert practitioner observer was more accurate than the specific peer observer who made the ratings in the present study. Instead, it is more reasonable to suggest that experience might impact the willingness of educators to take risks in identifying anxious behaviour due to heightened awareness of the cues. Expert practitioner observers who are concerned about language anxiety in their classrooms are more likely to be assessing the anxiety of their students in real time. Teachers who actively take nonverbal emotional cues into consideration in the classroom, for example by asking learners about their reactions to classroom activities, seem more likely to be able to develop a higher probability of correctly identifying their learners' anxiety.

There are several limitations to the present study. First, given the focus on individual-level data, formal hypothesis testing with estimates of statistical significance is not available in this research design. In its place, patterns of variability become the focus of the study. A second issue might be identified by noting the potential biases in self-reporting. Although we assume that the variability in the self-ratings reflects a presenter's access to internal sources of anxiety-related experiences (e.g. their unexpressed thoughts or the emotions they recalled feeling), it is possible that the self-ratings are more variable than peer ratings for some other, unknown reason. The presenters used the same procedure as the observers in rating anxiety; that is, the presenters did not rate the anxiety directly *in situ* but did so after the fact, using video. Does this procedure simply produce more variability in the ratings? Both the interview data and the physiological data reported from Phase One (Gregersen *et al.*, 2014) provide some reassurance that the idiodynamic variability is meaningful, but the idiodynamic method is new and such issues have not been fully worked out. Finally, in the present study, we were limited to one expert practitioner and one peer observer; their ratings might reflect uniquely personal skills and nonverbal perception tendencies rather than tendencies indicative of teachers and peers more generally. We especially want to draw attention to the small size of our sample as it is highly plausible that substantial within-group variation exists among expert and peer observers, making our results more exploratory than generalisable.

Pedagogical Implications

Language practitioners (both teachers and language teacher educators) might find it beneficial to carefully examine Table 7.3, which contains the cues on which the presenter and both observers converged, and to closely compare Tables 7.4 and 7.6, in which we catalogued the nonverbal indicators of rising anxiety that the expert practitioner observer saw but the peer observer did not (Table 7.4) and vice versa (Table 7.6). Table 7.3 shows which of the nonverbal cues are most easily judged. A careful analysis of Table 7.4 can provide teacher educators with the cues that were missed by the inexperienced observer. Drawing pre-service teachers' attention to these cues in particular and encouraging them to be on the look out for these specific nonverbal manifestations of anxiety may provide affective decoding skills that are usually gained through experience. Because Table 7.6 contains the cues that were picked up by the peer observer but not the expert practitioner, a thorough examination by all language teachers would put them on the alert for those cues that classmates might decode, as a near peer, but occur under the radar of more expert practitioners.

In the present data, most nonverbal behaviours indicative of anxiety occurred during times of rising anxiety. Language teachers who are experienced at continuously observing nonverbal cues might be more likely to assume the presence of higher anxiety than lower anxiety. If there is a bias towards false positives (seeing more anxiety than students are feeling) or false negatives (not seeing anxiety when it is present), the false positive bias is less problematic. Working to lower the anxiety is unlikely to be detrimental to the learning experience. Pedagogically speaking, it is better to assume the presence of anxiety and build in classroom 'safety nets' such as supportive interactive environments and effective error correction, than to miss negative affect when it is present and risk its negative effects.

A final suggestion for interested teachers is to replicate the present study as an activity for learners. Teachers and students who have access to recording equipment, including video cameras, webcams or even mobile phone cameras, can record students using the target language, load the footage onto a computer and ask students to idiodynamically rate themselves. A one-on-one and/or group discussion could consider student reactions to the idea of a spotlight effect and self-exacerbating syndrome associated with language anxiety arousal. Savitsky and Gilovich (2003) have demonstrated that merely reminding speakers that they might be exaggerating their audiences' ability to 'read' their 'leaked' cues is helpful;

imagine how much more effective it would be to actually *show* learners their oversensitivity via the same idiodynamic process used in this study! There is a need for classroom-oriented research that considers the dynamics of emotions and their effects on learning processes.[1]

Conclusion

Affect goes up and down. It is dynamic, and influenced by a myriad of different variables. Language anxiety, in particular, is vulnerable to extenuating circumstances such as teachers' behaviour and the social milieu of the classroom. Because of the debilitating effects of language anxiety on learners' linguistic growth as well as emotional and psychological wellbeing, it behoves language practitioners to help feed the benevolent wolf that resides inside each learner. To successfully supply the most wholesome nutrients, those learners who suffer from language anxiety need to be identified – a challenging process, even for expert practitioners. This identification process is facilitated through the effective interpretation of learners' nonverbal cues, as emotion is conveyed most prevalently through body language and vocalics.

Note

(1) For a free copy of the idiodynamic software and instructions on its use, see http://petermacintyre.weebly.com/idiodynamic-software.html#/.

References

Burgoon, J.I. and Koper, R.J. (1984) Nonverbal and relational communication associated with reticence. *Human Communication Research* 10 (4), 601–626.
Clément, R., Dörnyei, Z. and Noels, K. (1994) Motivation, self-confidence, and group cohesion in the foreign language classroom. *Language Learning* 44 (3), 417–448.
Collier, G. (1985) *Emotional Experience*. Hillsdale, NJ: Erlbaum.
Crookall, D. and Oxford, R.L (1991) Dealing with anxiety: Some practical activities for language learners and teacher trainees. In E.K. Horwitz and D.J. Young (eds) *Language Anxiety: From Theory and Research to Classroom Implications* (pp. 141–150). Englewood Cliffs, NJ: Prentice Hall.
Ely, C.M. (1986) An analysis of discomfort, risktaking, sociability, and motivation in the L2 classroom. *Language Learning* 36 (1), 1–25.
Gardner, R.C. (1985) *Social Psychology and Second Language Learning: The Role of Attitudes and Motivation*. London: Edward Arnold.
Gilovich, T., Savitsky, K. and Medvec, V.H. (1998) The illusion of transparency: Biased assessments of others' ability to read one's emotional states. *Journal of Personality and Social Psychology* 75 (2), 332–346.
Gilovich, T., Medvec, V.H. and Savitsky, K. (2000) The spotlight effect in social judgement: An egocentric bias in estimates of the salience of one's own actions and appearance. *Journal of Personality and Social Psychology* 78 (2), 211–222.
Gilovich, T., Kruger, J. and Medvec, V.H. (2002) The spotlight effect revisited: Overestimating the manifest variability of our actions and appearance. *Journal of Experimental Social Psychology* 38 (1), 93–99.

Gregersen, T.S. (2003) To err is human: A reminder to teachers of language-anxious students. *Foreign Language Annals* 36 (1), 25–32.

Gregersen, T.S. (2005) Non-verbal cues: Clues to the detection of foreign language anxiety. *Foreign Language Annals* 38 (3), 388–397.

Gregersen, T.S. (2007) Breaking the code of silence: A study of teachers' nonverbal decoding accuracy of foreign language anxiety. *Language Teaching Research* 11 (2), 209–221.

Gregersen, T.S. (2009) Recognizing visual and auditory cues in the detection of foreign-language anxiety. *TESL Canada Journal/Revue TESL Du Canada* 26 (2), 46–64.

Gregersen, T.S. (2010) Content-based instruction. In M. Al-Hamly, C. Coombe, P. Davidson, A. Shehadeh and S. Troudi (eds) *English in Learning; Learning in English* (pp. 19–24). Dubai: TESOL Arabia.

Gregersen, T.S. and Horwitz, E.K. (2002) Language learning and perfectionism: Anxious and non-anxious language learners' reactions to their own oral performance. *The Modern Language Journal* 86 (4), 562–570.

Gregersen, T. and MacIntyre, P.D. (2014) *Capitalizing on Language Learners' Individuality: From Premise to Practice*. Bristol: Multilingual Matters.

Gregersen, T., MacIntyre, P.D. and Meza, M.D. (2014) The motion of emotion: Idiodynamic case studies of learners' foreign language anxiety. *The Modern Language Journal* 98 (2), 574–588.

Horwitz, E.K. (2010) Foreign and second language anxiety. *Language Teaching* 43 (2), 154–167.

Horwitz, E.K., Horwitz, M. and Cope, J. (1986) Foreign language classroom anxiety. *The Modern Language Journal* 70 (2), 125–132.

Jussim, L. and Eccles, J. (1995) Naturalistic studies of interpersonal expectancies. *Review of Personality and Social Psychology* 63, 947–961.

Krashen, S. (1981) *Second Language Acquisition and Second Language Learning*. Oxford: Pergamon Press.

Leathers, D. and Eaves, M.H. (2008) *Successful Nonverbal Communication: Principles and Applications*. Boston, MA: Pearson Education.

MacIntyre, P.D. (1999) Language anxiety: A review of literature for language teachers. In D.J. Young (ed.) *Affect in Foreign Language and Second Language Learning* (pp. 24–43). New York: McGraw Hill Companies.

MacIntyre, P.D. (2012) The idiodynamic method: A closer look at the dynamics of communication traits. *Communication Research Reports* 29 (4), 361–367.

MacIntyre, P.D. and Gardner, R.C. (1991) Investigating language class anxiety using the focused essay technique. *The Modern Language Journal* 75 (3), 296–304.

MacIntyre, P.D. and Gardner, R.C. (1994) The subtle effects of language anxiety on cognitive processing in the second language. *Language Learning* 44 (2), 283–305.

MacIntyre, P.D. and Legatto, J. (2011) A dynamic system approach to willingness to communicate: Developing an idiodynamic method to capture rapidly changing affect. *Applied Linguistics* 32 (2), 149–171.

MacIntyre, P.D. and Gregersen, T. (2012) Affective responses to language learning. In S. Mercer, S. Ryan and M. Williams (eds) *Psychology for Language Learning: Insights from Research, Theory and Practice* (pp. 103–118). Basingstoke: Palgrave.

MacIntyre, P.D., MacKay, E., Ross, J., Abel, E. (in press) The emerging need for methods appropriate to study dynamic systems. In L. Ortega and Z. Han (eds) *Complexity Theory and Language Development: In Celebration of Diane Larsen-Freeman*. Amsterdam: John Benjamins.

Pappamihiel, E. (2002) English as a second language students and English language anxiety: Issues in the mainstream classroom. *Research in the Teaching of English* 36 (3), 327–355.

Pittam, J. and Scherer, K.R. (1993) Vocal expression and the communication of emotion. In M. Lewis and J. Haviland (eds) *Handbook of Emotions* (pp. 185–197). New York: Gilford Press.

Price, M. (1991) The subjective experience of foreign language anxiety: Interviews with highly anxious students. In E.K. Horwitz and D.J. Young (eds) *Language Anxiety: From Theory and Research to Classroom Implications* (pp. 101–108). Englewood Cliffs, NJ: Prentice Hall.

Richmond, V.P., McCroskey, J.C. and Hickson, M.L. (2012) *Nonverbal Behavior in Interpersonal Relations*. Boston, MA: Allyn & Bacon.

Savitsky, K. and Gilovich, T. (2003) The illusion of transparency and the alleviation of speech anxiety. *Journal of Experimental Social Psychology* 39, 618–625.

Snyder, M. (1984) When beliefs create reality. In L. Berkowitz (ed.) *Advances in Experimental Social Psychology* (pp. 247–305). New York: Academic Press.

8 Towards an Ecological Understanding of Language Anxiety

Christina Gkonou

Introduction

Research on individual differences in second language acquisition (SLA) has been the dominant paradigm for several decades, and the affective dimension of language learning in particular has interested scholars in the field. The term 'individual differences' indeed suggests that each learner is different in their approach to learning a foreign language. Traditional research and its emerging theoretical models and epistemologies have concentrated on similarities and differences among learners and how these influence their acquisition and use of the target language. Strong emphasis has also been placed on examining general patterns among learners and then looking at individual learner idiosyncrasies (Dewaele, 2009).

In light of the social turn (Block, 2003), the need for more interdisciplinary and socially informed approaches to SLA was emphasised. Previous research largely relied on group averages and statistics, which tell us something about characteristics of learners, but as Ushioda (2009: 216) succinctly puts it, they do so 'in an abstract collective sense', thereby 'depersonalising learners' (Ushioda, 2011: 12). However, it should be acknowledged that mixed methods research has made use of quantitative data to help uncover trends among learners which, combined with subsequent qualitative data where learners probed into possible causes for these trends, brought to the foreground a strong emic perspective. In addition, new insights into SLA research are largely informed by a view of learners as agents, whose learning and affect is largely contextualised, and it is this context that 'is relevant and necessary to gain a fuller, more ecological understanding of the individual's abilities, traits, behaviours, and knowledge' (Duff, 2008: 38). This echoes Dörnyei's (2005) claims about the importance of context in recent research into individual differences:

The most striking aspect of nearly all the recent ID [i.e. individual difference] literature is the emerging theme of *context*: It appears that cutting-edge research in all these diverse areas has been addressing the same issue, that is, the situated nature of the ID factors in question. Scholars have come to reject the notion that the various traits are context-independent and absolute, and are now increasingly proposing new dynamic conceptualisations in which ID factors enter into some interaction with the situational parameters rather than cutting across tasks and environments. (Dörnyei, 2005: 218)

More recently, the focus has been shifted to a 'person-in-context' view of the learner (Ushioda, 2009: 218), which reveals complex and dynamic patterns among individuals, their contexts and their personal histories (Benson, 2005; Lantolf & Pavlenko, 2001; Larsen-Freeman, 2001; Mercer, 2011a, 2011b; Mercer *et al.*, 2012; Skehan, 1991; Williams & Burden, 1997). 'Context' here refers to a range of external variables that are likely to influence individual differences or learner-internal variables, such as language anxiety. Ushioda (2015: 47) clarifies that this relationship between context and the learner is not necessarily unidirectional, but rather 'dynamically evolving [...] as each responds and adapts to the other. Moreover, through this process of co-adaptation, the learner necessarily becomes an integral part of the unfolding context of the interaction'.

Ecological perspectives on language learning have the potential to contribute towards conceptualising this mutually constitutive relationship between learners, their individual characteristics (see e.g. Peng [2012] for a proposition of an ecological model of willingness to communicate) and the sociocultural settings containing them (Ushioda, 2015). In this chapter, I undertake a novel exploration of language anxiety through the lens of Brofenbrenner's (1979, 1989, 1993) nested ecosystems model.

Theoretical Background

Language anxiety

Both within psychology and SLA, language anxiety is viewed as a negative emotion that shackles learner interaction and inhibits the acquisition, retention and production of the target language (Gregersen & MacIntyre, 2014; Horwitz, this volume). In their seminal research into foreign language classroom anxiety, Horwitz *et al.* (1986: 128) defined anxiety as 'a distinct complex of self-perceptions, beliefs, feelings, and behaviors related to classroom language learning, arising from the uniqueness of the language learning process'. Early research into language anxiety has therefore attempted to identify it in terms of two broad approaches: (1) as a transfer of anxieties from other domains (e.g. stage fright) and (2) as a unique emotional experience stemming from aspects which are characteristic of language learning as opposed to learning other skills or studying other academic subjects (Horwitz & Young, 1991). However, as MacIntyre (1999: 26) suggested, 'these two approaches are not necessarily opposing positions but represent different perspectives from which to define language anxiety'.

An important difference in approaches to language anxiety is the extent to which it is regarded as dynamic or stable. Within psychology-based research, two perspectives have been identified: trait and state anxiety (Spielberger, 1983). Trait anxiety is viewed as a distinct personality trait, which remains stable over time and across a variety of situations. By contrast, state anxiety is 'the moment-to-moment experience of anxiety; it is the transient emotional state of feeling nervous that can fluctuate over time and vary in intensity' (MacIntyre, 1999: 28). Croznier (1997) included descriptions of both trait and state anxiety in his discussion about anxiety:

> Personality theorists distinguish state and trait anxiety. Many situations, like examinations, public speaking, interviews, and going to the dentist are likely to evoke a state of anxiety in most people. The trait position proposes that some people are more prone to anxiety than others, in that they react to more situations with anxiety or react to particular situations with more intense emotion. (Croznier, 1997: 124)

The intensity of both state and trait anxiety depends on the vulnerability of each person (Rachman, 1998). For example, personality-wise, individuals can be either emotionally stable or more neurotic and, anxiety-wise, they can be either a little vulnerable or very vulnerable.

SLA researchers have suggested that language anxiety could best be conceived of as situation-specific (Dewaele, 2002; MacIntyre, 1999), given that it manifests within particular settings (i.e. language classrooms) where learners are expected to perform through limited linguistic means. In other words, language anxiety may be stable over time but not necessarily applicable to all situations, as it only refers to the specific context of learning and using a foreign language. Students anxious about language learning may be confident and resilient in most other contexts, for example their history or maths classes. MacIntyre and Gardner (1989, 1991a, 1991b) argued that, at the initial stages of language learning, anxiety as perceived by the learner constitutes an undifferentiated, stable personality trait, which is not specific to the language learning situation. Students who are still at those stages of learning a language are therefore not expected to be able to differentiate their anxiety, 'because their experiences in language class have not had sufficient time to become reliably discriminated from other types of anxiety experiences' (MacIntyre & Gardner, 1991b: 303). However, after repeated experiences with the second language environment, students may begin to associate feelings of anxiety with the language class. If the learner has negative experiences in the classroom, foreign language anxiety is likely to develop. Thus, the nature of language anxiety is not merely a question of either/or, but rather a combination of both trait/stable and situation-specific/dynamic dichotomies of language anxiety that are likely to be realised in language classrooms. It is worth noting that, although language anxiety may not just be a personality trait but might also be specific to the learning/teaching situation, certain personality traits such as neuroticism, introversion (see Dewaele, 2002, 2013) and social initiative (see Dewaele & Al-Saraj, 2015) were found to be significantly related to language anxiety.

Previous research has shown that language anxiety might be caused by a range of individual and situational factors, including, among others, competitiveness and peer pressure (Bailey, 1986; Horwitz *et al.*, 1986), speaking in a foreign language and a subsequent fear of negative evaluation (Aida, 1994; Gregersen & Horwitz, 2002; Horwitz *et al.*, 1986; Kitano, 2001; Mak, 2011) and weak self-concepts (Kitano, 2001; MacIntyre *et al.*, 1997). Through an interview-based study with learners at different anxiety levels, Yan and Horwitz (2008) also identified 12 affinities related to language anxiety, namely regional differences; language aptitude; gender, interest and motivation; class arrangements; teacher characteristics; language learning strategies; test types; parental influence; comparison with peers; and achievement. All these studies included plenty of contextual information, given that data were collected from students of specific nationalities studying specific foreign languages at clearly defined institutions. The present study will add to this body of research by exploring both in-class and out-of-class settings and the key role that contexts or ecosystems learners are embedded in might play on their levels of language anxiety. It is this ecosystemic model of human behaviour and development that I now turn to.

The nested ecosystems model

The term 'ecology' comes from the Greek οίκος ('house') and –λογία ('the study of X') and denotes the scientific study of environments and the organisms that live within them. To my mind, and being Greek myself, ecology would refer to aspects of the environment or a particular area such as animals, plants, water, land, air, microbes and so on, and the relationships among them, and not to classrooms and, more generally, societies or cultures that consist of and are shaped by humans. It was highly unlikely that I would have ever made the link between ecology and language classrooms.

However, in my own readings, I noticed that, within psychology, the notion of ecological environments is used for the study of the development of human behaviour, and that these ecological settings describe a set of complex, nested systems, each residing inside the next, 'like a set of Russian dolls', to use Bronfenbrenner's (1979: 3) excellent metaphor. Within SLA, the idea of adopting an ecological orientation to the study of how and why people learn languages has already been put forward by Van Lier (2000, 2002, 2004), who proposed a relational view of language and linguistics, and by Kramsch (2002, 2008) and Kramsch and Whiteside (2008), who discussed ecological perspectives on language acquisition, language socialisation and multilingualism. This chapter aims at viewing language anxiety from an ecological perspective by applying Bronfenbrenner's (1979) nested ecosystems model to the study of highly anxious Greek English-as-a-foreign-language (EFL) learners. In what follows, I describe the components of Bronfenbrenner's ecological model of human development.

According to Bronfenbrenner (1979), ecological environments stretch beyond the boundaries of the immediate setting(s) that directly influence a developing person. Therefore, human behaviour is structured over four layers: the microsystem, the mesosystem, the exosystem and the macrosystem. The most immediate situation or context for an individual is called the microsystem. This is the innermost of the four layers forming the nested ecosystems model. What is of paramount importance here is the whole environment of this setting, including connections between people that are also present within the same setting as well as how these connections are created and subsequently define the developing person. At the next layer is the mesosystem, which concentrates on the interrelatedness between a variety of settings in which a person participates or has participated. Contrary to the mesosystem, the exosystem represents the interrelatedness among settings in which the developing person may never enter but in which events and changes that take place can potentially influence what happens in the person's immediate setting. The fourth layer, the macrosystem, refers to overarching ideological and organisational patterns of social institutions (e.g. higher education, governmental bodies) that shape a particular culture.

Implementing an ecological approach to research into SLA implies that all these four subsystems are taken into account in the data collection as well as the data analysis and interpretation stages, in order to elucidate how context might inform understandings of a range of SLA aspects. As Van Lier (2002: 144) explains, the primary requirement of ecological approaches is 'by definition, that the context is central, it cannot be reduced, and it cannot be pushed aside or into the background'. Later, I will also argue that, apart from research, the four ecosystems should also be taken into account in order to inform classroom practice.

Motivated by Bronfenbrenner's nested ecosystems model and subsequent discussions about the significance of context in SLA, the present chapter will examine language anxiety ecologically, thus adding a fresh empirical perspective to the investigation of this construct. The study will address the following two research questions:

(1) In what way(s) do the four ecological subsystems (i.e. the micro-, meso-, exo- and macrosystem) influence language anxiety?
(2) In what way(s) do the four ecosystems interact with each other?

Method

Research design

This study draws on the qualitative data set of a larger, mixed-method research project on the language anxiety of students learning EFL in private language schools in Greece. The research design adopted in the present study follows that of Horwitz and Gregersen (2002). For the quantitative phase of the project, the Foreign Language Classroom Anxiety Scale (FLCAS; Horwitz *et al.*, 1986) was administered to 197 students, and those who received the highest total language anxiety scores were identified. The results obtained from this quantitative stage informed the collection of data for the second, qualitative phase, part of which constitutes the focus of this chapter. This subsequent qualitative phase involved collecting weekly diary entries from highly anxious students and interviewing them at the end of the diary study. Both these qualitative methods helped towards understanding the reasons why this specific group of students deviated significantly from the rest.

Participants

Seven adult Greek EFL learners who were enrolled in general English classes in two private language schools in Northern Greece participated in the qualitative strand of the study. Their level of proficiency ranged from B1 (i.e. pre-intermediate) to C1 (i.e. upper intermediate) (Common European Framework of Reference for Languages [CEFR]; Council of Europe, 2001). Their minimum length of exposure to English was two years, with a maximum length of six years. The participants were classified as highly anxious on the basis of their total anxiety score on the FLCAS. All students consented to participate in the study. Table 8.1 summarises the information about the participating students (the students' names in the table are pseudonyms).

Instruments

Students kept a weekly learner diary, which they were asked to return electronically at the end of each teaching week. The diary study spanned three months. Participants attended a training session prior to

Table 8.1 Information about the student participants

Participant	Total language anxiety score (min.=33, max.=165)	Age	Proficiency level	Reason for learning English
Natassa	147	26	C1	Job prospects
Sophia	144	19	B1	Importance of English as an international language
Nikos	126	30	B2	Job prospects
Kiki	113	35	C1	Job prospects
Zoe	112	27	B2	Academic goals abroad
Danae	107	18	B1	Importance of English as an international language
Maria	93	23	C1	Love of foreign languages

the commencement of diary writing, where they were informed about the aims of the project and were given a list of prompts. These were intended to suggest ideas about aspects of their EFL learning experience that they were expected to comment on in their entries. Examples of prompts included questions such as 'What is the most/least anxiety-provoking aspect of the lesson?', or 'How do you feel when you work in pairs or groups in class?' Students were given the option to write their entries in English or Greek, although the benefits of writing a diary in the target language were emphasised as this was considered as a means of urging students to persist with the study. All diary entries were written in English.

An in-depth, follow-up, semi-structured interview was conducted with each diarist in Greek one week after the end of the diary study. Students were given the option to speak in English, but they opted for Greek as they felt more confident articulating thoughts and emotions in their first language. An interview guide formed the basis of this phase of the study. However, the guides were slightly modified to ensure that interesting points made by each student in their diary entries were covered and to account for themes that were of particular significance to each student. Examples of questions that were part of the interview protocol were 'What makes you anxious about English?', 'How do your language learning experiences influence your learning?' and 'What are your strengths and weaknesses in English?'

Data analysis

The diary and interview data were analysed, combining deductive and inductive approaches (Lincoln & Guba, 1985; Strauss, 1987). A categorical scheme for analysing the data was created on the basis of the quantitative analysis of students' questionnaires and existing language anxiety frameworks in the literature (e.g. Horwitz *et al.*, 1986). The scheme comprised topics such as fear of negative evaluation, concern over errors, self-concepts and language learning experiences, which helped to develop an awareness of possible themes that may emerge from the data. The data were also analysed in line with an inductive approach, which does not rely on preconceived assumptions but rather on an analysis that takes into account the situated nature of the data and any themes that are constructed as meaningful to the diarists/interviewees with regard to the topic under investigation. The data were coded in two stages: (1) first-level coding, where themes were created, revised, and defined and (2) pattern (or second-level) coding, which allowed the researcher to group the already identified codes into manageable sets (Miles & Huberman, 1994). The themes of the categorical scheme, which emerged from the quantitative data analysis and the review of the literature, were compared and contrasted to the codes identified during the process of first- and second-level coding.

Findings

The findings will be presented in relation to each of the four ecosystems discussed in the theoretical background.

The microsystem

The microsystem, which is the innermost layer in a nested ecosystem, is operationalised through what is going on in actual EFL classrooms. For the purposes of this study, and given space constraints, I will focus on the five most recurrent aspects of the microsystem, namely speaking anxiety, peer pressure, significant others, fear of negative evaluation and self-beliefs.

Speaking anxiety constituted the most frequently mentioned characteristic of the microsystem. Many students discussed the critical role that mainly peers and occasionally tutors played in their levels of speaking anxiety in class, implying that classroom dynamics and the classroom atmosphere could influence the amount, quality and type of spoken interactions. These distinctive dynamics interacted with weakened self-related constructs, in particular students' sense of self-efficacy and self-confidence, while at the same time increased students' fear of negative evaluation. Although more than capable of producing an accurate sentence as she was a C1-level student, Natassa recollected the following classroom event during her interview:

> We were chatting in class, and my classmate asked me something and I answered 'Because I am foolish'. Then she asked me what this word

meant. And the others were laughing. So this situation influenced me negatively and then I was wondering if I had made a mistake or said something wrong. And above all it made me feel embarrassed about speaking in English. I just doubt myself and my abilities and I believe that the other students are better than me.

Natassa also offered a glimpse into the influence of peer pressure on her decision to speak in class, confessing in her interview that she even postponed speaking until she was absolutely certain that what she had to say was accurate:

I get nervous when my peers make fun of me. However, the thing is that I never speak in class unless I am 100% sure that I have the answer. I think there is an element of anxiety there too. And also I don't want them to judge me, or to think less of me, because this will make me worry about my performance and I won't be able to do well in the next lesson.

Sophia also had very strong views about her classmates, thinking that their behaviour was the main source of her language anxiety. In her interview, she recounted the following:

Classmates can make me anxious in two different ways. First, they are anxious too, they are getting hysterical, and they make me anxious, and this is something very common. I mean you are on your way to the lesson and you are relaxed, but as soon as you enter the school you realise how anxious they are, so you become anxious too. Second, they can be a bit of a snob and you know that they are stronger students than you actually are. So, you try to be like them, but by the time you realise that that's not possible, your feelings of anxiety overwhelm you.

As illustrated by Sophia, peer pressure may lead to competitiveness and tension. Confronted with a similar problem, Zoe believed that her classmates could do better than her and feared facing derision if she said something wrong. Kiki, in turn, considered that the discrepancy between the level of proficiency of students within the same class seemed to generate most competitiveness-stemming problems. In her interview, Danae spoke about how she invoked her own anxiety in order to avoid her peers' severe criticism:

I sometimes feel that I put pressure on myself, because I don't want to show to my peers that I am not good at English or that I can't do it. And I don't like being laughed at, so I try to study hard to avoid making mistakes.

Another emotionally laden account of the effects of peer pressure was offered by Natassa in her diary:

> I usually check what other people are doing in class instead of focusing on my own work. If they are writing and I am not, I become very anxious. At that point, I may even forget everything I know, and I will perform badly.

By contrast, Nikos explained why his classmates did not ignite feelings of anxiety, a statement which partly resonates with Kiki's opinion reported previously:

> My peers don't make me anxious. First, one of them is my sister so I am aware of her reactions. The other students are of the same level of proficiency as me, perhaps even of a lower level, so neither anxiety nor competitiveness can affect me.

When given the hypothetical situation of perceiving himself as less capable than his classmates, Nikos said that this would definitely be hurtful and would influence his language anxiety in class. Maria offered important insights into this aspect, adding that negative evaluation and criticisms were most often initiated by the weakest members of the group she belonged in.

Of the participants who referred to their English teachers as assessors of their performance in class, most agreed that their comments were much appreciated and well-received, and indeed maintained that giving feedback formed an integral part of a teacher's job. However, Kiki's point of view appeared to be at odds with the general picture. In an attempt to avoid becoming weak in the eyes of her teacher, Kiki summarised the precaution expressively:

Kiki: I really fear making mistakes, not because I've made a mistake and that means that I haven't studied enough, but rather because I tremble from my teacher's and my peers' reaction to it. I know that my teacher calls on us in a predictable order and I know when it is my turn to speak. So I read my question again and again to make sure that I can give as accurate an answer as possible, but I ignore everything else that goes on in the classroom at that time.

Christina: From your experience, what could your teacher's reaction be like?

Kiki: I don't know. I think that my teacher will have a condescending attitude and will tell me that I am not well prepared. And that my classmates will laugh at my mistake.

Christina: Does this happen in the end?

Kiki: Well, I think that in a class there will possibly be one or two students that you don't like or they don't like you. That's why I am expecting them to laugh at my mistake. As for the teacher, I think I want to show him that I am doing my best. But now that I come to think about it, maybe it's just a situation I've created in my mind. It may be something like a phobia.

Whether it was a real or an imaginary situation, Kiki's fear of being negatively evaluated by her teacher ignited speaking anxiety in class. She also felt that the EFL classroom was as hierarchically structured an entity as a company, with the teacher holding a high status in class, much in the same way as a boss is leading a company. In her diary, she wrote:

> I see my teacher as my boss. When I know I am seeing someone who is superior to me and I know that I will be judged by the way I'll answer his/her questions, I get nervous. I am not self-confident and I feel that my level of English is low.

Zoe also thought that the interactional context generates feelings of speaking anxiety. The following excerpt comes from her interview:

> In speaking, I first need to check what the communication with my interlocutor is like, if s/he is friendly and easy-going, or if s/he is strict. The latter is definitely stressful and makes me not want to speak much or even not at all.

Difficult interactional situations in class, where students notice that they cannot get their message across, were also referred to by the students. When interviewed, Sophia said:

> I become anxious when the others do not understand what I am saying. Then I try to use other words to explain it.

Kiki shared a similar feeling in her diary:

> I am anxious when I realise that Joanna [i.e. her teacher] cannot understand what I am talking about, which means that I cannot get my message across.

The comments included in this section are indicative of the importance that highly anxious students attach to significant others' opinions about them and of the influence of classroom interaction and dynamics on the participating students' language anxiety levels.

The mesosystem

The second level, the mesosystem, reflects the interrelatedness between the classroom and other settings containing the students. Students' past EFL learning experiences that occurred outside the current classroom but that exerted an influence on language anxiety in the present class are grouped under this level. These past language-learning experiences concern past teachers' judgmental attitudes towards students as well as instances of failure in formal exams in the past, which are likely to endanger students' current self-beliefs.

The participants commented on negative past occurrences that clearly controlled their anxiety over EFL learning. First, it is notable that the English language tutors' attitude has made quite an impact on the students' present levels of language anxiety. Former EFL teachers who were very anxious themselves or who had a condescending manner were mentioned as a major source of learners' anxiety in class. The extracts below, from Sophia's interview and Maria's diary, further illustrate this point.

> I think that teachers transfer their stress to their students. I had an English teacher a few years ago who was so anxious in class that I always hoped for the lesson to finish in order to calm myself down. She was flicking through the book nervously, telling us what we will do now, in one month, in three months, when we will write our tests. And I also believe that this is bad for a teacher's image too.

> The teacher I had was very tough and demanding, and had a judgmental attitude towards students. You were afraid of him just by looking at him. He was always asking us to do the difficult exercises in the book, because he was saying that the easier ones are only for idiots. I believe he was a qualified teacher, but he should really work on his manner.

The second aspect of prior EFL learning experiences concerns instances of failure in formal examinations in the past or having scored marks on tests that were approaching the borderline. Both were shown to induce feelings of fear of upcoming failure among learners and to consequently increase their anxiety. Nikos recollected the following account:

> **Nikos**: Anxiety is part of my life that I can't get rid of. It follows me in almost everything I do. With relation to English, I am anxious because I believe that I am not good enough to succeed.

Christina: Why not?

Nikos: Because I once failed the Michigan preliminary exams, I got 21 instead of 23 which was the pass mark.

This extract reveals how language anxiety is shaped by the mesosystem. It also demonstrates that anxiety is dynamic, resulting from a process of interaction between different conditions. Global anxiety pre-exists within the learner and is a stable personality trait, presumably manifesting under stressful circumstances including language learning and production. This leads to a situation-specific form of anxiety (i.e. classroom language anxiety), which dramatically increases due to an inherent fear of failure stemming from an unlucky past examination event. In addition, receiving a low mark can add extra feelings of despair to one's affective state.

Students also reported feelings of self-consciousness and low self-confidence, which stemmed from interpersonal interactions in the past and engendered speaking-specific classroom anxiety and low willingness to communicate in the present classroom, as Sophia said:

In my previous language school, I would make a pronunciation mistake and I would be laughed at for the next couple of weeks. And I really wonder if those students were considering themselves so expert to criticise the level of English of others. I was so young back then and couldn't understand how such an event could affect my willingness to speak now. Now I always think that someone will make fun of me and of my English.

This student's account is indicative of how a present, weak self-belief has been shaped by negative group dynamics and by the way peers in a previous language school reacted to others' mistakes. The excerpt also reveals the extent to which a past negative experience about pronunciation mistakes might further stifle present and future oral attempts.

The exosystem and the macrosystem

These two subsystems will be discussed in conjunction, as both represent settings that individuals do not actively participate in or have not participated in but which can have a profound impact on language anxiety in the present classroom (i.e. the microsystem). Local, success-oriented beliefs about language learning and the Greek foreign language education system are grouped under these levels.

In the extract that follows, Natassa comments on the extent to which her past teacher's attitude, and the fact that the teacher was exerting enormous pressure on students to succeed, augmented her own present feelings of language anxiety. This comment could in fact exemplify how the mesosystem, in the form of past teachers' attitudes, could influence students' language anxiety in the microsystem. However, I eschewed listing this comment under the section on the mesosystem as I felt that it reflects more prominently one form of the exosystem. For this decision, I also took into account the fact that this exosystemic aspect was indeed emphasised by the participating student in the interview. Natassa attributed this particular teacher's attitude to her teacher's personality and also, interestingly, to a range of success-oriented beliefs that apparently foreign language school owners in rural areas seem to possess. Specifically, she argued in her interview:

> I used to hate English, but the teacher was to blame for that. She was weird. [...] She was demoralising me, and I was avoiding classes, I wasn't doing my homework. [...] That school was in my hometown, you know, it's a small town in a remote area, and she wanted us to pass the exam to prove that her institute is good. All this was putting pressure on me. Then I failed the exam and stopped studying English. I registered again for English lessons when I came here to go to university. Now I like English, but I still feel I have a kind of fear of it.

For one thing, local, success-oriented beliefs about language learning govern small institutions in remote, provincial areas. For another, locality and its emergent beliefs about foreign language learning success shape one's experiences and influence one's levels of language anxiety in present encounters with the language within instructional settings, thereby affecting performance and emotions in the microsystem that is the current EFL classroom.

Another interesting finding that emerged from the study revealed that the Greek foreign language education system exerted an influence on students' anxiety about EFL learning. Zoe said:

> Why do we need to get so many certificates? I mean, I may be able to speak English without holding the proficiency or the first certificate. It would really be interesting to see if this is the case in other countries too. My friends in France do not even know what proficiency and first certificate mean. They don't have to have a collection of foreign language certificates as we do. This causes lots of stress.

Despite taking issue with the structure and requirements of the Greek foreign language education system, the participating students realised that English language learning was necessary for professional advancement within Greece. This condition broadly dictated that failure was not an option for them, as Danae and Kiki emphatically stated:

When I was younger, I was lazy and I wasn't studying English. I can now understand how important having certified knowledge of English is. I mustn't fail. I need the points to have more chances to get a job in a state school.

My anxiety stems from all the effort I am expending and from the possibility of failure. The reason why I am learning English, apart from the fact that I like it, is also connected with my profession, because quite often employers ask for an excellent knowledge of the English language. And this again relates with failure. It means that if you fail, you will not get the certificate, and therefore you will not meet the person specification criteria for that specific job that requires that certificate.

Thus, the fact that certified knowledge of English (and of other foreign languages) is a prerequisite for getting a good job increased students' need for achievement, fear of failure and, consequently, language anxiety.

Discussion

The findings of the current study have revealed that the language anxiety of Greek EFL learners is influenced by a range of aspects evident across all four layers of Bronfenbrenner's nested ecosystems model. The microsystem, which is the innermost layer and is operationalised through events that take place in actual EFL classrooms, consisted of speaking anxiety, peer pressure, significant others, fear of negative evaluation and negative self-beliefs. These aspects lead to differential levels of classroom language anxiety and have been extensively discussed in previous research (e.g. Horwitz *et al.*, 1986; Kitano, 2001; Mak, 2011; Woodrow, 2006), albeit not from a microsystemic or, more generally, ecosystemic perspective *per se*. However, the findings of the present study highlighted the remaining three subsystems. The discussion of the findings will therefore centre on these three aspects of the nested ecosystems model.

The second level, the mesosystem, reflects the interrelatedness between the classroom and other settings containing the students. Students' past EFL learning experiences that have occurred outside the current classroom but exert an influence on language anxiety in the current classroom are grouped under this level. The mesosystemic level in this study was found to comprise aspects such as prior EFL achievement, significant others' feedback and appraisals, and past teachers' attitude in the form of having a judgmental manner towards students, all of which influenced students' present degree of in-class language anxiety. Prior language anxiety was found to influence future academic achievement and prior academic achievement was found to affect language anxiety development. Daly (1991: 10) claimed that 'people who previously have had positive experiences learning languages are, in all likelihood, less anxious about conquering another one than are those who recollect nothing but fear, anxiety and failure from prior attempts'.

In the context of the present study, and in particular in Natassa's and Nikos's case, negative past experiences with failure and with strict teachers influenced learners' subsequent language learning experience to the point that they were anxious about failing the course or being taught by a tutor with a similar attitude to teaching. Therefore, acknowledging prior experience as an influence on how language anxiety develops is a perspective that should be taken into account when attempting to conceptualise anxiety. Language anxiety and achievement were often found to have a bidirectional relationship (Horwitz, 2001; Kitano, 2001; Marcos-Llinás & Garau, 2009; Onwuegbuzie et al., 1999; Pappamihiel, 2002; Phillips, 1992; Woodrow, 2006) and, in fact, measures of achievement were extensively used in correlational studies investigating the relationship between these two variables. The present findings therefore support existing research, with the exception of Yan and Horwitz's (2008) study, whose model did not indicate any influence of achievement on the anxiety of Chinese EFL learners and vice versa. According to the authors (Yan & Horwitz, 2008: 173), 'they [i.e. the learners] only commented on how anxiety kept them from achieving and did not mention lack of achievement as contributing to their anxiety'.

From this ecological approach to language anxiety, though, the most interesting finding concerns the existence of a third systemic level that could be conceived of as situated somewhere between the exosystem and the macrosystem. At this level, the exosystem and the macrosystem encapsulate two important dimensions: Natassa's – the most anxious student in this cohort – concerns over local, success-oriented beliefs about language learning having a subtle effect on student affective behaviour in class; and the nature and structure of the Greek foreign language education system, which influences students' language anxiety levels. These two aspects will be discussed next.

Natassa explained that her teacher owned a language school in a rural area in Greece; students' success at learning English would be a means of advertising the quality of teaching offered by the school. Overall, a student's success at foreign language learning mirrors a school's high quality of education programmes. As such, teachers' and school owners' anxiety and their expectations of their students are likely to engender anxiety within the latter. Concomitantly, a country's foreign language education system extends to educational policies implemented by each language school. It is therefore important not to lose sight of the big picture when assessing teaching and learning practices and their detrimental effect on students' stress. Students admit feeling controlled by the teacher and having their anxiety augmented. By the same token, teachers also feel controlled by higher-order factors and administrative bodies. Thus, exosystemic and macrosystemic factors influence not only students' language anxiety but also teacher behaviour that often impacts on student affective behaviour within the microsystem.

With reference to the Greek foreign language education system (i.e. the second exosystemic/macrosystemic component), instrumental reasons stemming from higher education norms and the indigenous culture of learning put much pressure on learners. The education system in general, and not just the foreign language education system, revolves around formal examinations. Foreign language learning also targets exams from international acclaimed examination boards or national standardised English testing centres. The public sector, where an overwhelming majority of citizens aspire to work, is monitored by the Supreme Council for Civil Personnel Selection (ASEP) and is structured on the basis of a point-factor system, where many points go to English and other foreign language certification as a prerequisite for securing the top jobs there. It thus seems that the Greek foreign language education system, which shares both exosystemic and macrosystemic features, might have increased learners' sense and exercise of agency (Gkonou, 2014) but also boosted their language anxiety in the microsystem, the immediate EFL classroom.

A final note concerns the fact that the microsystem is strongly influenced by the remaining three ecosystems and that there is a complex and dynamic interplay among all four ecosystems. Thus, delimiting the notion of context to the microsystem only would be a shortcoming for research (Bronfenbrenner, 1979) and teaching practice. As Larsen-Freeman and Cameron (2008: 76) argued, 'as agents in multiple, nested, complex systems, the decisions that we make as individuals cannot help but be influenced by our connections into all kinds of social groupings'. Raising awareness of the existence of the four systems could thereby benefit language teachers, urging them to scrutinise their students' ecosystemic behaviour in an attempt to alleviate their stress in the classroom. Teachers could become aware of the realities of the different contexts that surround their students and engage in pedagogical decision-making aimed at enhancing their learners' options and learning potential. In particular, from a mesosystemic perspective, language educators should be reminded that learners should not be viewed as *tabula rasa* and that prior foreign language learning experiences can shape present classroom behaviour in a distinctive manner. As Kramsch (2002: 19) explained, research that takes an ecological approach 'recognizes […] that linguistic phenomena […] are also indissociable from an individual's memory of past phenomena and his/her anticipation of future ones; they retain the sedimented traces of experiences that a person's body has given meaning and relevance to'. In addition, teachers should be informed that the wider context and external influences emanating from research can also contribute to the development and maintenance of language anxiety among learners.

Conclusion

The findings of the present study offer a fresh approach to making language anxiety research more ecological. As Williams and Burden (1997: 190) pointed out, 'what is of particular significance to us here is that ecological or systems approaches emphasise the importance of taking into account the total environment of the learner if we are to explain adequately how and why people learn'. The idea of the importance of context and of viewing language learners holistically is not new to SLA (see, for example, Ushioda [2009, 2011]). What is new, though, is the application of Bronfenbrenner's nested ecosystems model to the empirical investigation of language anxiety, which has revealed the salience of interaction between multiple settings and has shown that environments which are not prominently linked to the microsystem or the present classroom (i.e. the mesosystem, the exosystem and the macrosystem) can play a key role in the experience of language anxiety in the microsystem. It is hoped that the present study will encourage researchers to incorporate this theoretical framework in the examination of language anxiety and other emotions in different contexts.

References

Aida, Y. (1994) Examination of Horwitz, Horwitz, and Cope's construct of foreign language anxiety: The case of students of Japanese. *The Modern Language Journal* 78 (2), 155–168.

Bailey, K.M. (1983) Competitiveness and anxiety in adult second language learning: Looking *at* and *through* the diary studies. In H.W. Seliger and M.H. Long (eds) *Classroom-Oriented Research in Second Language Acquisition* (pp. 67–103). Rowley, MA: Newbury House.

Benson, P. (2005) (Auto)biography and learner diversity. In P. Benson and D. Nunan (eds) *Learners' Stories: Difference and Diversity in Language Learning* (pp. 4–21). Cambridge: Cambridge University Press.

Block, D. (2003) *The Social Turn in Second Language Acquisition*. Edinburgh: Edinburgh University Press.

Bronfenbrenner, U. (1979) *The Ecology of Human Development: Experiments by Nature and Design*. Cambridge, MA: Harvard University Press.

Bronfenbrenner, U. (1989) Ecological systems theory. In R. Vasta (ed.) *Six Theories of Child Development: Revised Formulations and Current Issues* (pp. 187–250). London: Jessica Kingsley Publishers Ltd.

Bronfenbrenner, U. (1993) Ecological models of human development. In M. Gauvain and M. Cole (eds) *Readings on the Development of Children* (pp. 37–43). New York: Freeman.

Council of Europe (2001) *Common European Framework of Reference for Languages: Learning, Teaching, Assessment*. Cambridge: Cambridge University Press.

Croznier, W.R. (1997) *Individual Learners: Personality Differences in Education*. London: Routledge.

Daly, J.A. (1991) Understanding communication apprehension: An introduction for language educators. In E.K. Horwitz and D.J. Young (eds) *Language Anxiety: From*

Theory and Research to Classroom Implications (pp. 3–15). Upper Saddle River, NJ: Prentice Hall.
Dewaele, J.-M. (2002) Psychological and sociodemographic correlates of communicative anxiety in L2 and L3 production. *International Journal of Bilingualism* 6 (1), 23–38.
Dewaele, J.-M. (2009) Individual differences in second language acquisition. In W.C. Ritchie and T.K. Bhatia (eds) *The New Handbook of Second Language Acquisition* (pp. 623–646). Bingley: Emerald.
Dewaele, J.-M. (2013) The link between foreign language classroom anxiety and psychoticism, extraversion, and neuroticism among adult bi- and multilinguals. *The Modern Language Journal* 97 (3), 670–684.
Dewaele, J.-M. and Al-Saraj, T.M. (2015) Foreign language classroom anxiety of Arab learners of English: The effect of personality, linguistic and sociobiographical variables. *Studies in Second Language Learning and Teaching* 5 (2), 205–228.
Dörnyei, Z. (2005) *The Psychology of the Language Learner: Individual Differences in Second Language Acquisition*. Mahwah, NJ: Lawrence Erlbaum Associates.
Duff, P. (2008) *Case Study Research in Applied Linguistics*. New York: Lawrence Erlbaum Associates.
Gkonou, C. (2014) Agency, anxiety and activity: Understanding the classroom behaviour of EFL learners. In P. Deters, X. Gao, E.R. Miller and G. Vitanova (eds) *Theorizing and Analyzing Agency in Second Language Learning: Interdisciplinary Approaches* (pp. 195–212). Bristol: Multilingual Matters.
Gregersen, T.S. and Horwitz, E.K. (2002) Language learning and perfectionism: Anxious and non-anxious language learners' reactions to their own oral performance. *The Modern Language Journal* 86 (3), 562–570.
Gregersen, T. and MacIntyre, P.D. (2014) *Capitalizing on Language Learners' Individuality: From Premise to Practice*. Bristol: Multilingual Matters.
Horwitz, E.K. (2001) Language anxiety and achievement. *Annual Review of Applied Linguistics* 21, 112–126.
Horwitz, E.K. and Young, D.J. (eds) (1991) *Language Anxiety: From Theory and Research to Classroom Implications*. Upper Saddle River, NJ: Prentice Hall.
Horwitz, E.K., Horwitz, M.B. and Cope, J. (1986) Foreign language classroom anxiety. *The Modern Language Journal* 70 (2), 125–132.
Kitano, K. (2001) Anxiety in the college Japanese language classroom. *The Modern Language Journal* 85 (4), 549–566.
Kramsch, C. (2002) Introduction: "How can we tell the dancer from the dance?" In C. Kramsch (ed.) *Language Acquisition and Language Socialisation: Ecological Perspectives* (pp. 1–30). London: Continuum.
Kramsch, C. (2008) Ecological perspectives on foreign language education. *Language Teaching* 41 (3), 389–408.
Kramsch, C. and Whiteside, A. (2008) Language ecology in multilingual settings: Towards a theory of symbolic competence. *Applied Linguistics* 29 (4), 645–671.
Lantolf, J. and Pavlenko, A. (2001) (S)econd (L)anguage (A)ctivity theory: Understanding second language learners as people. In M. Breen (ed.) *Learner Contributions to Language Learning: New Directions in Research* (pp. 141–158). London: Longman.
Larsen-Freeman, D. (2001) Individual cognitive/affective learner contributions and differential success in second language acquisition. In M.P. Breen (ed.) *Learner Contributions to Language Learning* (pp. 12–24). Harlow: Pearson Longman.
Larsen-Freeman, D. and Cameron, L. (2008) *Complex Systems and Applied Linguistics*. Oxford: Oxford University Press.
Lincoln, Y.S. and Guba, E.G. (1985) *Naturalistic Inquiry*. Beverly Hills, CA: Sage.
MacIntyre, P.D. (1999) Language anxiety: A review of the research for language teachers. In D.J. Young (ed.) *Affect in Foreign Language and Second Language Learning:*

A Practical Guide to Creating a Low-Anxiety Classroom Atmosphere (pp. 24–45). Boston, MA: McGraw-Hill.
MacIntyre, P.D. and Gardner, R.C. (1989) Anxiety and second language learning: Toward a theoretical clarification. *Language Learning* 39 (2), 251–275.
MacIntyre, P.D. and Gardner, R.C. (1991a) Methods and results in the study of anxiety and language learning: A review of the literature. *Language Learning* 41 (1), 85–117.
MacIntyre, P.D. and Gardner, R.C. (1991b) Language anxiety: Its relation to other anxieties and to processing in native and second languages. *Language Learning* 41 (4), 513–554.
MacIntyre, P.D., Noels, K.A. and Clément, R. (1997) Biases in self-ratings of second language proficiency: The role of language anxiety. *Language Learning* 47 (2), 265–287.
Mak, B. (2011) An exploration of speaking-in-class anxiety with Chinese ESL learners. *System* 39 (2), 202–214.
Marcos-Llinás, M. and Garau, M.J. (2009) Effects of language anxiety on three proficiency-level courses of Spanish as a foreign language. *Foreign Language Annals* 42 (1), 94–111.
Mercer, S. (2011a) Language learner self-concept: Complexity, continuity and change. *System* 39 (3), 335–346.
Mercer, S. (2011b) Understanding learner agency as a complex dynamic system. *System* 39 (4), 427–436.
Mercer, S., Ryan, S. and Williams, M. (eds) (2012) *Psychology for Language Learning: Insights from Research, Theory and Practice*. Basingstoke: Palgrave Macmillan.
Miles, M.B. and Huberman, A.M. (1994) *Qualitative Data Analysis*. Thousand Oaks, CA: Sage.
Onwuegbuzie, A.J., Bailey, P. and Daley, C.E. (1999) Factors associated with foreign language anxiety. *Applied Psycholinguistics* 20 (2), 217–239.
Pappamihiel, N.E. (2002) English as a second language students and English language anxiety. *Research in the Teaching of English* 36 (3), 327–355.
Peng, J.-E. (2012) Towards an ecological understanding of willingness to communicate in EFL classrooms in China. *System* 40 (2), 203–213.
Phillips, E.M. (1992) The effects of language anxiety on students' oral test performance and attitudes. *The Modern Language Journal* 76 (1), 14–26.
Ranchman, S. (1998) *Anxiety*. Hove: Psychology Press.
Skehan, P. (1991) Individual differences in second language learning. *Studies in Second Language Acquisition* 13 (2), 275–298.
Spielberger, C.D. (1983) *Manual for the State-Trait Anxiety Inventory (STAI)*. Palo Alto, CA: Consulting Psychologists Press.
Strauss, A. (1987) *Qualitative Analysis for Social Scientists*. Cambridge: Cambridge University Press.
Ushioda, E. (2009) A person-in-context relational view of emergent motivation, self and identity. In Z. Dörnyei and E. Ushioda (eds) *Motivation, Language Identity and the L2 Self* (pp. 215–228). Bristol: Multilingual Matters.
Ushioda, E. (2011) Motivating learners to speak as themselves. In G. Murray, X. Gao and T. Lamb (eds) *Identity, Motivation and Autonomy in Language Learning* (pp. 11–24). Bristol: Multilingual Matters.
Ushioda, E. (2015) Context and Complex Dynamic Systems Theory. In Z. Dörnyei, P.D. MacIntyre and A. Henry (eds) *Motivational Dynamics in Language Learning* (pp. 47–54). Bristol: Multilingual Matters.
Van Lier, L. (2000) From input to affordance: Social-interactive learning from an ecological perspective. In J. Lantolf (ed.) *Sociocultural Theory and Second Language Learning* (pp. 245–259). Oxford: Oxford University Press.

Van Lier, L. (2002) An ecological-semiotic perspective on language and linguistics. In C. Kramsch (ed.) *Language Acquisition and Language Socialisation: Ecological Perspectives* (pp. 140–164). London: Continuum.

Van Lier, L. (2004) *The Ecology and Semiotics of Language Learning: A Sociocultural Perspective*. Dordrecht: Kluwer Academic.

Williams, M. and Burden, R.L. (1997) *Psychology for Language Teachers: A Social Constructivist Approach*. Cambridge: Cambridge University Press.

Woodrow, L. (2006) Anxiety and speaking English as a second language. *RELC Journal* 37 (3), 308–328.

Yan, J.X. and Horwitz, E.K. (2008) Learners' perceptions of how anxiety interacts with personal and instructional factors to influence their achievement in English: A qualitative analysis of EFL learners in China. *Language Learning* 58 (1), 151–183.

9 Exploring the Relationship between Anxiety and Advanced Hungarian EFL Learners' Communication Experiences in the Target Language: A Study of High- vs Low-Anxious Learners

Zsuzsa Tóth

Introduction

It is a well-established fact that, for many individuals, learning and using a second or foreign language (L2) is an anxiety-provoking experience. In the past 30 years, language learning anxiety has become one of the major, most highly examined psychological variables in L2 research, documented in learners in various instructional settings (cf. Horwitz, 1986, 2010; MacIntyre, 1999; MacIntyre & Gardner, 1991; Young, 1991, 1994). However, until fairly recently (Ewald, 2007; Horwitz, 1996; Phillips, 2003; Tóth, 2010), most research has tended to focus on foreign language (FL) learning at the earlier levels because of the tacit assumption that L2-related anxiety is specific to learners at lower levels of language competence.

In this chapter, I examine the issue of foreign language anxiety (FLA) in English as a foreign language (EFL) learners at high levels of proficiency. Specifically, I seek to explore how FLA impacts on and shapes advanced learners' experiences of using the target language (TL), focusing on what is considered to be the most anxiety-provoking of FL activities: oral communication. While previous research has provided many insights into anxious learners' feelings about L2 speaking in general (e.g. Bailey, 1983; Cohen & Norst, 1989; Ewald, 2007; Hilleson, 1996; McCoy, 1979; Price,

1991; Tóth, 2011), few studies have looked at learners' reactions to actual L2 interactions they took part in (Gregersen & Horwitz, 2002; Gregersen, 2003; Phillips, 1992). The study I report here aims to do just that.

English major students with high and low levels of FLA were first asked to have one-on-one conversations with a native-speaking interlocutor and then to reflect on this experience immediately after the conversational encounter. Comparing high-anxious and low-anxious learners' perceptions of and affective reactions to this specific L2 interaction, I hope to shed light on the role of anxiety in the subjective experience of conversing in the TL and to seek a better understanding of the concept of FLA in the case of advanced learners.

Why a Study of Advanced Learners?

FLA has been described as a 'distinct complex of self-perceptions, beliefs, feelings, and behaviours related to classroom language learning arising from the uniqueness of the language learning process' (Horwitz et al., 1986: 128). What lies at the heart of Horwitz et al.'s classic definition is the idea that the multifaceted construct of anxiety arising in the context of instructed language learning and other L2 situations is rooted in the very experience of learning and using a language other than one's native tongue. Using a foreign language we are not fully proficient in is an intrinsically risky enterprise, a minefield of potential misunderstandings and problems with making oneself understood, hence its potential to provoke feelings of tension, apprehension, nervousness and worry, all leading to anxiety. This anxiety, however, is not merely about the linguistic challenges and difficulties posed by the complexity of L2 use. Because of the intimate relationship between language and self-expression, communication in an FL may also arouse feelings of personal inadequacy as it can make us feel that we cannot present what we believe to be our 'true' selves in the foreign language (Horwitz et al., 1986: 128). This is what explains the unique psychological experience shared by many language learners, that 'one feels like a different person when speaking a second language' (Guiora & Acton, 1979: 199). Perhaps it is this potential of FL learning/use to touch on one's identity that makes FLA a unique type of anxiety, which can also affect individuals not characteristically anxious in other situations (Horwitz et al., 1986; Young, 1992).

In light of this, it seems intuitively sound to suggest that the more proficient in an FL the learners are, the more efficiently they can use it as a means of communication; consequently, the less likely they are to experience the above feelings of inadequacy precipitating anxiety. Logical as it may seem that language anxiety should be more pervasive at the earlier stages of learning a new language than at more advanced levels, empirical findings suggest that the relationship between proficiency and anxiety is not as straightforward as it seems.

In a number of studies, beginning learners were indeed found to carry higher levels of L2-related anxiety than intermediate- and advanced-level learners (e.g. Gardner et al., 1977, 1979). On the basis of such findings, it has been posited that 'as experience and proficiency increase, anxiety declines in a fairly consistent manner' (Gardner & MacIntyre, 1991: 111), which implies that anxiety levels are highest at the earlier stages of learning a new language and anxiety becomes less of a problem for more advanced learners.

While some investigations have lent further empirical support to this view (e.g. Frantzen & Magnan, 2005; Liu, 2006), evidence to the contrary was found in others. A number of studies reported no significant differences in the anxiety levels of beginning, intermediate and advanced FL learners (Cheng, 2002; Onwuegbuzie et al., 1999; Pichette, 2009; Saito & Samimy, 1996); what is more, in other investigations, advanced learners scored higher on FLA than their peers at lower levels of instruction. In a study of learners of Spanish, advanced-level participants were significantly more anxious than beginners (Marcos-Llinas & Garau, 2009) and my own research on FLA in Hungarian EFL learners at the tertiary level has shown similar results (Tóth, 2009). Advanced learners, English major students, reported significantly higher anxiety than pre-intermediate level non-English majors at the same institution, despite having studied English for a longer period of time and having a higher proficiency in the TL.

Furthermore, in follow-up interviews with highly-anxious English majors (Tóth, 2011), I have found that the interviewed learners did not experience FLA at the earlier stages of their language learning career but reported having developed their anxiety in their advanced-level university English classes. This is in line with what has been reported by students of Spanish in upper-level classes (Ewald, 2007), many of whom claimed to experience more anxiety in advanced-level courses than in their beginning and intermediate language classes. Feelings of anxiety in both contexts were found to be related to factors like (1) learners' perceptions of a linguistically more challenging learning environment, (2) feelings of pressure to do well, (3) fears of not living up to higher expectations, (4) doubts about their own L2 competence and (5) worry about classmates' proficiency and abilities.

These conflicting findings show that anxiety does not necessarily decline as learners become more proficient in a new language, and may even appear for the first time at more advanced levels of learning. What is more, it might even affect non-native language teachers, as evidenced by a relatively new line of research into teacher/trainee teacher anxiety (Kunt & Tüm, 2010; Mousavi, 2007; Rajagopalan, 2005; Tüm, 2012), set off by Horwitz's (1996) seminal article introducing this seemingly paradoxical view.

Although the need to pay greater attention to anxiety at higher levels of proficiency has been realised and repeatedly called for (Ewald, 2007; Horwitz, 1996; Phillips, 2003), few studies have focused specifically on learners at more advanced stages of language learning. Therefore, relatively little is known about the nature and characteristics of anxiety experienced by high-proficiency L2 speakers. This was the motivation behind my studies of advanced Hungarian EFL learners, including the one reported here.

Focus and Aims

Research has consistently shown that, of all FL activities, it is oral communication that provokes most anxiety in learners, and this is true even for learners at more advanced levels of proficiency (Ewald, 2007; Horwitz, 1996; Tóth, 2011). A consistent, negative relationship has been documented between anxiety and oral test scores (Hewitt & Stephenson, 2011; Phillips, 1992; Woodrow, 2006; Young, 1986), speaking course grades (Cheng et al., 1999) and performance variables related to the quantity and quality (Hewitt & Stephenson, 2011; MacIntyre & Gardner, 1994; Phillips, 1992) as well as the content and elaboration of L2 speech (Steinberg & Horwitz, 1986). Taken together, these findings indicate that anxiety affects learners' oral performance, specifically both the quantity and quality of their L2 output.

But how does it affect the learners themselves? Rather than focusing on anxiety's impact on linguistic performance and achievement, as most previous research has done, this study aims to explore how anxiety affects the subjective experience of conversing in the TL. Although prior qualitative investigations have yielded valuable insights into anxious learners' fears and worries related to L2 speaking (e.g. Bailey, 1983; Cohen & Norst, 1989; Hilleson, 1996; McCoy, 1979; Price, 1991), most of them relied on learners' accounts of their in-class experiences, i.e. they tapped into general/overall attitudes/feelings rather than concrete/specific reactions to actual L2 interactions (e.g. Gregersen, 2003; Gregersen & Horwitz, 2002; Phillips, 1992). Studies of advanced learners, likewise, have mainly unearthed classroom-related sources of anxiety, including ones specific to upper-level courses such as higher expectations on the part of teachers; the heavier linguistic demands of a TL-only environment; competition with peers; classmates' experience in TL countries or the very idea of being a language specialist student/would-be expert of the TL (Ewald, 2007; Tóth, 2009, 2011).

The study I report on in this chapter examines advanced Hungarian EFL learners' feelings on using the TL in conversation with a native-speaking interlocutor outside of the classroom, in a quasi-naturalistic communicative setting. I compare the experiences of English specialist students with high FLA with those of their peers with low anxiety in order to identify potential differences in their reactions to the same L2 encounter and thereby gain insights into the nature of FLA in the case of advanced-level learners. My research questions are as follows:

- What do high- and low-anxious learners have to say about the experience of having a conversation with a native speaker (NS) of English?
- What are the differences between high- and low-anxious learners' reactions to the same experience?
- What are the characteristics of the anxiety of advanced-level learners?

Method

Participants

The participants were 16 English major students from a Hungarian university. They were selected from a larger group of EFL majors ($n=117$) participating in a series of studies comprising different aspects of a large-scale research project into anxiety at high levels of proficiency. Based on their scores on the Hungarian language validated version of Horwitz *et al.*'s (1986) Foreign Language Classroom Anxiety Scale (FLCAS) (Tóth, 2008), these 16 students were identified as the 8 most anxious and the 8 least anxious learners in the examined sample of English specialist students (Tóth, 2009). While the mean FLA score for the 117 students was 84.59 (standard deviation [SD]=19.34), the FLA scores of the 8 high-anxious participants ranged from 108 to 136 and those of the 8 low-anxious ones from 49 to 59. Of the 16 students, 13 were female and 3 were male. All participants were between the ages of 18 and 22. They had studied English for an average of 9.5 years before entering university, and they were preparing to become English teachers or other EFL professionals. Of the 16 students, 14 had never visited an English-speaking country. The interlocutor was a young lecturer from England, whose classes had not been attended by any of the students involved in the study. This allowed student participants to look on their conversation partner just as an NS rather than an instructor.

Procedures

To allow an examination of the relationship between anxiety and advanced learners' subjective experience of conversing in the TL, a two-phase study was designed. In the first phase, participants took part in 10–15 minute, one-on-one conversations with the native-speaking lecturer on the same preset topics. First, they were invited to exchange information about themselves and the interlocutor in a lead-in free phase (where they come from, interests, studies and career goals). Second, they were asked to express their opinion on a controversial issue presented on a situation card (whether the amount of tuition fees to be paid for university studies should depend on students' academic results). Finally, they had to describe and interpret an ambiguous picture (a close-up of a mother and her child with terrified faces in a situation open to different interpretations).

In the second phase, immediately after each conversation, short individual interviews were conducted with the students to have a quick survey of their immediate affective reactions. I invited them to reflect freely on their experiences, i.e. to express any thoughts or feelings concerning the conversation. They were only prompted by simple, open-ended questions like 'What was it like?' and 'How did you feel during the conversation?' to allow them maximum freedom in deciding what they chose to talk about. This approach was supposed to better serve the purpose of finding out how prominently anxiety figured in their experiences of interacting with the NS than asking them about anxiety directly.

After the interviews, the participants were also asked to complete a short, affective questionnaire (see Appendix). They had to indicate, on three 10-point rating scales, (1) how they felt during the conversation (1=very unpleasant, 10=very pleasant); (2) how much anxiety they experienced (1=I was totally calm, 10=I was very anxious and all but panicked); and (3) what they thought of their performance (1=it was very poor, 10=it was very good). The aim of quantifying the extent/quality of these feelings was merely to supplement and verify the qualitative data gained through the interviews.

The interviews were conducted in Hungarian and lasted between 5 and 10 minutes. They were audio-recorded with the consent of the participants, who were ensured that their responses would be treated as confidential and that their performances would not affect their grades in any way. The transcripts were coded for recurring themes and analysed qualitatively using the constant comparative method (Maykut & Morehouse, 1994). To compare high- and low-anxious participants' responses to the affective questionnaire, I computed the frequencies and averages (means) of students' ratings in the two anxiety groups.

Findings and Discussion

Participants' numerical answers to the first questionnaire item revealed that students with high vs low levels of FLA differed considerably with regard to how pleasant or unpleasant an experience conversing with the NS appeared to them. In response to how they felt during the conversation, seven out of the eight low-anxious students gave a rating of 8, 9 or 10 on the 10-point scale ($M_{low\text{-}anx}$=8.57), indicating that, for them, interacting with the NS was a pleasant experience, whereas high-anxious students' noticeably lower rating ($M_{high\text{-}anx}$=5.57) showed that the same conversational encounter, for them, was a less positive experience. In what follows, I look at the differences the retrospective interviews brought to light between high- and low-anxious learners' perceptions of and affective reactions to the same L2 experience.

First reactions

The interviewees' immediate reactions after the conversation – prompted by the questions 'What was it like?' and 'How did you feel?' – proved to be very revealing. Students' responses in the two anxiety groups appeared to differ not only in how positive or negative they were but also in terms of content or focus. While participants with low anxiety tended to express their feelings about the conversation with the NS as a 'conversation', i.e. communication between two people on various topics, high-anxious interviewees' responses centred around themselves; specifically, how they performed in English and how anxious or embarrassed they felt while doing so.

Most students in the low-anxiety group started to talk about the atmosphere of the conversation, describing it in enthusiastic terms such as 'good, really good', 'a pleasant conversation', 'it cheered me up, now I feel switched on', 'wasn't a bad conversation at all', 'it was OK, I didn't feel bad' or 'I enjoyed it'. Other students talked about the interlocutor and the impression he made on them. To quote some responses: 'the conversation partner was very pleasant, absolutely open and helpful', 'I felt he was genuinely interested in what I was saying, not just asking questions without really caring about the answers' and 'I enjoyed talking to him; he was very pleasant to talk to'. Finally, some low-anxious participants commented on the topics: 'interesting', 'thought-provoking', 'stimulating', 'dry', 'artificial', or 'too serious'; and on which was easier or more difficult to talk about and why. In short, personal feelings about the (1) atmosphere, (2) conversation partner and (3) topics were the main themes of low-anxious students' first reactions.

In contrast, high-anxious participants' first sentences were reflective of a preoccupation with themselves. So preoccupied were these students with their own performance and feelings of uneasiness that they started to talk about these issues *in medias res*, before any questions could have been asked, as shown by the following quotes: 'I'm not satisfied with myself, my own performance', 'I made very stupid mistakes, appalling ones', 'It was extremely difficult, I feel I did very poorly, I didn't find the words, and I always had to ask him [i.e. the interlocutor] to repeat what he had said', 'There were words, many words I couldn't recall and, unfortunately, I couldn't really pay attention to grammar', 'It was horrible, I spoke incoherently, my vocabulary is disappointing, my sentences had no subject and predicate', 'What I want to say: It was terrible when I couldn't properly understand the text' [i.e. the situation card], 'The problem is I was too anxious' and 'I'm so pathetic, I feel awful, I couldn't find the words

I needed, couldn't come up with ideas'. As evidenced by these agitated comments, what seemed to be uppermost in high-anxious students' minds was worry over how poorly they came across, how many mistakes they had made, what difficulties they encountered and what an uncomfortable experience the encounter was.

Interpretation of the situation

Students' initial remarks in the two anxiety categories were indicative of two very different responses to the same situation. High-anxious participants tended to see the interaction with the NS more as a language task or exam than a real conversation, which was evident from their recurring remarks on their 'language performance'. Low-anxious students' comments, in contrast, were not restricted to linguistic matters. While talking about their feelings regarding the three stages of the conversation (lead-in chat, situation card, ambiguous picture), students in the high-anxiety group tended to reflect on these phases in terms of how demanding they were linguistically and how successful they felt in 'performing' them, whereas low-anxious students generally commented on the topics and the ideas discussed.

To illustrate this with examples, the lead-in free conversation about personal matters was seen by most high-anxious students as 'the best' or 'the easiest' part because 'talking about yourself is an easy *task*', 'it doesn't present so many difficulties as other *tasks*' or 'it's a *topic* in language and entrance *exams* as well' (emphasis added). By contrast, a low-anxious student referred to the same introductory chat as the 'best part' for a very different reason: 'because this was the one closest to a real conversation, through which you can learn things about someone you don't know and reveal something about yourself'. Another participant in the low-anxiety group expressed a similar attitude when talking about how happy he felt during the lead-in phase on learning that the English interlocutor had not only heard of but had been to his hometown in Transylvania, and this was why he liked this part the most: 'From this point on it wasn't a mock conversation any longer like those in language exams; we genuinely exchanged views and feelings about my country'. What these learners appeared to value was the authenticity of the interaction: the fact that they used the language for real communication.

Similarly, the second stage (expressing an opinion on whether university students should pay a certain level of tuition fee if they do not achieve a given end-of-term grade point average) was regarded by high-anxious participants as 'the most difficult', 'the most demanding' or 'the worst of all three', for reasons such as 'it would have required more sophisticated language', 'it made it clear for me that OK I can speak English, but I can't yet talk about *any* topic in English', 'the text [i.e. the situation card] was difficult to understand' or 'I can't react to something I've read so quickly'. By contrast, students in the low-anxiety group differed in how positively or negatively they felt about this part of the conversation, but this depended on whether they liked the topic or not rather than linguistic considerations. For example, one student said he found it 'a bit dry or artificial' and this is why he 'couldn't engage with the subject'. Another low-anxious participant, in contrast, considered the same issue 'very easy to talk about' as she 'felt personally affected by the very thought of the idea' on the situation card, saying: 'if such a fee was indeed introduced, I could say good-bye to university, as I wouldn't be able to achieve such a good grade point average'.

High- and low-anxious students' reactions to the ambiguous picture reflected the same difference in focus. While high-anxious participants were concerned with the language demands of describing the picture and their personal problems with it, e.g. 'not being able to recall appropriate words to describe facial expressions', low-anxious students again gave non-linguistic reasons for liking or disliking the picture or for finding it easier or more difficult to talk about. To quote a low-anxious participant: 'The picture was interesting. I put myself into the shoes of the mother and felt really involved in what I imagined to be happening. It was good; I enjoyed it'. Remarks like this showed that low-anxious students got personally involved in the topics, i.e. their responses were content rather than language oriented. This was in contrast with high-anxious participants' apparent preoccupation with linguistic rather than other aspects of the conversation, which is consistent with the findings of a previous study (Gregersen, 2003), whose high-anxious participants were also more concerned with form rather than the message they were trying to convey in the L2.

Feelings about performance

The interviewed advanced-level learners with high vs low levels of FLA also differed in terms of how they felt about their performance, how much importance they attached to mistakes and other limitations in the TL and what they attributed them to. As evidenced by some of the comments quoted thus far, high-anxious participants tended to see their performance in a rather negative light and repeatedly express dissatisfaction with it, which was also confirmed by their rating it as low as 3.87, approaching the 'very poor' end of the 10-point scale. Low-anxious participants' evaluation of their own performance, in contrast, was considerably higher ($M_{low\text{-}anx}=6.5$ vs $M_{high\text{-}anx}=3.87$).

Students with low anxiety – as evidenced by the interviews – were, by and large, satisfied with themselves, if not completely: 'more or less', 'relatively', 'on the whole', 'under the circumstances'. Although they mentioned problems such as 'sometimes not finding the right word', 'passive vocabulary', 'hesitating more than desirable' or 'not comprehending one or two things in what the interlocutor said', they did not seem to worry about such issues. Some of them talked about these aspects of their performance as 'natural' and 'understandable' in view of how rarely they had a conversation with an NS. To quote a low-anxious participant: 'Considering that I'm not surrounded with native speakers, that I practically don't speak English with anyone, not counting my classmates, it's not surprising that sometimes I have to search for words, that they don't come automatically'. Other low-anxious students explained these problems by not being able to 'switch' to English in the short time-span of the interaction. For example, one student said that 'of course' he 'would have been able to speak much better' if he 'had watched ten cartoons or two movies in English' before the conversation to 'spur' his 'sleeping [i.e. passive] English into action', but 'given that' he 'had to walk in and start to speak English', he said he was 'quite happy' with how he did. Others offered explanations such as 'not having any language classes' that day or 'not having spoken with a NS of English for ages'. Remarks like these showed that low-anxious students accepted their limitations in the TL and tended to ascribe them to circumstances beyond their control, namely, limited contact with an NS and the fact that they spoke English almost exclusively in the classroom only.

A similar, fairly easy-going attitude was displayed by these learners towards mistakes. Some low-anxious students openly admitted that they did 'not worry too much about accuracy'. One of them described himself as 'the opposite of students, girls in particular, who have an excellent knowledge of grammar and do very well in writing but score one point out of ten in an oral exam, as they don't dare to say a word for fear of being inaccurate'. He, by contrast, as he put it, 'was never afraid of grammatically incorrect sentences', and indeed he seemed fairly pleased with his performance despite the mistakes he was aware of making during the conversation.

Participants' reflections in the high-anxiety group showed a very different picture. Out of the eight students, none said they were satisfied with themselves. The words they used to describe their performance were all reflective of negative affect, e.g. 'bad', 'horrible', 'awful', 'very poor' and 'weak', and the same applied to their choice of adjectives when referring to the mistakes they perceived to have made during the interaction, e.g. 'catastrophic', 'tragic', 'appalling', 'colossal' and 'very serious'. This is indicative of a notably greater concern over accuracy than that which was expressed by students in the low-anxiety group, which supports previous findings on the differences between high- and low-anxious learners' level of error tolerance (Gregersen, 2003; Gregersen & Horwitz, 2002).

Another observable difference the interviews revealed was that students in the high-anxiety group were far more critical of themselves and talked about their language performance in highly pessimistic terms, for example 'I wouldn't be able to name one thing I was satisfied with, not a single moment during the whole *exam*' (emphasis added) and 'Lack of vocabulary, no grammar in my sentences, so I can't say I'm satisfied with anything, I did very poorly indeed'. What is more, several high-anxious participants said they were left with a feeling of disappointment after the conversation, as reflected in the following comment: 'It's a bad feeling to realise how poorly I did, that I don't do as well as I should, as it is expected of me. After so many years of learning English I would expect more from myself'. What this high-anxious participant expresses here is a growing impatience or feeling of frustration over her unsatisfactory command of the TL, despite long years of commitment to learning it – a feeling likely to be typical at more advanced levels.

Related to this is the finding that students with high anxiety had a tendency to see the difficulties they encountered in conversation with the NS as a personal shortcoming or deficiency. When talking about these in the interviews, none of them mentioned any 'mitigating circumstances', as participants with low anxiety did, but tended to blame themselves for their performance level: their linguistic deficiencies (e.g. not having a wide enough range of vocabulary) and their anxiety, which they saw as an important factor in how they 'performed' as well as how they felt during the interaction.

Anxiety

Students' ratings of their actual anxiety level on the 10-point scale showed that learners with high scores on the Hungarian FLCAS were indeed more anxious while interacting with the NS than their peers with low FLA scores, and the difference between the two groups' mean anxiety level was substantial ($M_{high\text{-}anx}=6.25$ vs $M_{low\text{-}anx}=3.37$). In the interviews, low-anxious participants referred to anxiety only sparingly and mainly to express their satisfaction at staying 'calm' and 'confident' during the interaction. Although some of them admitted they felt 'a little embarrassed' when they realised that they 'said something that wasn't correct' or 'used a wrong word', they said 'it wasn't too bad' and 'didn't last long' because they 'moved on as quickly as possible, not even correcting what was wrong'. In short, they took pride in not getting 'distracted by worries and doubts'.

As for high-anxious participants, although they said they were less anxious than 'usual' when taking a 'real oral exam' 'with serious consequences' as what they experienced 'was just the anxiety you feel when you talk to a NS', they felt inhibited and negatively affected by their anxious reactions during the interaction. As one of the participants put it: 'I feel I know much more than what I managed to show here; in a more relaxed state of mind it would have been different'. Others referred to specific problems they saw as being related to their feelings of anxiety, specifically difficulty (1) understanding the interlocutor: 'As

I felt anxious, I didn't really understand what he was asking precisely'; (2) understanding the situation card: 'When I'm very anxious I don't understand what I'm reading, the letters are blurred before my eyes, I can't see words or sentences, just letters'; (3) retrieving vocabulary: 'In such an anxious state, words simply don't come; actually, I think they don't come because I'm afraid they won't'; and (4) generating ideas (pros and cons for the controversial issue, alternative interpretations about the picture): 'It was not merely a language problem: that I didn't remember how to say something in English, but that I had no idea whatsoever, nothing came to my mind'.

Anxiety was in part related to high-anxious students' concern over the interlocutor's reactions, due to which they found it difficult to focus on what they were doing at a given moment. For instance, when reading the situation card, some of them reported worrying about not being able to react fast enough, which hindered them in their efforts to understand what they were reading, as the following comment shows: 'I wanted to read it quickly so that I wouldn't take up the interlocutor's time, and I tried really hard to understand it, but I felt I just couldn't concentrate'. Others worried about not being able to give 'interesting' or 'clever' answers: 'I was so anxious about being able to say something, something intelligent that I couldn't come up with anything'.

Perceptions of self as L2 speaker

Another concern related to the interlocutor is shown by the following excerpt, in which a high-anxious participant discusses at length the frustration she felt because of the difference between her own and the interlocutor's English:

> It was good talking to him in that I always enjoy listening to someone who speaks English well [ironically laughs implying that she does not], at the same time it puts you to shame: 'how does your pronunciation compare to his and everything else: he speaks so elegantly and with the greatest ease, while you, poor thing, are struggling and sweating and racking your brains so that you can recall words, even basic ones. And all your efforts are in vain, you stumble over every other sentence, and it's so embarrassing, my God!, and disturbing. The contrast is just too strong!'

As this sample comment shows, the native-speaking interlocutor himself was a source of anxiety for the high-anxious participants of the study. His 'beautiful'/'perfect English' pronunciation made them feel uneasy about their own 'Hunglish accent', and they found his easy and natural command of English 'frustrating'/'intimidating'.

The passage gives a graphic description of how this high-anxious student was feeling about herself as an L2 speaker compared with the NS. She referred to herself as 'poor thing', and other high-anxious interviewees used similar derogatory phrases when talking about themselves, such as 'a poor little student babbling in English', 'a pitiable Hungarian schoolgirl', 'poor wretch', 'a ridiculous little fellow trying so hard', etc. These self-deprecatory remarks, all related to feeling diminished or deprived in some sense – age/maturity ('little', 'schoolgirl', 'babbling'), personality ('thing', 'wretch', 'fellow'), effectiveness/sophistication ('poor', 'ridiculous', 'pitiable') – are reflective of a negative L2 self-image, resulting from negative feelings and self-perceptions related to TL communication.

What most high-anxious students complained about was a feeling that they were unable to communicate their ideas as clearly and effectively as they wanted to, as a result of which they felt uncomfortable in front of the interlocutor: 'I couldn't express my thoughts and feelings as well/ as precisely as I would have liked to'; 'What I said was very often different from what I wanted to say; I found this embarrassing'. Some students said they did not feel 'clever' or 'intelligent' but rather 'a bit silly', 'slow' and 'awkward' in English, as if their 'English-speaking-self did not have the same intellectual capacity', which made them feel uneasy. Others talked about perceiving themselves as 'dull', 'plain' or 'colourless', which contributed to their negative feelings during the conversation.

High-anxious participants' self-perceptions of being less articulate, less intelligent/sophisticated or less interesting/attractive a person in the L2 are clear manifestations of what is described in the literature as a feeling of 'disparity between the "true" self as known to the language learner' and a 'more limited self' they felt to be projecting during the conversation (Horwitz *et al.*, 1986: 31). The vocabulary these students used to describe themselves when speaking English also supports the view that 'language and self are so closely bound, if indeed they are not one and the same thing, that a perceived attack on one is an attack on the other' (Cohen & Norst, 1989: 76). Experiencing their limitations in conversation with the native-speaking interlocutor (i.e. the perceived 'attack' on language) was indeed an 'attack' on their self/identity, as a result of which they felt infantilised, ineffective and unable to show their individual 'colours' (i.e. their personality) in the TL. The severity of the 'attack' is shown by a high-anxious student's comment, in which she appears to identify herself with her L2 output: 'Me in his [i.e. the interlocutor's] eyes? Probably strong Hungarian accent, lots of hesitations and *ers* on end, poor grammar, wrong words, etc'.

As for low-anxious participants, no student in this category made any mention of feeling ashamed because of their English, nor did they talk about being frustrated by the native-speaking interlocutor's superior language skills, and nobody made any reference to feeling less efficient, less intelligent or less pleasant a person in English. This finding shows that the same situation did not provoke high anxiety and other negative feelings in students categorised as low-anxious. Being aware of mistakes and other limitations when speaking the TL did not seem to prevent these learners from enjoying the conversation and from getting interested in the topics and ideas discussed. Furthermore, it did not make them feel inferior as conversation partners, which appeared to be the case with their high-anxious peers. The absence of self-derogatory statements in the low-anxiety group would appear to indicate a more positive L2 self-concept among learners in this category. Comments like the ones quoted below stand in stark contrast with those of highly-anxious interviewees. They show that participants with low anxiety tended to be 'quite happy' with their English-speaking self: 'I think I was a rather confident conversation partner', 'I enjoyed talking to him [i.e. the interlocutor], so I guess he enjoyed talking to me too' and 'I think it was a refreshing change for him to converse with me, I think he liked my sense of humour'.

As evidenced by these remarks, far from feeling frustrated, unequal or inferior in conversation with the native-speaking interlocutor, some low-anxious participants even expressed pride in what they considered as their positive qualities as conversation partners such as being confident, cheerful, or having a good sense of humour. What is clear from these findings is that the participating advanced-level learners with high vs low levels of FLA also differed in how they felt about themselves as L2 speakers.

Conclusion

In this chapter, I examined the relationship between anxiety and advanced learners' oral communication experiences. In particular, I was interested in finding out how important an issue anxiety is for learners at this proficiency level when using the TL outside the classroom walls and how it affects their experiences of face-to-face communication with an NS.

The study of Hungarian EFL majors showed that, for high scorers on the Hungarian FLCAS, having a conversation with an NS in a quasi-naturalistic communicative setting was an anxiety-provoking experience. Notwithstanding the non-evaluative nature of the situation and the friendly interlocutor, they felt markedly more anxious during the interaction than their peers with low FLA scores. They experienced negative thoughts and feelings concerning their language competency as well as themselves as L2 speakers (e.g. self-consciousness, uneasiness, worry, self-blame, shame, frustration, disappointment), and they felt their anxious reactions had negatively affected their performance. As a result, the experience of interacting with an NS was for them far less pleasant than for their low-anxious counterparts.

A comparison of participants' retrospective comments in the two anxiety categories revealed important differences between high- and low-anxious students, which are likely to be related to how much anxiety they experienced during the conversation as well as to their overall affective reactions to it. These concern their (1) interpretation of the situation, (2) tendency to focus on linguistic vs other aspects of the conversation, (3) attitudes to and attributions of mistakes and other limitations in the TL and (4) perceptions of themselves as L2 speakers. High-anxious students' negative emotional responses can be linked to the following factors:

- The situation is perceived as an evaluative one, more like a test or exam than a casual conversation.
- Speaking in the L2 feels more like a task or exercise than real communication.
- There is a strong focus on language (i.e. linguistic form) rather than content (i.e. topics, ideas discussed).
- Mistakes and other limitations in the L2 are seen as a personal failure or deficiency rather than natural/inevitable.
- Negative *self*-evaluation based on self-perceptions of L2 performance.
- Perceived inability to be themselves/present their true self in the TL.
- Idealisation of the NS, feeling inferior.

High-anxious participants' internal experiences emerging from the interviews provide clear evidence that long years of commitment to learning an FL and a relatively high level of proficiency do not necessarily confer a sense of confidence in using the TL on every learner. Therefore, this study supports the findings of previous research which challenge the view that language anxiety is specific to learners at lower levels of proficiency. Advanced learners, such as the EFL majors in this study, may be relatively proficient in the language; however, their own personal expectations of themselves as L2 speakers are also higher. As evidenced by the interviews with high-anxious students, rather than being satisfied with making themselves understood, these learners wanted to speak the TL correctly, elaborately and easily; consequently, discrepancies between this ambition and their actual L2-related self-perceptions were an important source of anxiety and frustration for them. Face-to-face with the native-speaking interlocutor, these learners felt inhibited by what they perceived as an unbridgeable gap between the NS's and their own English and also frustrated by the feeling that, despite their best efforts, they might never attain the same level of proficiency.

These findings indicate that learners' higher expectations towards themselves as L2 speakers, together with a fear of not being able to achieve the desired level of competence after long years of language study, are key elements of anxiety at more advanced levels of proficiency. This can be particularly acute for learners who specialise in FL study to become language teachers or other FL professionals, like the English major participants in this research.

Providing in-depth insights into high- vs low-anxious EFL specialist participants' experiences of the same conversational encounter in the TL, this study has gone some way towards enhancing our understanding of language anxiety in the case of advanced learners. However, its limitations must also be noted. As the study was based on a small sample of English majors from one Hungarian university, whose reactions to conversing with an NS were only examined in one particular situation, more research is needed to further explore the role of anxiety in the language learning and communication experiences of learners at high levels of proficiency. Specifically, future studies could ascertain the extent to which the sentiments expressed by the high-anxious participants in this study are shared by learners with similar L2 proficiency in other cultural and language learning contexts. Likewise, future research will also need to verify whether and to what extent the observed differences between high- and low-anxious Hungarian EFL majors apply to advanced learners in other settings. Furthermore, future investigations might explore the relationship between anxiety and different communication settings (e.g. quasi-naturalistic vs naturalistic, native-speaking vs non-native-speaking [NNS] interlocutor or NNS interlocutor with the same vs another L1, etc.). Finally, another area worthy of further research would be the role of learning goals/career choices in the anxiety of high proficiency learners (e.g. FL majors vs learners not specialised in FL study or language teacher trainees vs students in non-teaching programmes).

References

Bailey, K.M. (1983) Competitiveness and anxiety in adult second language learning: Looking *at* and *through* the diary studies. In H.W. Seliger and M.H. Long (eds) *Classroom-Oriented Research in Second Language Acquisition* (pp. 67–102). Rowley, MA: Newbury House.
Cheng, Y. (2002) Factors associated with foreign language writing anxiety. *Foreign Language Annals* 35, 647–656.
Cheng, Y., Horwitz, E.K. and Schallert, D.L. (1999) Language anxiety: Differentiating writing and speaking components. *Language Learning* 49, 417–446.
Cohen, Y. and Norst, M.J. (1989) Fear, dependence and loss of self-esteem: Affective barriers in second language learning among adults. *RELC Journal* 20, 61–77.
Ewald, J.D. (2007) Foreign language learning anxiety in upper-level classes: Involving students as researchers. *Foreign Language Annals* 40 (1), 122–142.
Frantzen, D. and Magnan, S.S. (2005) Anxiety and the true beginner – false beginner dynamic in beginning French and Spanish classes. *Foreign Language Annals* 38 (2), 171–190.
Gardner, R.C., Smythe, P.C. and Brunet, G.R. (1977) Intensive second language study: Effects on attitudes, motivation and French achievement. *Language Learning* 27, 243–261.

Gardner, R.C., Smythe, P.C. and Clément, R. (1979) Intensive second language study in a bicultural milieu: An investigation of attitudes, motivation and language proficiency. *Language Learning* 29, 305–320.

Gregersen, T.S. (2003) To err is human: A reminder to teachers of language-anxious students. *Foreign Language Annals* 36, 25–32.

Gregersen, T.S. and Horwitz, E.K. (2002) Language learning and perfectionism: Anxious and non-anxious language learners' reactions to their own oral performance. *The Modern Language Journal* 86, 562–570.

Guiora, A. and Acton, W. (1979) Personality and language: A restatement. *Language Learning* 29, 193–204.

Hewitt, E. and Stephenson, J. (2011) Foreign language anxiety and oral exam performance: A replication of Phillips's *MLJ* study. *The Modern Language Journal* 96 (2), 170–189.

Hilleson, M. (1996) 'I want to talk with them, but I don't want them to hear': An introspective study of second language anxiety in an English-medium school. In K. Bailey and D. Nunan (eds) *Voices from the Language Classroom* (pp. 248–275). Cambridge: Cambridge University Press.

Horwitz, E.K. (1996) Even teachers get the blues: Recognizing and alleviating non-native teachers' feelings of foreign language anxiety. *Foreign Language Annals* 29, 365–372.

Horwitz, E.K. (2010) Foreign and second language anxiety. *Language Teaching* 43 (2), 154–167.

Horwitz, E.K., Horwitz, M.B. and Cope, J. (1986) Foreign language classroom anxiety. *The Modern Language Journal* 70, 125–132.

Kunt, N. and Tüm, D.Ö. (2010) Non-native student teachers' feelings of foreign language anxiety. *Procedia, Social and Behavioral Sciences* 2 (2), 4672–4676.

Liu, M. (2006) Anxiety in Chinese EFL students at different proficiency levels. *System* 34, 301–316.

MacIntyre, P.D. (1999) Language anxiety: A review of the research for language teachers. In D.J. Young (ed.) *Affect in Foreign Language and Second Language Learning: A Practical Guide to Creating a Low-Anxiety Classroom Atmosphere* (pp. 24–45). Boston, MA: McGraw-Hill.

MacIntyre, P.D. and Gardner, R.C. (1991) Methods and results in the study of anxiety and language learning: A review of the literature. *Language Learning* 41, 85–117.

MacIntyre, P.D. and Gardner, R.C. (1994) The subtle effects of language anxiety on cognitive processing in the second language. *Language Learning* 44, 283–305.

Marcos-Llinás, M. and Garau, M.J. (2009) Effects of language anxiety on three proficiency-level courses of Spanish as a foreign language. *Foreign Language Annals* 42 (1), 94–111.

Maykut, P. and Morehouse, R. (1994) *Beginning Qualitative Research: A Philosophic and Practical Guide*. London: The Falmer Press.

McCoy, I.R. (1979) Means to overcome the anxieties of second language learners. *Foreign Language Annals* 12, 185–189.

Mousavi, E.S. (2007) Exploring 'teacher stress' in non-native and native teachers of EFL. *English Language Teacher Education and Development* 10, 33–41. See http://www.elted.net/uploads/7/3/1/6/7316005/v10mousavi.pdf (accessed 29 November 2016).

Onwuegbuzie, A.J., Bailey, P. and Daley, C.E. (1999) Factors associated with foreign language anxiety. *Applied Psycholinguistics* 20, 217–239.

Phillips, E.M. (1992) The effects of language anxiety on students' oral test performance and attitudes. *The Modern Language Journal* 76, 14–26.

Phillips, J. (2003) Foreign languages, literatures, cultures: Moving toward unity. *ADFL Bulletin* 35 (1), 15–19.

Pichette, F. (2009) Second language anxiety and distance language learning. *Foreign Language Annals* 42 (1), 77–93.

Price, M.L. (1991) The subjective experience of foreign language anxiety: Interviews with anxious students. In E.K. Horwitz and D.J. Young (eds) *Language Anxiety: From Theory and Research to Classroom Implications* (pp. 101–108). Englewood Cliffs, NJ: Prentice-Hall.

Rajagopalan, K. (2005) Non-native speaker teachers of English and their anxieties: Ingredients for an experiment in action research. In E. Llurda (ed.) *Non-Native Language Teachers: Perceptions, Challenges and Contributions to the Profession* (pp. 283–304). New York: Springer.

Saito, Y. and Samimy, K. (1996) Foreign language anxiety and language performance: A study of learning anxiety in beginning, intermediate, and advanced-level college students of Japanese. *Foreign Language Annals* 29, 239–251.

Steinberg, F.S. and Horwitz, E.K. (1986) The effect of induced anxiety on the denotative and interpretive content of second language speech. *TESOL Quarterly* 20, 131–136.

Tóth, Zs. (2008) A foreign language anxiety scale for Hungarian learners of English. *Working Papers in Language Pedagogy* 2, 55–78.

Tóth, Zs. (2009) Foreign language anxiety – For beginners only? In R. Lugossy, J. Horváth and M. Nikolov (eds) *UPRT 2008: Empirical Studies in English Applied Linguistics* (pp. 225–246). Pécs: Lingua Franca Csoport.

Tóth, Zs. (2010) *Foreign Language Anxiety and the Advanced Language Learner: A Study of Hungarian Students of English as a Foreign Language*. Newcastle upon Tyne: Cambridge Scholars.

Tóth, Zs. (2011) Foreign language anxiety and advanced EFL learners: An interview study. *Working Papers in Language Pedagogy* 5, 39–57.

Tüm, D.Ö. (2012) Feelings of language anxiety amongst non-native student teachers. *Procedia, Social and Behavioral Sciences* 47, 2055–2059.

Woodrow, L. (2006) Anxiety and speaking English as a second language. *RELC* 37 (3), 308–328.

Young, D.J. (1986) The relationship between anxiety and foreign language oral proficiency ratings. *Foreign Language Annals* 19, 439–445.

Young, D.J. (1991) Creating a low-anxiety classroom environment: What does language anxiety research suggest? *The Modern Language Journal* 75, 426–439.

Young, D.J. (1992) Language anxiety from the foreign language specialist's perspective: Interviews with Krashen, Omaggio Hadley, Terrell, and Rardin. *Foreign Language Annals* 25, 157–172.

Young, D.J. (1994) New directions in language anxiety research. In C.A. Klee (ed.) *Faces in a Crowd: The Individual Learner in Multisection Courses* (pp. 3–45). Boston, MA: Heinle & Heinle Publishers.

Appendix

Affective questionnaire

(1) How did you feel during the conversation?
    1 2 3 4 5 6 7 8 9 10

    (1=very unpleasant; 10=very pleasant)

(2) How much anxiety did you experience during the conversation?
    1 2 3 4 5 6 7 8 9 10

    (1=I was totally calm; 10=I was very anxious, all but panicked)

(3) What did you think of your performance?
    1 2 3 4 5 6 7 8 9 10

    (1=it was very poor; 10=it was very good)

Part 3

Implications for Practice

10 Anxious Language Learners Can Change Their Minds: Ideas and Strategies from Traditional Psychology and Positive Psychology

Rebecca L. Oxford

> *Dare to live*
> ('Vivere', Trovato *et al.*, 2007)

Introduction

Most learners with language anxiety would be puzzled or even shocked by the concept 'Leap, and the net will appear' (Cameron, 1992: 66) for language learning. For them, there is no social safety net. In fact, they actively distrust social situations in which they are expected to interact or perform in front of others in the target language because they anticipate severe scrutiny and embarrassment. In the language learning environment, highly anxious learners are the centre of their own swirling, pressured, negative world, which seems particularly focused on what they believe they cannot do. They are 'worried about being so worried' (Comer, 2014: 113), yet they frequently feel they cannot escape the compulsion to worry. They are likely to experience 'insidious' outcomes (Dewaele & MacIntyre, 2014: 238), such as reductions in the following: cognition, self-confidence, personal agency, control, willingness to communicate and ability to express and recognise emotions (Dewaele, 2010; Dewaele & MacIntyre, 2014; Horwitz, 2001; Horwitz & Young, 1991; MacIntyre, 2002). Perhaps for less severely anxious learners, there are cases in which anticipatory anxiety is beneficial for (1) stimulation and alertness (Marcos-Llinas & Juan Garau, 2009), (2) the focus of action (Dewaele & MacIntyre, 2014) and (3) the process of resilience (Oxford *et al.*, 2007).

Because of their negative assumptions and lack of social skills (Comer, 2014), individuals with social anxiety, which is usually the basis of language anxiety, often use avoidance behaviours (Rosenberg et al., 2010) such as wishful thinking, denial, distractions, escapism and giving up (Carver et al., 2011). I observed avoidance behaviours in language classrooms, where learners with serious language anxiety sweated, shook and failed to speak even a few words in the target language for fear of censure. I also witnessed the avoidance behaviours of certain military officers assigned to learn the Spanish language in Costa Rica. Because of fear of scrutiny and humiliation, along with possible low motivation, these seasoned officers chose to 'hang out' with each other, speaking English and never interacting with the local Costa Ricans despite the extrinsic, career-related incentives that were built into their language education system.

This chapter centres on knowledge and interventions from the fields of traditional psychology (first section) and positive psychology (second section), followed by the conclusion (third section). Besides being a language education specialist, I teach traditional psychology and have presented and published on positive psychology, so I am aware of the riches these fields offer learners with language anxiety. In this chapter, the basic information is in regular print and possible interventions are in italics.

What We Know from Traditional Psychology

Traditional psychology treats anxiety as a set of clinical 'disorders', including, among others, social anxiety disorder and generalised anxiety disorder. Rather than viewing these phenomena as clinical conditions or implying that those who experience them are emotionally ill, I refer to them simply as 'social anxiety' and 'generalised anxiety' and note that many people around the world experience them. In this section, I apply what we know about anxiety from traditional psychology to language learners and make suggestions for relevant interventions.

Social anxiety

Individuals with social anxiety are persistently, irrationally and often severely fearful of engaging in any social or performance situations in which scrutiny by others and embarrassment might occur (American Psychiatric Association, 2013; Comer, 2014). Social anxiety is often described as the primary root of language anxiety, although I contend that generalised anxiety might also play a role in certain instances.

Maladaptive assumptions are the main cognitive explanation for social anxiety (Comer, 2014; Heimberg et al., 2010; Hofmann, 2007). For language learners, such social anxiety-related assumptions often include the following (based on Comer, 2014): (1) 'I must perform perfectly in social situations in the target language, whether in class or elsewhere'; (2) 'I am unattractive, unskilled, inadequate, and/or incompetent in social situations where the target language is used'; (3) 'My inept social behaviors will inevitably lead to terrible consequences'; and (4) 'I have no control over my feelings of social anxiety'. In addition to having these debilitating beliefs, individuals who suffer from social anxiety often literally 'lack skill at starting conversations, communicating their needs, or meeting the needs of others (Beck, 2010)' (Comer, 2014: 134).

Interventions to increase the calmness of learners whose language anxiety is clearly a matter of social anxiety, without generalised anxiety:

- *Modelling is a social cognitive approach (Bandura, 1997) often used with people who have social anxiety. The therapist or teacher models desirable behaviours for individuals with social anxiety and then encourages those individuals to imitate the behaviours. For example, the language teacher might model deep breathing, use of humour and visualisation techniques (Oxford, 1990) to help anxious learners relax.*
- *In exposure therapy (Antony & Roemer, 2011), the therapist or teacher encourages people with social anxiety to expose themselves gradually and repeatedly to the fearsome situation until their fears subside. Exposure usually includes assigned homework to be done in the social situation. In the case of anxious learners, exposure therapy would consist of (1) continually allowing themselves to be exposed to language performance situations rather than avoiding those situations and (2) using cognitive and affective techniques to face those situations (Oxford, 1990, 2011).*
- *Rational-emotive therapy and other cognitive therapies are helpful in treating social anxieties (Boden et al., 2012; Ellis, 2003; Kim et al., 2011). In Ellis' (2003) rational-emotive therapy, a person would do a homework assignment in which she identifies her negative assumptions, and then in a social situation, she forces herself to speak up and express herself in order to defeat these negative assumptions.*
- *Biological approaches such as relaxation training and biofeedback can be combined with cognitive therapies (Comer, 2014). One relaxation exercise is deep breathing: 'First, breathe in deeply while imagining that you are taking in all the fresh, healthy, positive energies that your body and soul crave. Next, let your breath out while imagining that you are releasing old, unhealthy, and negative energies and emotions, such as anxiety, that no longer serve you – if they ever did. Go through this cycle several times and experience the serenity and calmness that come. Your body shows you that you cannot feel anxious when you fill yourself with positive, sustaining breaths'. Another exercise is progressive relaxation: 'Relax your muscles step by step. First, systematically tense a particular muscle group in your body, such as your shoulders. Then release any tension. Tense and relax that muscle group a few more times, noticing that your muscles in that area are becoming become increasingly relaxed. Now go to another nearby muscle group and do the same thing, tensing and relaxing a few times and experiencing the wonderful feeling that relaxation brings. Keep going until your body is totally relaxed. When you are this relaxed,*

it is impossible to feel anxiety or other stressful emotions'. Relaxation training takes no equipment and is readily available to language learners (Oxford, 1990, 2011), while biofeedback requires equipment that is often unavailable in language education settings.
- Because social anxiety typically includes low social skills as well as negative assumptions, it is frequently necessary to use social skills training to treat social fears.
  - Social skills training is a therapeutic process that helps people learn or improve social skills and assertiveness through role playing and rehearsing of desirable behaviours while receiving correction and praise (Comer, 2014).
  - Social skills training groups and assertiveness training groups often produce better results than working just with a therapist or teacher (Kim et al., 2011). It is possible for learners with language anxiety based on social anxiety to learn new social skills with the help of the teacher and other students.

Generalised anxiety

For most anxious language learners, language anxiety is thought to be strictly a matter of social anxiety localised in language performance settings. However, some language learners might also experience anxiety that is more generalised. Though I usually steer clear of the clinical term 'disorder', it is useful to note that 4% – not a negligible number – of the population in the USA, Canada, Britain and other Western countries has generalised anxiety disorder (Kessler et al., 2010a, 2010b; Ritter et al., 2010, in Comer, 2014).

Generalised anxiety consists of broad, persistent feelings of worry and anxiety in most circumstances in reference to almost anything – including, of course, performing in the target language in a social situation. Individuals with generalised anxiety usually feel restless, physically tense, exhausted and unable to concentrate, and they have intense physical reactions to stress (Comer, 2014). Research shows that generalised anxiety, like social anxiety, is often due to maladaptive assumptions. For generalised anxiety, such assumptions include: 'If something might be dangerous or scary, I should be terribly concerned about it and should keep dwelling on the possibility of its happening' and 'I must be completely competent, adequate, and high-achieving in all possible respects if I want to consider myself worthwhile' (paraphrased from Ellis, 1962). Other dysfunctional assumptions for generalised anxiety include 'A situation or a person is unsafe until proven to be safe' and 'It is always best to assume the worst' (Beck & Emery, 1985; Clark & Beck, 2012, in Comer, 2014: 119).

Research also supports three 'new-wave' cognitive theories about generalised anxiety (Comer, 2014). First, the metacognitive theory argues that individuals with generalised anxiety hold both positive and negative beliefs about worrying. Generally anxious individuals assume that worrying helps them appraise and cope with threats in life, yet they simultaneously believe that worrying is harmful and uncontrollable (Wells, 2011). Second, the theory of intolerance of uncertainty states that some generally anxious individuals cannot bear the possibility that bad things *might* happen, even if the likelihood is very small. These individuals worry in the effort to find supposedly 'correct' solutions to gain certainty in uncertain situations (Fisher & Wells, 2011). Third, the physical arousal theory suggests that people with generalised anxiety experience intensely negative physical arousal (e.g. heart rate, respiration and perspiration) and that worrying paradoxically reduces this unpleasant arousal (Borkovec *et al.*, 2004).

Interventions to increase the calmness of learners whose language anxiety is likely based on or influenced by generalised anxiety:

- *Rational-emotive therapy, mentioned earlier, is a successful cognitive process in which the therapist (and this could be a teacher) helps the individual identify his/her maladaptive assumptions, after which the individual practices changing these assumptions in settings that would ordinarily stimulate the person's anxiety.*
- *Some cognitive therapists guide individuals who have generalised anxiety to recognise their anxiety in relation to physical arousal (Comer, 2014). This involves educating individuals about the role of worrying and their misconceptions about worrying, having them observe their physical arousal and the triggers to their anxiety and helping them see the world as less threatening and hence less anxiety-provoking. This multistep procedure could be managed by the language teacher to help learners whose anxiety is generalised.*
- *Relaxation training and biofeedback can be used for generalised anxiety, as well as for social anxiety.*

Let us now turn to positive psychology, which offers its own useful ideas for dealing with factors related to language anxiety.

What We Know from Positive Psychology

Positive psychology sheds light on emotions, flow, agency, hope and optimism (see Oxford, 2016). All of these factors are likely to be associated with language anxiety.

Emotions

For positive psychologists, anxiety is viewed as a 'negative' emotion. Negative emotions cause a narrowing of the individual's response options to survival behaviours (Fredrickson, 2001, 2003, 2004). Seligman (2011: 139) stated that '[n]egative emotions warn us about a specific threat: when we feel fear, it is almost always preceded by a thought of danger'. He specifically cautioned that negative emotions lead to the restrictive fight-or-flight behaviours: '[T]he negative, firefighting emotions... identify, isolate, and combat external irritants' (Seligman, 2011: 66). Working with learner narratives, my colleagues and I (e.g. Ma & Oxford, 2014; Oxford, 1996, 2014; Oxford *et al.*, 1996, 2005, 2007) encountered certain negative emotions, including anxiety, anger and shame, underscoring the statement that learning a language is sometimes considered 'a profoundly unsettling psychological proposition' (Guiora, 1983: 8). Positive psychologists have little good to say about negative emotions, despite the fact that anticipatory anxiety has some advantages (see earlier).

Positive psychologists emphasise that positive emotions, such as happiness, curiosity, interest, pleasure and joy, broaden learners' response options and build up new skills for the future (Cohn & Frederickson, 2011; Frederickson, 2001, 2003, 2004). Above, I mentioned some negative emotions found in learner narratives, but in these narratives (e.g. Kao & Oxford, 2014; Ma & Oxford, 2014; Oxford, 1996, 2014; Oxford & Cuéllar, 2014; Oxford *et al.*, 1996, 2005, 2007, 2014) we also discovered positive emotions, such as excitement, pleasure, pride, contentment, satisfaction, joy and love. The narratives showed that some hitherto anxious learners were able to reduce their own anxiety, one through writing poetry, another through positive self-talk and another through doing something altruistic (Oxford *et al.*, 1996, 2007).

Emotional intelligence is 'the ability to understand feelings in the self and others and to use these feelings as informational guides for thinking and action' (Salovey *et al.*, 2011: 238). It has been shown to reduce anxiety, stress and conflict; improve relationships; and increase achievement, stability, self-motivation, social awareness and harmony (Goleman, 2005). Individuals with high language anxiety tend to have low emotional intelligence and vice versa. Dewaele *et al.* (2008; also Dewaele, 2013) found that adult multilinguals with higher emotional intelligence had generally lower levels of foreign language anxiety. These researchers discovered that, during communication, individuals with higher emotional intelligence, compared with those with lower emotional intelligence, perceived themselves as more capable of (1) gauging the emotions of their interlocutor, (2) controlling their own stress and (3) feeling self-confident.

Interventions to increase positive emotions and emotional intelligence in learners with language anxiety:

- *Positive psychology's ABCDE macro-strategy (Seligman, 2006, 2011), drawing on rational-emotive therapy (Ellis, 1962, 2003), contains a set of interlocking strategies, which can help learners overcome language anxiety.*
  - *The learner uses ABCDE to recognise that beliefs about adversity cause consequent negative feelings (e.g. anxiety), but disputation, that is, presenting counter-evidence, results in energisation or a positive change of mind (Seligman, 2006).*

- Within the ABCDE macro-strategy, the strategy of identifying irrational beliefs – 'I must/should' (dogmatic demands), 'It's terrible' (awfulising), 'I can't stand it' (low frustration tolerance) and 'I'm worthless and incompetent' (self/other rating) – is necessarily matched with the strategies of (1) identifying counter-evidence and (2) creating a new, lower-anxiety mindset.
  - ABCDE combats the pessimistic explanatory style (see later) and can therefore reduce language anxiety, which is associated with the pessimistic explanatory style.
  - ABCDE reveals that 'emotions don't follow inexorably from external events but from what you think about those events, and you can actually change what you think' (Seligman, 2011: 90).
- Hyper-reflection, or gloomily anxious attention to one's failures or difficulties (Frankl, 1984), harms the progress of language learners. They can develop the ability to take their minds off failure or difficulties and instead visualise something interesting in the language activity or text. Visualisation is a powerful tool for guiding emotions.
- A situation-analysis technique involves (1) thinking about a time/event when positive emotion, such as pride, gratitude, pleasure, satisfaction, interest or hope, were felt; (2) recalling situational details; (3) giving the situation a name; and (4) specifying the emotion(s). With this information, learners can be aided in 'setting up moments of genuine positivity' for themselves (Seligman, 2011: 141).
- Emotion-release activities include (1) letting go of emotional icebergs, which are 'deeply held beliefs that often lead to out-of-kilter emotional reactions' (Seligman, 2011: 168) and (2) 'letting go of grudges' (Seligman, 2011: 91).
- The technique of 'paradoxical intention' in Frankl's (1984) logotherapy (meaning therapy) is useful for students with very strong anticipatory anxiety. Employing this technique, learners focus precisely on that which they fear and make a paradoxical wish. For example, they resolve to fail an upcoming test or decide to act ridiculously when talking aloud in the target language. Paradoxical intention gives learners a capacity for self-detachment and humour and diminishes negative emotions.

Flow

Flow is an optimal psychological state that combines intrinsic motivation (described as autotelism) with the confidence that comes from complete immersion in a task (Csíkszentmihályi, 2008). Flow also includes a balance between challenge and competence (the perception that the task is neither too easy nor too hard), a merging of action and awareness without distractions, heightened control (security and lack of worry about failure), effortlessness, lack of self-consciousness and an altered perception of time (slowing down or speeding up). As mentioned, flow involves intrinsic motivation:

Intrinsically motivated learners are deeply concerned to learn things well, in a manner that is intrinsically satisfying and that arouses a sense of optimal challenge appropriate to their current level of skill and competence. Compared to their extrinsically motivated counterparts [or to unmotivated learners], . . . such learners are likely to display much higher levels of involvement in learning, engage in more efficient and creative thinking processes, use a wider range of problem solving strategies, and interact with and retain material more effectively. (Ushioda, 2008: 21–22)

Learners with language anxiety are usually the opposite of intrinsically motivated learners and hence lose the possibility of experiencing flow. Many anxious learners feel overwhelmed, overly challenged and fearfully withdrawn. Worry muddies their thinking, reduces their creativity, wreaks havoc with their strategies and lowers their effectiveness. It is unlikely for a highly anxious learner to switch into the flow mode, although there is evidence that it can occur under very special circumstances. One anxious learner, a native English speaker newly arrived in Spain, experienced flow. He used positive self-talk to shove aside his feelings of anxiety so that he could speak Spanish at a bar and mingle in the *movida* (street scene). He compared this to jumping out of a helicopter for the first time (Oxford *et al.*, 1996).

Interventions to increase flow and intrinsic motivation[1] *in learners with language anxiety:*

- *Positive self-talk*, such as 'I want to learn this language because it is interesting and challenging', 'I love _____ about this language', 'My favorite part of the language is _____' and 'I will stop worrying about the outcome and instead focus on _____' (see Oxford, 1990, 2011), can increase the possibility of flow by increasing intrinsic motivation.
- *Savouring* increases intrinsic motivation and flow. Learners can develop the ability to savour positive events, share interesting aspects of language learning with others, build memories by taking a mental photograph, sharpen perceptions by focusing on positive elements and blocking out negative ones and become totally absorbed or immersed in the learning process (see Peterson, 2006).
- *The elements of hardiness* or *existential courage* can help learners develop flow and intrinsic motivation. Hardiness involves three attitudes, that is, commitment (committing to total involvement), control (desiring to influence outcomes) and challenge (accepting challenge positively); and several action patterns, such as coping transformationally (seeking new perspectives), finding social support and maintaining effective self-care (Maddi, 2006; see also Kobasa, 1979).
- *The 'thieves' technique* can help learners combat negativity. In this technique, learners visualise locking up the 'thieves' of happiness, such as anxiety, depression, shyness, anger and resentment (Lykken, 2000), all of which negatively affect flow and intrinsic motivation.

Agency

Learners with language anxiety usually feel a lack of agency, i.e. the 'capacity to act volitionally to affect outcomes' (Ryan & Irie, 2014: 113). Agency can also be defined as actively shaping the 'terms and conditions' of one's own learning (Lantolf & Pavlenko, 2001: 145) and purposefully assigning relevance and significance to language learning as a whole and to specific events in the process (Lantolf & Thorne, 2006). For Little *et al.* (2002), the agentic person is the

> origin of his or her actions, has high aspirations, perseveres in the face of obstacles, sees more and varied options for action, learns from failures, and overall, has a greater sense of well-being. In contrast, a non-agentic individual can be a pawn to unknown extra-personal influences, has low aspirations, is hindered with problem-solving blinders, often feels helpless and, overall, has a greater sense of ill-being. (Little *et al.*, 2002: 390)

I would modify this by saying that, for many anxious individuals, their agency is reduced because of their overly high (rather than low) standards and lofty aspirations, veering on perfectionism (see earlier).

Interventions to increase agency in learners with language anxiety:

- *Becoming proficient in the target language requires that learners take responsibility for their own learning. Learners can be aided by the teacher in understanding that they are the authors of the 'terms and conditions' of their own learning and that they have power in controlling their own thoughts and actions.*
- *The classroom can become a community of practice in which learners are cognitive apprentices (Collins, 1988), increasingly gaining agency and feeling less anxious. In the words of Vygotsky (1978), learners can come to feel that their teachers are mediators who help them confidently traverse the 'zone of proximal development' (zone of potential learning). Social assistance helps learners develop agency.*
- *Agency is increased when learners become familiar with and employ a range of learning strategies relevant to learning tasks. Some of these strategies are cognitive, while others are metacognitive, social and affective (emotion-related). Teachers can teach students how to select and use strategies intentionally (Oxford, 1990, 2011).*
- *Anxious learners' agency can be strengthened when they learn to deal with catastrophic thinking, which is usually 'paralyzing and unrealistic' (Seligman, 2011: 133, 169). This involves gathering evidence about specific situations, becoming more optimistic about these situations (see optimism later) and putting the situations in perspective (by identifying the worst case, the best case and the most likely case).*

- *Humour is a mature defence mechanism that 'reframes reality without denying it'* (Peterson, 2006: 240). Humour, such as joking, can help anxious learners deal with negative emotions and difficult experiences (see Vaid, 2006, for cross-cultural joking) and increase agency.
- *'Signature strengths' are the individual's most frequently employed character strengths, such as kindness or creativity. Identifying and using signature strengths can stimulate greater agency in the learner. After identifying the signature strengths, the learner can then apply the greatest strength in a new way or work on developing a new strength* (Peterson & Seligman, 2004). For lists and descriptions of strengths, see Peterson (2006: 137–164), Seligman (2011: 243–265) and the VIA Institute of Character (2014).
- *A sense of agency and balance is found in Reinhold Niebuhr's Serenity Prayer: 'God give me the serenity to accept the things which cannot be changed; give me the courage to change things which must be changed; and the wisdom to distinguish one from the other'* (Sifton, 2003, in Peterson, 2006: 241). This prayer can be the focus of a discussion about what can be changed and what cannot, thus clarifying the parameters of agency for learners with language anxiety.
- *Agency in communicating and building relationships can be increased via three means: (1) employing active-constructive responding, that is, responding enthusiastically and in detail to specific elements of favourable news from someone else* (Gable et al., 2004); *(2) praising someone effectively by using specific details* (Kamins & Dweck, 1999); *and (3) using a model of assertive communication* (Seligman, 2011).

Hope

Learners with language anxiety often lack a sense of hope, defined as 'desire accompanied by (reasonable) expectation' (Clarke, 2003: 164; also see Schrank *et al.*, 2008; Snyder *et al.*, 2011). For developmental psychologist Erik Erikson, '[h]ope became the very foundation block of all human development' (Vaillant, 2008: 110). The opposite of hope/hopefulness is hopelessness, which is quite often linked with negative distortions of reality (Clarke, 2003), with despair and anxiety (Vaillant, 2008) and with demoralisation (Clarke, 2003). Demoralisation, like anxiety, is marked by a subjective sense of incompetence (Clarke, 2003).

Brown Kirschman *et al.* (2011) reported that (1) adolescents at risk of dropping out of high school were less likely to do so if they had higher hope; and (2) higher levels of trait hope (long-term hope) related to greater academic success, such as higher grade point averages and higher graduation rates for college students, after controlling for intelligence, previous academic performance, college entrance-exam scores and self-esteem. In addition, high-hope college students reported being more energised, inspired, goal-oriented and confident than their low-hope compatriots (Snyder et al., 1991), and they experienced greater self-worth and less depression (Snyder et al., 1997).

For Vaillant (2008) and Lazarus (1999), hope is primarily emotion based, but the best-known hope theory in positive psychology is highly cognitive. Snyder and colleagues (Snyder, 1994, 2000, 2002; Snyder et al., 1997) defined hope as a cognitive set, including a person's beliefs in:

- his/her capacity to produce workable *pathways* to goals, which are mental targets or desired future conditions that guide actions;
- his/her *agency*, i.e. ability and intention to initiate and sustain movement via pathways toward those goals. The theory also defines agency as a greater probability of using chosen pathways in the goal pursuit.

This theory asserts that human behaviour is largely goal directed. Goals can be expressed in words (e.g. 'I want to talk intelligibly in Spanish') or mental images (e.g. an image of oneself engaged in a spirited, fully intelligible discussion in Spanish). Goals can be 'approach goals' (e.g. 'I will pass my Mandarin test') or 'avoidance goals' (e.g. 'I will try hard not to fail my Mandarin test') (see Snyder, 2002). Goals can be short term or long term.

Agency thinking and pathways thinking are both particularly important when an originally planned route or pathway is blocked (Rand & Cheavens, 2011). An example of agency thinking is to use energetic, positive statements like 'I can do this' and 'I will keep going'. Pathways thinking helps the learner generate new routes or pathways towards the goal. When facing a stressor, higher-hope people, compared with lower-hope people, create more pathways for dealing with the stressor, show more agency, use cognitive flexibility and positive self-talk and stay fully engaged, while low-hope individuals (including highly anxious learners, I contend) merely use avoidance strategies and ruminate about being stuck (see Oxford, 2016).

Interventions to increase hope in learners with language anxiety:

- *In language learning, where temporary blockages toward goals occur with some frequency, it would be very useful to teach learners how to generate alternative pathways towards a particular goal (pathways thinking) and how to use positive self-talk (Oxford, 1990, 2011) for agency thinking.*
- *Hope-based interventions are currently being tested on university campuses, and self-help texts based on hope theory have been written for adults (Rand & Cheavens, 2011). There are many self-help books on how to learn a foreign language, and authors can start including chapters or sections on how to increase hope through pathways thinking and agency thinking, especially for learners with language anxiety.*

- *Some hope interventions help individuals to do the following: (1) identify hopeful versus unhopeful language, (2) form partnerships called 'hope buddies' to share future goals and (3) write hope stories (Brown Kirschman et al., 2011; Pedrotti et al., 2008). These could readily be used with learners who have language anxiety.*
- *Clarke (2003) provided a research-based system of interventions to ameliorate the demoralisation that is linked with hopelessness (and I would add language anxiety). The system includes offering reassurance and help, teaching problem-solving skills, being quietly and supportively present with the individual and exploring personal meaning. Language teachers could implement this system with anxious learners.*

Optimism

Learners with language anxiety lack dispositional optimism, i.e. a pattern of generalised positive expectations for the future (Carver & Scheier, 2012; Carver et al., 2011). Optimists are more likely than pessimists to believe they can achieve a valued goal, and they confidently persevere even when facing adversity. Conversely, pessimists doubt that the goal can be reached and are therefore hesitant or reluctant when dealing with adversity (Carver et al., 2011). While optimists anticipate good outcomes, despite difficulties, and show excitement and eagerness, pessimists expect bad outcomes and experience negative emotions such as anxiety, sadness, despair and anger. In longitudinal studies of college students, stronger optimism at the start of college predicted less distress at the end of the first semester and greater development of friendship networks (Carver et al., 2011). Some learners are pessimistic (and anxious) because they are perfectionistic and their high standards simply cannot be met, but not all pessimists are perfectionistic.

Pessimists and optimists use different coping strategies. According to Carver et al. (2011), pessimists revert to the avoidance behaviours mentioned earlier. Optimists, in contrast, keep on trying to solve the problem at hand, and if they cannot solve it, they use other strategies, such as acceptance, positive reframing and humour. If the worst happens, optimists readjust themselves, look to the future and keep on going. 'Thus, optimists appear generally to be approach copers, and pessimists appear to be avoidant copers' (Carver et al., 2011: 305).

I just described optimism or pessimism as a disposition or generalised expectancy. However, it is also possible to view optimism or pessimism as an explanatory style, i.e. the habitual way that people, looking backwards, explain causes of events in their lives. An explanatory style refers to how an individual considers an event's causality in terms of three dimensions: stability (permanent/stable vs temporary/unstable effects), globality (universal vs specific scope) and internality (internal cause=self vs external cause=others or environment). 'An explanatory style characterised by internal, stable, and global explanations for bad events has been described as "pessimistic", and the opposite style – external, unstable [temporary], and specific explanations for bad events – has been described as "optimistic"' (Peterson & Steen, 2011: 315). Thus, for a pessimist (who might well have language anxiety), defeat seems permanent, destroys everything and appears caused by the person himself or herself. For an optimist, defeat is viewed as temporary, restricted to a specific case and not his or her fault. Compared with those who use a pessimistic explanatory style, people with an optimistic explanatory style perform better academically, have better physical and mental health, are more active, do not give up as easily and may live longer (Peterson *et al.*, 1988; Seligman, 1991, 2006). 'Invariably, those with an optimistic explanatory style fare better than those with a pessimistic explanatory style' (Peterson & Steen, 2011: 316).

Interventions to increase optimism in learners with language anxiety:

- *In language classrooms, it would be wise to help learners to deal optimistically and effectively with difficulty through realistically accepting the problem, reframing to gain a new perspective and using humour (see affective strategies in Oxford, 1990, 2011).*
- *Rather than undergoing optimism training, pessimistic-anxious learners who are perfectionistic need help in setting realistic goals and disposing of implausible, unrealistic goals (Carver & Scheier, 2003). Language teachers and language textbooks can teach how to create realistic goals.*
- *Cognitive therapies, such as rational-emotive therapy, described earlier, can help change pessimists to optimists by altering negative thoughts. 'The therapies aim to make the cognitions more positive, thereby reducing distress and fostering renewed effort' (Carver et al., 2011: 309). Techniques such as identifying the problem, determining the associated feelings and beliefs related to the problem and adjusting dysfunctional feelings and beliefs, are useful when a pessimistic-anxious learner comes to the teacher complaining of a problem.*
- *Attributions of success and failure can be changed in order to develop an optimistic explanatory style. Learners can be taught to make more positive attributions, i.e. not viewing negative situations as permanent, widespread and caused by the learner. Teachers can help learners reconsider their inner explanations for failures and successes, focusing more on success factors that they control and therefore telling more self-empowering stories.*
- *The 'Three-Good-Things Exercise' can increase optimism. It involves 'writing down daily three good things that happened each day for a week', and writing beside each one the answer to one of the following: 'Why did this good thing happen?', 'What does this mean to you?' or 'How can you have more of this good thing in the future?' (Seligman, 2011: 84).*

- *When relationships are improved, optimism is enhanced and anxiety is often reduced.*
  - For instance, optimism is strengthened when a learner writes a letter of gratitude and sends the letter, fostering the relationship (Seligman, 2011).
  - In Algoe's (2012) find-remind-and-bind theory, gratitude inspires people to strengthen their relationships with helpful and responsive partners, and this enhances optimism.
  - Loving-kindness meditation, in which learners imagine someone whom they love unconditionally and then cultivate the same feelings toward self, friends, acquaintances, rivals and even strangers (Hutcherson et al., 2008), increases optimism.
  - Similarly, learners can do altruistic things for other people on a regular basis (Keltner, 2009; Peterson, 2006; Schwartz et al., 2003; Seligman, 2011), thus developing greater optimism. An example is the behaviour of Yaru, a young Chinese woman with severe anxiety about speaking English. When her English teacher was being evaluated by the external inspector, Yaru altruistically realised that if she communicated in English, despite her terror, the inspector would give the teacher a good rating. Anxious Yaru stood up and spoke in understandable English, saved her teacher, and expanded her own optimism and confidence (Oxford, 2013). Today she is a professor of English.
- *An increase in optimism and reduction of anxiety can occur when learners are taught to control intrusive thoughts and images and when they share their feelings through constructive self-disclosure (Seligman, 2011) in a safe environment.*

Conclusion

I explained above that serious language anxiety is typically related to social anxiety, as applied specifically in the language setting, but that in some learners it can also be associated with a more generalised form of anxiety. I described some interventions for learners whose language anxiety comes from either of these sources. Drawing on positive psychology, I contended that anxiety is a negative emotion that can be tied to low emotional intelligence and lack of flow, agency, hope and optimism. Therefore, I offered an array of interventions for dealing with these factors.

I now close by mentioning some ideas from acceptance and commitment therapy (ACT, Hayes & Lillis, 2012). ACT helps anxious individuals 'become aware of their streams of thoughts, including their worries, as they are occurring and to *accept* such thoughts as mere events of the mind. By accepting the thoughts rather than trying to eliminate them, the [individuals] are expected to be less upset and affected by them' (Comer, 2014: 122, emphasis in original). 'Worrying about worrying' will diminish, and learners can focus on using additional techniques in this chapter to help them more often experience positive emotions, flow, agency, hope and optimism. With assistance, anxious language learners can develop acceptance, along with the commitment to continue learning.

ACT reminds me of the poem 'The Guest House' by Jelaluddin Rumi, the 13th-century Persian poet and Sufi mystic. Rumi encouraged us, not only to face our emotions, but to welcome them as guides. He did not specifically mention anxiety, but every emotion was meant to be considered. Here are a few verses (Rumi, 1997):

> This being human is a guest house.
> Every morning a new arrival.
>
> A joy, a depression, a meanness,
> some momentary awareness comes
> as an unexpected visitor.
>
> Welcome and entertain them all!
> Even if they are a crowd of sorrows,
> who violently sweep your house
> empty of its furniture,
> still, treat each guest honorably.
>
> ... Be grateful for whatever comes,
> because each has been sent
> as a guide from beyond. (Rumi, 1997: 77)

Rumi stressed emotional self-acceptance. If language learners can interpret anxiety as a guide and can use it to become more self-compassionate and self-accepting, they will have a better chance of becoming proficient. As the saying goes, only when one accepts oneself can change occur. Teachers can help learners with language anxiety to discover this reality.

Note

(1) Another aspect of language learning motivation is possible selves (Dörnyei, 2009; Ryan & Irie, 2014) and a connected element is learner resilience (Masten *et al.*, 2011; Oxford *et al.*, 2007). Unfortunately, this chapter does not have the space to deal with these topics. See Oxford (2016).

References

Algoe, S.B. (2012) Find, remind, and bind: The functions of gratitude in everyday relationships. *Social and Personality Psychology Compass* 6, 455–469.

American Psychiatric Association (APA) (2013) *Diagnostic and Statistical Manual of Mental Disorders* (5th edn). Washington, DC: Author.

Antony, M.M. and Roemer, L. (2012) *Behavior Therapy*. Washington, DC: American Psychological Association.

Bandura, A. (1997) *Self-Efficacy: The Exercise of Control*. New York: Freeman.

Beck, A.T. and Emery, G. with Greenberg, R.L. (1985) Differentiating anxiety and depression: A test of the cognitive content-specificity hypothesis. *Journal of Abnormal Psychology* 96, 179–183.

Beck, J.G. (2010) *Interpersonal Processes in the Anxiety Disorders: Implications for Understanding Psychopathology and Treatment*. Washington, DC: American Psychological Association.

Boden, M.T., John, O.P., Goldin, P.R., Werner, K., Heimberg, R.G. and Gross, J.J. (2012) The role of maladaptive beliefs in cognitive-behavioral therapy: Evidence from social anxiety disorder. *Behavior Research and Therapy* 50 (5), 287–291.

Borkovec, T.D., Alcaine, O.M. and Behar, E. (2004) Avoidance theory of worry and generalized anxiety disorder. In R.G. Heimberg, C.L. Turk and D.S. Mennin (eds) *Generalized Anxiety Disorder: Advances in Research and Practice* (pp. 77–108). New York: Guilford Press.

Brown Kirschman, K.J., Johnson, R.J., Bender, J.A. and Roberts, M.C. (2011) Positive psychology for children and adolescents: Development, prevention, and promotion. In S.J. Lopez and C.R. Snyder (eds) *The Oxford Handbook of Positive Psychology* (pp. 133–148). New York: Oxford University Press.

Cameron, J. (1992) *The Artist's Way: A Spiritual Path to Higher Creativity*. New York: Tarcher/Putnam.

Carver, C.S. and Scheier, M.F. (2003) Three human strengths. In L.G. Aspinwall and U.M. Staudinger (eds) *A Psychology of Human Strengths: Fundamental Questions and Future Directions for a Positive Psychology* (pp. 87–102). Washington, DC: American Psychological Association.

Carver, C.S. and Scheier, M.F. (2012) *Perspectives on Personality* (7th edn). Boston, MA: Pearson.

Carver, C.S., Scheier, M.F., Miller, C.J. and Fulford, D. (2011) Optimism. In S.J. Lopez and C.R. Snyder (eds) *The Oxford Handbook of Positive Psychology* (pp. 303–311). New York: Oxford University Press.

Clark, D.A. and Beck, A.T. (2012) *Cognitive Therapy of Anxiety Disorders: Science and Practice*. New York: Guilford Press.

Clarke, D. (2003) Faith and hope. *Australian Psychiatry* 11 (2), 164–168.

Cohn, M.A. and Fredrickson, B.L. (2010) In search of durable positive psychology interventions: Predictors and consequences of long-term positive behavior change. *Journal of Positive Psychology* 5, 355–366.

Collins, A. (1988) Cognitive Apprenticeship and Instructional Technology. Technical Report No. 6899. Cambridge, MA: BBN Laboratories.

Comer, R.J. (2014) *Abnormal Psychology* (8th edn). New York: Worth.

Csíkszentmihályi, M. (2008) *Flow: The Psychology of Optimal Experience* (2nd edn). New York: Harper.

Deci, E.L. and Ryan, R.M. (2000). The "what" and "why" of goal pursuits: Human needs and the self-determination of behavior. *Psychological Inquiry* 11, 227–268.

Dewaele, J.-M. (2010) *Emotions in Multiple Languages*. Basingstoke: Palgrave Macmillan.

Dewaele, J.-M. (2013) Emotions and language learning. In M. Byram and A. Hu (eds) *Routledge Encyclopedia of Language Teaching and Learning* (2nd edn; pp. 217–220). London: Routledge.

Dewaele, J.-M. and MacIntyre, P. (2014) Two faces of Janus? Anxiety and enjoyment in the foreign language classroom. In P. MacIntyre and S. Mercer (eds) *Positive Psychology in SLA*. Special issue, *Second Language Learning and Teaching* 4 (2), 237–274.

Dewaele, J.-M., Petrides, K.V. and Furnham, A. (2008) The effects of trait emotional intelligence and sociobiographical variables on communicative anxiety and foreign language anxiety among adult multilinguals: A review and empirical investigation. *Language Learning* 58, 911–960.

Dörnyei, Z. (2009) The L2 motivational self system. In Z. Dörnyei and E. Ushioda (eds) *Motivation, Language Identity and the L2 Self* (pp. 9–42). Bristol: Multilingual Matters.

Ellis, A. (1962) *Reason and Emotion in Psychotherapy*. Secaucus, NJ: Lyle Stuart.

Ellis, A. (2003) Early theories and practices of rational-emotive behavior therapy and how they have been augmented and revised during the last three decades. *Journal of Rational-Emotive and Cognitive-Behavior Therapy* 21 (3/4), 219–243.

Fisher, P.L. and Wells, A. (2011) Conceptual models of generalized anxiety disorders. *Psychiatric Annals* 41 (2), 127–132.

Frankl, V.E. (1984) *Man's Search for Meaning: An Introduction to Logotherapy*. Trans. I. Lasch. Boston, MA: Beacon.

Frederickson, B.L. (2001) The role of positive emotions in positive psychology: The broaden-and-build theory of positive emotions. *American Psychologist* 56, 218–226.

Frederickson, B.L. (2003) The value of positive emotions: The emerging science of positive psychology looks into why it's good to feel good. *American Scientist* 91, 330–335.

Frederickson, B.L. (2004) The broaden-and-build theory of positive emotions. *Philosophical Transactions of the Royal Society of London (Biological Sciences)* 359, 1367–1377.

Gable, S.L., Reis, H.T., Impett, E.A. and Asher, E.R. (2004) What do you do when things go right? The intrapersonal and interpersonal benefits of sharing good events. *Journal of Personality and Social Psychology* 87, 228–245.

Goleman, D. (2005) *Emotional Intelligence: Why It Can Matter More Than IQ* (2nd edn). New York: Bantam.

Guiora, A.Z. (1983) Introduction: An epistemology for the language sciences. *Language Learning* 33 (1), 6–11.

Hayes, S.C. and Lillis, J. (2012) *Acceptance and Commitment Therapy: Theories of Psychotherapy Series*. Washington, DC: American Psychological Association.

Heimberg, R.G., Brozovich, F.A. and Rapee, R.M. (2010) A cognitive-behavioral model of social anxiety disorder: Update and extensions. In S.G. Hofmann and P.M. DiBartolo (eds) *Social Anxiety: Clinical, Developmental, and Social Perspectives* (2nd edn; pp. 395–422). New York: Academic Press.

Hofmann, S.G. (2007) Cognitive factors that maintain social anxiety disorder: A comprehensive model and its treatment implications. *Cognitive Behaviour Therapy* 36 (4), 193–209.

Horwitz, E. (2001) Language anxiety and achievement. *Annual Review of Applied Linguistics* 21, 112–126.

Horwitz, E. and Young, D.J. (eds) (1991) *Language Anxiety: From Theory and Research to Classroom Implications*. Englewood Cliffs, NJ: Prentice Hall.

Hutcherson, C.A., Seppala, E.M. and Gross, J.J. (2008) Loving-kindness meditation increases social connectedness. *Emotion* 8, 720–724.

Kamins, M.L. and Dweck, C. (1999) Person versus process praise and criticism: Implications for contingent self-worth and coping. *Developmental Psychology* 35, 835–847.

Kao, T-A. and Oxford, R.L. (2014) Learning language through music: A strategy for building inspiration and motivation. In R.L. Oxford and C. Griffiths (eds) *Language Learning Strategy Research in the Twenty-First Century*. Special issue, *System: International Journal of Educational Technology and Applied Linguistics* 43, 114–120.

Keltner, D. (2009) *Born to Be Good: The Science of a Meaningful Life*. New York: Norton.

Kessler, R.C., Gruber, M., Hettema, J.M., Hwang, I., Sampson, N. and Yonkers, K.A. (2010a) Major depression and generalized anxiety disorder in the National Comorbidity Survey follow-up survey. In D. Goldberg, K.S. Kendler, P.J. Sirovatka and D.A. Regier (eds) *Diagnostic Issues in Depression and Generalized Anxiety Disorder: Refining the Research Agenda for DSM-V* (pp. 139–170). Washington, DC: American Psychiatric Association.

Kessler, R.C., Ruscio, A.M., Shear, K. and Wittchen, H.-U. (2010b) Epidemiology of anxiety disorders. In M.B. Stein and T. Steckler (eds) *Behavioral Neurobiology of Anxiety and its Treatment: Current Topics in Behavioral Neurosciences* (pp. 21–35). New York: Springer Science.

Kim, K.L., Parr, A.F. and Alfano, C.A. (2011) Behavioral and cognitive behavioral treatments for social anxiety disorder in adolescents and young adults. In C.A. Alfano and D.C. Beidel (eds) *Social Anxiety in Adolescents and Young Adults: Translating Developmental Science into Practice* (pp. 245–264). Washington, DC: American Psychological Association.

Kobasa, S.C. (1979) Stressful life events, personality, and health: An inquiry into hardiness. *Journal of Personality and Social Psychology* 37, 1–11.

Lantolf, J.P. and Pavlenko, A. (2001) (S)econd (L)anguage (A)ctivity theory: Understanding second language learners as people. In M.P. Breen (ed.) *Learner Contributions to Language Learning* (pp. 141–158). London: Longman.

Lantolf, J.P. and Thorne, S.L. (2006) *Sociocultural Theory and the Genesis of Second Language Development*. Oxford: Oxford University Press.

Lazarus, R.S. (1999) Hope: An emotion and a vital coping resource against despair. *Social Research* 66, 653–678.

Little, T.D., Hawley, P.H., Henrich, C.C. and Marsland, K. (2002) Three views of the agentic self: A developmental synthesis. In E.L. Deci and R.M. Ryan (eds) *Handbook of Self-Determination Research* (pp. 389–404). Rochester, NY: University of Rochester Press.

Lykken, D. (2000) *Happiness: The Nature and Nurture of Joy and Contentment*. New York: St. Martin's.

Ma, R. and Oxford, R.L. (2014) A diary study focusing on listening and speaking: The evolving interaction of learning styles and learning strategies in a motivated, advanced ESL learner. In R.L. Oxford and C. Griffiths (eds) *Language Learning Strategy Research in the Twenty-First Century*. Special issue, *System: International Journal of Educational Technology and Applied Linguistics* 43, 101–113.

MacIntyre, P.D. (2002) Motivation, anxiety, and emotion in second language acquisition. In P. Robinson (ed.) *Individual Differences and Instructed Language Learning* (pp. 45–68). Amsterdam: John Benjamins.

Maddi, S.R. (2006) Hardiness: The courage to grow from stresses. *The Journal of Positive Psychology* 1 (3), 160–168.

Marcos-Llinas, M. and Juan Garau, M. (2009) Effects of language anxiety on three proficiency-level courses of Spanish as a foreign language. *Foreign Language Annals* 42 (1), 94–111.

Masten, A.S., Cutuli, J.J., Herbers, J.E. and Reed, M.-G.J. (2011) Resilience in development. In S.J. Lopez and C.R. Snyder (eds) *The Oxford Handbook of Positive Psychology* (pp. 117–131). New York: Oxford University Press.

Oxford, R.L. (1990) *Language Learning Strategies: What Every Teacher Should Know*. Boston, MA: Heinle.

Oxford, R.L. (1996) When emotion meets (meta)cognition in language learning histories. In A. Moeller (ed.) *The Teaching of Culture and Language in the Second Language Classroom: Focus on the Learner.* Special issue, *International Journal of Educational Research* 23 (7), 581–594.

Oxford, R.L. (2011) *Teaching and Researching Language Learning Strategies.* Harlow: Pearson Longman.

Oxford, R.L. (2013) Understanding language learner narratives. In J. Arnold and T. Murphey (eds) *Meaningful Action: Earl Stevick's Influence on Language Teaching* (pp. 95–110). Cambridge: Cambridge University Press.

Oxford, R.L. (2014) What we can learn about strategies, language learning, and life from two extreme cases. *Studies in Second Language Learning and Teaching* 4 (4), 593–615.

Oxford, R.L. (2015) How language learners can improve their emotional functioning: Important psychological and psychospiritual theories. *Applied Language Learning* 25 (1/2), 1–15.

Oxford, R.L. (2016) Toward a psychology of well-being for language learners: The "EMPATHICS" vision. In T. Gregersen, P. MacIntyre and S. Mercer (eds) *Positive Psychology in Second Language Acquisition* (pp. 10–87). Bristol: Multilingual Matters.

Oxford, R.L. and Cuéllar, L. (2014) Positive psychology in cross-cultural narratives: Mexican students discover themselves while learning Chinese. *Studies in Second Language Learning and Teaching* 4 (2), 173–203.

Oxford, R.L., Lavine, R.Z., Felkins, G., Hollaway, M.E. and Saleh, A. (1996) Telling their stories: Language students use diaries and recollection. In R.L. Oxford (ed.) *Language Learning Strategies Around the World: Cross-Cultural Perspectives* (pp. 19–34). Honolulu, HI: University of Hawaii, Second Language Teaching and Curriculum Center.

Oxford, R.L., Massey, K.R. and Anand, S. (2005) Transforming teacher–student style relationships: Toward a more welcoming and diverse classroom discourse. In C. Holten and J. Frodesen (eds) *The Power of Context in Language Learning and Teaching* (pp. 249–266). Boston, MA: Heinle & Heinle.

Oxford, R.L., Meng, Y., Zhou, Y., Sung, J. and Jain, R. (2007) Uses of adversity: Moving beyond L2 learning crises. In A. Barfield and S. Brown (eds) *Reconstructing Autonomy in Language Education: Inquiry and Innovation* (pp. 131–142). London: Palgrave Macmillan.

Oxford, R.L., Pacheco Acuña, G., Solís Hernández, M. and Smith, A.L. (2014, June 21) Positive Psychology in Action: Social and Psychological Themes Reflected in First-person Learner Histories of Bilingual Adults. Paper presented at the International Conference on Language and Social Psychology, Honolulu, Hawaii.

Pedrotti, J.T., Lopez, S.J. and Krieshok, T. (2008) Making hope happen: A program for fostering strengths in adolescents. Unpublished manuscript.

Peterson, C. (2006) *A Primer in Positive Psychology.* New York: Oxford University Press.

Peterson, C. and Seligman, M.E.P. (2004) *Character Strengths and Virtues: A Handbook and Classification.* New York: Oxford University Press.

Peterson, C. and Steen, T.A. (2011) Optimistic explanatory style. In S.J. Lopez and C.R. Snyder (eds) *The Oxford Handbook of Positive Psychology* (pp. 313–321). New York: Oxford University Press.

Peterson, C., Seligman, M.E.P. and Vaillant, G.E. (1988) Pessimistic explanatory style is a risk factor for physical illness: A thirty-five-year longitudinal study. *Journal of Personality and Social Psychology* 55, 23–27.

Rand, K.L. and Cheavens, J.S. (2011) Hope theory. In S.J. Lopez and C.R. Snyder (eds) *The Oxford Handbook of Positive Psychology* (pp. 323–333). New York: Oxford University Press.

Ritter, R.M., Blackmore, M.A. and Heimberg, R.G. (2010) Generalized anxiety disorder. In D. McKay, J.S. Abramowitz and S. Taylor (eds) *Cognitive-Behavioral Therapy for*

Refractory Cases: Turning Failure into Success (pp. 111–137). Washington, DC: American Psychological Association.

Rosenberg, A., Ledley, D.R. and Heimberg, R.G. (2010) Social anxiety disorder. In D. McKay, J.S. Abramowitz and S. Taylor (eds) *Cognitive-Behavioral Therapy for Refractory Cases: Turning Failure into Success* (pp. 65–88). Washington, DC: American Psychological Association.

Rumi, J. (1997) The guest house. Trans. C. Barks. Illus. M. Green. *The Illustrated Rumi*. New York: Broadway Books.

Ryan, R.M. and Deci, E.L. (2001) Self-determination theory and the facilitation of intrinsic motivation, social development, and well-being. *American Psychologist* 55, 68–78.

Ryan, S. and Irie, K. (2014) Imagined and possible selves: Stories we tell about ourselves. In S. Mercer and M. Williams (eds) *Multiple Perspectives on the Self in SLA* (pp. 109–126). Bristol: Multilingual Matters.

Salovey, P., Mayer, J.D., Caruso, D. and Yoo, S.H. (2011) The positive psychology of emotional intelligence. In S.J. Lopez and C.R. Snyder (eds) *The Oxford Handbook of Positive Psychology* (pp. 237–248). New York: Oxford University Press.

Schrank, B., Stanghellini, G. and Stade, M. (2008) Hope in psychiatry: A review of the literature. *Acta Psychiatrica Scandinavica* 118 (6), 421–433.

Schwartz, C., Meisenhelder, J.B., Ma, Y. and Reed, G. (2003) Altruistic social interest behaviors are associated with better mental health. *Psychosomatic Medicine* 75, 778–785.

Seligman, M.E.P. (1991) *Learned Optimism*. New York: Alfred A. Knopf.

Seligman, M.E.P. (2002) *Authentic Happiness: Using the New Positive Psychology to Realize Your Potential for Lasting Fulfillment*. New York: Free Press/Simon and Schuster.

Seligman, M. (2006) *Learned Optimism: How to Change your Mind and your Life*. New York: Vintage.

Seligman, M.E.P. (2011) *Flourish: A Visionary New Understanding of Happiness and Well-Being*. New York: Atria/Simon & Schuster.

Sifton, E. (2003) *The Serenity Prayer: Faith and Politics in Times of War and Peace*. New York: Norton.

Snyder, C.R. (1994) *The Psychology of Hope: You Can Get There from Here*. New York: Free Press.

Snyder, C.R. (2000) Hypothesis: There is no hope. In C.R. Snyder (ed.) *Handbook of Hope: Theory, Measures, and Applications* (pp. 3–21). San Diego, CA: Academic.

Snyder, C.R. (2002) Hope theory: Rainbows in the mind. *Psychological Inquiry* 13, 249–275.

Snyder, C.R., Harris, C., Anderson, J.R., Holleran, S.A., Irving, L.M., Sigmon, S.T. Yoshinobu, L., Gibb, J., Langelle, C. and Harney, P. (1991) The will and the ways: Development and evaluation of an individual-differences measure of hope. *Journal of Personality and Social Psychology* 60, 570–585.

Snyder, C.R., Hoza, B., Pelham, W.E., Rapoff, M., Ware, L., Danovsky, M., Highberger, L., Ribinstein, H. and Stahl, K.J. (1997) The development and validation of the Children's Hope Scale. *Journal of Pediatric Psychology* 22, 399–421.

Snyder, C.R., Lopez, S.J. and Pedrotti, J.T. (2011) *Positive Psychology: The Scientific and Practical Exploration of Human Strengths*. Thousand Oaks, CA: Sage.

Trovato, G., Anastasio, A. and Valli, C. (2007) Vivere (Dare to live). Sung by A. Bocelli and L. Pausini. *The Best of Andrea Bocelli*. London: Decca.

Ushioda, E. (2008) Motivation and good language learners. In C. Griffiths (ed.) *Lessons from Good Language Learners* (pp. 19–34). Cambridge: Cambridge University Press.

Vaid, J. (2006) Joking across languages: Perspectives on humor, emotion, and bilingualism. In A. Pavlenko (ed.) *Bilingual Minds: Emotional Experience, Expression and Representation* (pp. 152–182). Clevedon: Multilingual Matters.

VIA Institute (2014) VIA classification of character strengths. See http://www.viacharacter.org/www/Character-Strengths/VIA-Classification (accessed 2 January 2015).

Vygotsky, L.V. (1978) *Mind in Society*. Cambridge, MA: Harvard University Press.

Wells, A. (2011) Metacognitive therapy. In J.D. Herbert and E.M. Forman (eds) *Acceptance and Mindfulness in Cognitive Behavior Therapy: Understanding and Applying the New Therapies* (pp. 83–108). Hoboken, NJ: Wiley.

11 The Links Between Self-Esteem and Language Anxiety and Implications for the Classroom

Fernando D. Rubio-Alcalá

Introduction

An account of foreign language (FL) literature has revealed that probably no other affective factors exert so much influence in the FL classroom as self-esteem and anxiety do. Studies in this field (e.g. Ortega, 2007) have also shown that both factors are closely related and mutually interactive; in other words, a higher level of healthy self-esteem leads to a lower level of language anxiety. Furthermore, these affective factors have also shown to play a significant role in students' behaviour, leading to positive/negative attitudes which may result in a better/worse classroom atmosphere and higher/lower academic achievement. However, it seems that there is a gap between the recognition of the importance of self-esteem and anxiety and the actual implementation of teaching strategies and activities in the FL classroom. Anecdotal evidence of teaching practice and textbook analysis suggest that these factors still need to be highlighted in the school curriculum and teachers' methodology. Accordingly, this chapter aims to explain how to fill the gap between theory and practice and to analyse how self-esteem and anxiety interact in the FL classroom. It concludes by suggesting a range of teaching strategies and activities that can be implemented in the classroom in order to promote healthy self-esteem and reduce language anxiety to optimum levels.

The affective domain gained much attention at the end of last century. The seminal book that positioned the emotional factor as one of the key elements for language success was edited by Arnold (1999), who studied affective factors from a research, theoretical and classroom practice point of view, including one chapter devoted to anxiety (Oxford, 1999a) and another one to self-esteem (De Andrés, 1999). In part, this attention dedicated to the affective factor and the development of new methodological conceptions emerged from the study and research of anxiety in the 1980s, led primarily by Elaine Horwitz (Horwitz et al., 1986), and by Peter MacIntyre in the 1990s (MacIntyre & Gardner, 1991), among others. Until then, anxiety was not specific to the language context but related to clinical, social and general academic contexts. Horwitz et al. (1986) developed the first scale to measure anxiety (Foreign Language Classroom Anxiety Scale; FLCAS), which became the springboard that motivated research in this particular context. Language anxiety was also shown to be different from trait anxiety (i.e. anxiety as a stable personal trait, genetically endowed) and state anxiety (which is experienced in particular moments, such as speaking in public for the first time). A Japanese version of the FLCAS (Aida, 1994), a Spanish one (Pérez Paredes & Martínez Sánchez, 2000) and some others (see, for instance, a Hungarian version by Tóth, 2008) appeared later. Prior to that, Horwitz and Young (1991) edited a monograph in English addressing the issue with a series of chapters on different aspects of the influence of anxiety in the foreign language classroom (FLC), and the first monograph in Spanish that analysed the phenomenon from a global perspective, including research and teaching, was later published (Rubio, 2004).

The study on self-esteem and self-concept in the FLC started later than anxiety. It was generally referred to when other affective factors were analysed, such as anxiety and motivation (Arnold & Brown, 1999; Clément & Kruidenier, 1985[1]; Dörnyei, 2005). Krashen (1982) and Gardner (1985) were the contributions that had the most impact in the field. Krashen devised the Affective Filter Hypothesis as part of the Monitor Model. Despite not having been scientifically proven, he hypothesised that high levels of anxiety or low self-esteem created a filter or barrier that prevented FL input from being processed cognitively. Also, Gardner proposed the Socio-Educational Model, in which situational anxiety was one of the key elements to raise states of inhibition, impeding students to perform communicative activities appropriately, thus setting an obstacle to the optimal acquisition of the FL.

It was not until 2007 that the first publication that addressed self-esteem solely in the context of FL learning was published, including a conceptual approach, empirical research and ideas for teaching practice (Rubio, 2007a). Later on, Sarah Mercer (2010) studied self-concept, adopting a qualitative approach.

Second language acquisition (SLA) research has recently seen an upsurge in the study of the self. Mercer and Williams (2014) edited *Multiple Perspectives on the Self in SLA*, with chapters devoted to the study of the self, including its dynamics, relational views, neurological networking, etc. The self could thus be described as a complex dynamic system that is composed of multiple interrelated components. Ryan and Irie (2014) describe how the self is temporally situated through subjective interpretations of past, present and future events. According to Markus and Nurius (1986), self-concept is concerned with evaluations derived from the individuals' past experiences. However, when individuals envisage future events, the regulation of *possible* or *imagined selves* emerges, taking two possible forms on the basis of the ideas of who they would like to become (*ideal self*) or what they are afraid of becoming (*feared self*). These function as future self-guides, and the *ideal self* may be biased by the *ought-to self*, which filters wishes and hopes with duties, obligations or moral responsibilities, and how individuals would like to be seen by others (i.e. individuals tend to act according to what others expect from them).

Self-regulation studies explained different motivational theories. For example, Higgins' (1987) *self-discrepancy theory* posited that motivation arouses after the conflict among the *ideal, ought-to* and *actual self*, the latter being a key motivational component. In addition, Deci and Ryan's (1985, 2002) *self-determination theory* described how individuals internalise external responsibilities, and the role each self plays in that process. It is Dörnyei's (2005) *L2 motivational self-system* which has contextualised those theories in the field of SLA. Dörnyei reduced the model to the *ideal self* (the desired future state and the awareness of how to get there), the *ought-to* self (our understanding of what others want us to be – what we ought to be and do) and the L2 learning experience. Six steps are listed to promote positive motivational states (Dörnyei, 2009; Dörnyei & Kubanyiova, 2014; Hadfield & Dörnyei, 2013): (1) constructing the vision, (2) strengthening the vision, (3) substantiating the vision, (4) activating the ideal L2 self, (5) developing an action plan and (6) considering failure.

Other affective states are anxiety and self-esteem. Since both are complex constructs, they have been studied separately. However, some authors have attempted to establish links between them; for example, Young (1990) described the following relationship:

> Individuals with low self-esteem tend to have high levels of language anxiety, communication apprehension, and social anxiety. Low self-esteem can be particularly significant in a language class where students are expected to perform orally more often than in larger history, government or chemistry classes. (Young, 1990: 541)

A more recent comprehensive study of both factors was realised by Ortega (2007), including an analysis of the activation phase and its effects. Furthermore, Zare and Riasati (2012), in a study of Iranian FL university students, found that anxiety and self-esteem are negatively correlated; in other words, high levels of anxiety and low levels of self-esteem are related to low academic achievement in the FLC.

The aim of this chapter is to make the link between anxiety and self-esteem, explaining the differences between anxiety, fear, anguish or stress and self-esteem, self-concept and self-efficacy. It also intends to examine anxiety and self-esteem in an interrelated manner, starting from their causes and symptoms, and the effects and coping strategies that teachers and students use in these situations. Finally, it offers strategies for classroom implementation, including guidelines for teachers' rapport, methodological orientations and learning activities.

Conceptual Confusion

Both anxiety and self-esteem are phenomena studied within the field of psychology, but their use in popular science is often confused with the scientific one. Furthermore, some terms are also misunderstood and, indeed, practitioners tend to equate anxiety with fear, anguish and stress, and self-esteem with self-concept and self-confidence.

It is quite different for a student to be afraid of something (e.g. fear coming from a knowledgeable reason, such as fearing parents' actions when finding that one has failed an exam) than to be anxious, which is caused by non-specific factors not easily recognised by students. Fear is easily manageable, as a person may work directly with the causative agent and the appropriate measures can be employed, but anxiety is much less tangible. Therefore, when a student is afraid of something, he/she may tend to cope directly with the situation because the causing factor is known, since it is observable and recognisable (e.g. a shy student who avoids participating because he/she does not want to be the centre of attention in class). Actually, such a student just wants to elude feeling uncomfortable and reacts to protect his/her ego. If the same behaviour occurs but there are no logical reasons to account for it, then one would think that the student might be experiencing anxiety.

Anxiety is often confused with anguish. Actually, many people consider both phenomena synonymous; however, they are diagnosed differently in the clinical context (Rojas, 1989). Anguish is experienced as if time was slowed down and works as a blocking device, whereas anxiety is related to states of hypervigilance and restlessness; thus, the former is linked to depression and the latter to hyperactivity. When a student feels anguish, he/she has no energy and is apathetic, and these symptoms are precisely classified as the psychological symptoms of anxiety (see the fifth dimension in Rojas, 1989). Feeling low self-esteem or feelings of a loss are also part of this classification. Conversely, when a student is anxious, he/she tends to appear suspicious, distrustful and defiant. The symptoms have essentially a cognitive character (i.e. they emerge from a distorted perception and interpretation of reality).

However, probably the most frequent conceptual confusion occurs between stress and anxiety. The term stress comes from the field of physics and alludes to the idea of a body subjected to high tension by some recognisable factors. By the same token, a learner or a teacher who is stressed feels tense because, for example, they might have to perform many tasks in a limited, or perceived as insufficient, time. Again, it can be observed that anxiety is more complex and difficult to cope with, as the factors that intervene are hardly identifiable.

Confusion between the terms of self-esteem and self-concept is also common. In the literature, self-esteem is sometimes found to be linked to the affective sphere and self-concept to the cognitive one, as if self-concept was the thinker mechanism that produces a certain feeling, that is self-esteem. This description may be non-operative, because as Schumann (1997) pointed out, both processes are difficult to separate and operate in an interrelated and interdependent manner, as described by many neurocognitive studies (e.g. Damasio, 1994; LeDoux, 1996). Therefore, Dörnyei (2005) described self-esteem as the value or result of the evaluation of self-concept. Accordingly, the person constantly makes evaluations of different spheres of himself/herself, namely physical, personal, competential, interpersonal, etc. These dimensions form the self-concept and the resulting evaluation is self-esteem (Rubio, 2014). In fact, if both terms are semantically analysed, self-concept refers to an entity, dimension or, ultimately and rather obviously, a *concept*, while *to esteem* is actually to estimate or give a value, consequently leading to a measurable result.

In this line of conceptual analysis, self-efficacy also plays an important role. Self-efficacy was described by Bandura (1977) as the perception of competence or ability of a person while performing a task and after achieving the task goal. In this case, and considering the above description, competence is a dimension of the self-concept, and subsequently, self-efficacy is a self-concept subdomain.

Relationship Between Anxiety and Self-Esteem

The relationship between the two factors will now be explored in order to determine the causes, symptoms, effects and coping behaviours.

Causes

Onwuegbuzie *et al.* (1999) found seven predictors of anxiety in the context of FL learning: age, academic achievement, travel history to foreign countries, language learning prior experiences, mark or grades expectations, perceived academic competence and perceived self-worth. Also, Rubio (2004) draws on some researchers (Daly, 1991; Tsui, 1996; Young, 1991) to list the main sources of anxiety. In this case, the causes are found in contexts where an FL is learnt (i.e. the target language does not cohabit in the same context). These anxiety causes are going to be related to the five dimensions of self-esteem (security, identity, belonging, purpose and competence; Reasoner, 1983) and grouped into three intervening elements: students, teacher or context.

Causes centred on students

(1) Previous experience: If previous experiences have been negative, a student will expect those experiences to happen again (MacIntyre & Gardner, 1991). Rubio (2014) indicated that the self-concept is also influenced by biographical experiences. Those situations that hurt the self-concept in the past will likely be avoided when a similar situation is going to occur. Horwitz *et al.* (1986, 1991) pointed out that inhibition is a major cause of anxiety and it might arise from negative experiences when performing communicative tasks in the past.

(2) Low level of competence: If the student's proficiency level (actual or self-perceived) is below his/her peers, the student will feel uncomfortable and insecure in class, avoiding participation and probably adopting passive or disruptive behaviours. This matter is closely related to self-esteem in the dimension of competence. De Andrés and Arnold (2009) explained that students who consider themselves competent take more risks and employ greater effort in class. According to Horwitz *et al.* (1986), one of the main causes of anxiety is the fear of making mistakes or being evaluated negatively, which may stem in part from having a low level of competence but also from other self-esteem dimensions, such as a sense of security.

(3) Personality: There are personality traits that may predict the generation of anxiety and affect self-esteem. For instance, Dewaele (2013) found a significant link between neuroticism and anxiety and moderately significant relationships among psychoticism, extraversion and anxiety. Similarly, Costa *et al.* (1991) pointed out that self-esteem is influenced moderately by extraversion and is more closely linked to neuroticism, which is the tendency to feel nervous and easily vulnerable. People who score highly on neuroticism tend to feel inferior, worthless, hopeless, tense and anxious (Dewaele, 2013).

(4) Learning styles: As is also the case with personality, students with low tolerance for ambiguity (ability to deal with ambiguous situations) may experience anxiety because FL learning is prone to create ambiguous situations (Ehrman, 1996). Accordingly, Dewaele and Tsui Shan Ip (2013) found that students who were more tolerant of second language ambiguity were less anxious in their English as a foreign language (EFL) classes and also felt more proficient. Similarly, synthetic or global students (i.e. those who prefer to learn by getting the overall picture) are uncomfortable when the teacher adopts a deductive methodology and focuses on the details of the language, rather than the global use. Likewise, a conflict may occur when the learning style of the student and the teacher's style are opposite (Oxford, 1999b). For example, a perfectionist or an analytical

teacher may generate discomfort with students who conceive language learning as something global and practical; in other words, a teacher who emphasises grammar and accuracy frustrates those students who want to learn the language to communicate and focus on fluency rather than on accuracy. Moreover, perfectionism has been correlated with anxiety levels (Gregersen & Horwitz, 2002; see also Dewaele, this volume). In spite of all this, it is important to note that the idea that learners maintain a static style of learning across contexts and tasks has been widely debunked in recent years.

Causes centred on the teacher

(1) Intolerant attitude: Tsui (1996) describes the situation in which a teacher asks questions to students and does not give enough time to them to understand the question, think and answer. Sometimes, repeating the same question several times can make students more anxious because they might consider themselves incompetent or more tense because of the lack of time to think about the question, which may result in a low level of self-esteem (Rubio, 2004). Obviously, it is advisable to ask close-ended questions to beginners and, as students become more proficient, proceed to open-ended questions, which require a higher level of cognitive demand (assessment, analysis, opinion, etc.). Also, the discrepancy in wait time length expectations may also stem from cross-cultural misunderstandings about acceptable levels of silence during interactions.

(2) Interaction with students: The way in which the teacher communicates with his/her students, for example, to give feedback or correct a mistake, can cause anxiety. For example, if a teacher criticises a student in front of the class, he/she will likely use self-defence mechanisms to protect his/her self-concept (Rubio, 2001), using flight behaviour, confrontation, etc. What the student is actually doing is protecting his/her sense of identity, which is one of the self-esteem dimensions described by Reasoner (1993). In her study, Price (1991) found that the role of the teacher may also exert considerable influence, since highly anxious students reported feeling more relaxed with certain teachers whose role was that of a facilitator (i.e. the teacher not only focuses on teaching specific contents, but also attends to students' psychological well-being; Underhill, 1999).

(3) Methodology: A teacher-centred methodology creates more anxiety than a student-centred one because, in the latter, students do not feel observed or evaluated by the teacher or the class (Littlewood, 1981). The methodology centred on the teacher limits the chances of oral interaction, giving little opportunity to practice the language in a more natural, authentic way. For example, a common teacher-centred activity is to ask questions to students in front of the class, one by one, which is useful to check and correct pronunciation but is interactively poor. Horwitz *et al.* (1986) indicate that the fear of being evaluated is one of

three major causes of anxiety in the FLC, together with oral interaction inhibition and fear of exams. Another activity which is less focused on the learner and on skills improvement is reading out loud, which can hardly be used for reading comprehension but again just for checking out pronunciation.

Anxiety can also be activated by creating a climate of competition through the implementation of certain types of activities (e.g. games or projects; De Andrés & Arnold, 2009). Bailey (1983) explains that anxiety is generated when students compete because they make comparisons with others or with themselves. This can affect their self-concept (Rubio, 2014) and is closely related to the self-esteem dimension of identity.

(4) Evaluation: Examination is normally perceived as an anxiety-provoking activity because examinees give importance to the activity due to pressure from parents, reputation among peers, etc. However, anxiety can also come from a bad teaching practice, when the teacher's methodology is based primarily on the development of oral skills but the written exam is the main assessment tool, as may occur in many contexts (Rubio & Tamayo-Rodríguez, 2012). This can create confusion and a reduction in learning motivation, thus activating anxiety and lowering self-esteem by decreasing security.

Causes centred on the context

Finally, anxious situations can be generated because of group conflicts in peer relationships. De Andrés and Arnold (2009) explain that students need to feel accepted and connected to other people or groups and when this does not occur, the self-concept is damaged, thus creating a low sense of belonging. In this sense, a methodology based on cooperative learning can enhance self-esteem and lower levels of anxiety caused by interpersonal conflicts (Casal, 2007).

Symptoms

There are many different classifications of anxiety. In this chapter, Rojas's (1989) pentadimensional system is used, in which a person may experience symptoms of anxiety within the following dimensions: physical, cognitive, psychological, communicative (called assertive by Rojas) and behavioural (Rubio, 2004).

The physical symptoms of anxiety produce changes in the body organs, such as palpitations, sweating or stomach-ache. Therefore, they are difficult to recognise in the classroom, unless they are revealed through language or are seen in the form of nervous tics. Cognitive symptoms are difficult to detect too, but in this case, close links between anxiety and self-esteem can be established. Cognitive symptoms are related to how thoughts are subject to perception and interpretation. In anxious situations, such thoughts might be distorted. This coincides with the symptoms of low self-esteem, in which students appear oversensitive to criticism and become overtly suspicious, partly due to experiencing a state of physical or emotional insecurity (self-esteem dimension). This is also related to the dimension of belonging, when students avoid participating or being the centre of attention because they have the fear of being rejected by the group. In addition, a cognitive symptom of anxiety is difficulty in deciding; indecision is a characteristic of low self-esteem in the dimension of purpose, so a student constantly doubts what he/she should do in class (e.g. whether to participate or cooperate) and especially how he/she should set goals.

Finally, a relationship between anxiety and self-esteem can also be established by analysing the thoughts produced in situations where the sense of competence is put into play. This is actually related to self-efficacy, defined as the perception that a person has over his/her competence or skills when performing a task and about the possibilities of success (Bandura, 1977). When competence is challenged negatively, self-defence mechanisms may appear, such as projection, which involves attributing one's guilt or ineffectiveness to others (e.g. 'the teacher made me fail' instead of 'I failed'). Self-defence mechanisms have the function to keep a psychological homeostasis and protect the self-concept, but sometimes, as in this example, they are used immaturely. Rationalisation is another self-defence mechanism and serves to illustrate the connection between self-esteem and anxiety. It manifests when a student creates a belief about something, despite it being irrational (e.g. 'the teacher favours all students but me'). All these thoughts comprise a chain of cognitive symptoms of anxiety that can hardly be separated from the different dimensions of self-esteem. Other examples are pessimistic thinking ('I will fail no matter how hard I try'), cynicism ('What do I need English for? It's useless'), victimisation ('I am always unlucky') and other negative thoughts characterised by containing absolutist terms ('The teacher *always* asks what I don't know'; 'I *never* get the questions I know in the exam').

Rojas (1989c: 80) established a difference between the psychological symptoms of anxiety and the cognitive ones, by characterising the former as being part of the existential human dimension. Accordingly, these symptoms are experienced with feelings of insecurity, loss of energy, sadness, sense of emptiness and a number of other depressive correlates. Mruk (2006) connects these features with his self-esteem matrix. In fact, in one part of the matrix, he explains that when a person thinks of himself/herself as incompetent and also has a low sense of worthiness, then depressive feelings arise.

Psychological symptoms of anxiety can be observed in the language classroom when pupils adopt passive learning attitudes because they have feelings of incompetence and discomfort. In fact, Rojas (1989) lists as one of the main symptoms, the ego breakdown, as Littlewood (1981) also does to describe the process of depersonalisation that students experience; moreover, a sense of infantilisation may also occur when students see themselves as limited in their ability to speak the FL and feel embarrassed about their pronunciation. These descriptions have been also produced in various studies on the self, especially in the description of the self-concept (see, for instance, Mercer & Williams, 2014).

Communicative symptoms of anxiety appear when a person experiences inhibitions in conveying a message. These symptoms have been studied by several authors (Horwitz *et al.*, 1986; MacIntyre & Gardner, 1991; Rubio, 2004) who use different terminology, such as communicative apprehension or communicative anxiety, to describe situations in which students freeze and block when having to start a conversation, are very sensitive to error correction, avoid participating and generally adopt passive language learning attitudes. These behaviours have also been described within the dimensions of self-esteem, when students have a low sense of security, identity, belonging, purpose or competence.

Finally, behavioural symptoms of anxiety are clearly visible by just observing students, and are considered part of the effects generated by anxiety and low self-esteem. Caressing one's hair continually; wide eyes; clumsiness (uncoordinated movements); slurred speech (voice with high and low tones); facial gestures, such as tense or skewed jaw; and other nonverbal signs can easily be recognised when students perform the most anxiety-provoking tasks (e.g. communication activities, oral examination). In the FLC, these symptoms are also observed when students look downwards to avoid the teacher's look,[2] ignore the teacher's instructions (for example, when they have to use the FL) or make disapproval gestures for every new activity.

All these causes and effects of anxiety and low self-esteem lead to coping behaviours, which are described in the next section.

Coping behaviours

Broadly speaking, studies in the field of psychology accept the idea that perceptions and interpretations of an event, and not the event *per se*, are the drivers that can generate feelings of anxiety or damage the self-concept. Furthermore, certain studies (e.g. Gantiva Diaz *et al.*, 2010) report that people with moderate levels of anxiety employ more effective coping strategies by focusing specifically on the situation (not diverting to different sources) and reassessing the situation positively using various strategies to solve problems or conflicts, such as finding social support. Thus, the source is directly addressed, in contrast to the strategies commonly used by highly anxious subjects, which might include avoidance behaviours, thereby resulting in passive or non-adaptive attitudes that take the form of aggression or disruption (Lazarus & Folkman, 1984). Thus, Folkman and Lazarus (1985) propose the Transactional Model of Stress and Coping, which involves developing coping strategies focusing not only on the problem or situation but also on the emotion (i.e. individuals find strategies to relieve stress and control physiological arousal and emotional reactions).

However, coping strategies can also have an impact on psychological well-being, the way an individual judges his/her life in positive terms and makes associations to positive states of humour, high self-esteem and low depressive symptoms (Eronen & Nurmi, 1999). Psychological well-being has been linked to self-concept/self-esteem, along with other variables such as personality, quality of social interactions, positive family relationships or clinical symptoms (Fickova & Korcova, 2000), but this field of research is still relatively untouched in the context of FL learning.

Classroom Implementation

There are two approaches to deal with anxiety and self-esteem in the language classroom: a direct one and an indirect one. Implementing programmes, techniques or strategies to cope with high anxiety or low self-esteem can directly approach both phenomena, but they can also be tackled indirectly by implementing activities and other methodological procedures in which students learn the language and are likely to have a personal growth at the same time. Also, specific procedures can be used to create a less threatening environment.

A direct approach seems less practical and more difficult to implement, because it should be preferably applied to specific students that need help because they have reported low levels of self-esteem or high levels of anxiety. Moreover, the language teacher does not have the specialised training that requires this kind of psychopedagogic evaluation, which should be carried out by a psychologist or a special education teacher. Notwithstanding this, there are school programmes in some contexts which are devoted to training students to cope with anxious situations or develop self-esteem (see, for instance, Reasoner, 1983).

Therefore, an indirect application approach seems more practical and doable for language teachers, so that they can decide what kind of classroom climate they would rather promote in relation to their teaching methodology. Accordingly, three working elements may be highlighted, namely rapport, the type of teaching methodology and the learning activities.

Implementation based on rapport

The type of role that a teacher establishes with students can help to relieve anxiety. While it is true that the role may depend largely on the personality of the teacher, this does not mean that he/she has choices.

Learning an FL has been characterised as anxiety-provoking for many students (see previous sections), and therefore choosing the role of facilitator (Underhill, 1999) can be beneficial. This role requires being aware of different classroom situations – specifically, how students feel – and acting accordingly. Thus, when students see that the teacher cares about them, their emotional security is enhanced; a sense of security is one dimension of self-esteem.

The role of facilitator involves having discussions with students about the process of language learning so that some actions can be decided together as a group. An anecdote that exemplifies this happened to me on one occasion when I had to replace a teacher for a month to teach a language course. I came into class and started speaking to the class in English, and after a while, I started to see gestures and facial expressions of frustration and disapproval (i.e. behavioural symptoms of anxiety). Then, I realised that something was going wrong in this group, so I decided to stop the class and use the native language to inquire about their concerns. After students admitted that they were frustrated and conceived of FL learning as an uncomfortable experience, I explained that lessons should be enjoyable, that making errors was normal and part of the language learning process and that my role was to facilitate learning and not just to teach and assess. The class finished well, and occasionally, in other sessions, I promoted brief chats about how they felt and whether the language learning experience had changed. That class changed their attitude from passivity and fear to enthusiasm and participation. As a language teacher, I realised that the time which was used to facilitate learning and have a more human communication with students optimised the process. Therefore, introducing explicit discussions of anxiety and emotions in class can be beneficial for students.

The language for communication that teachers use can also help to reduce anxiety and promote self-esteem. In fact, the term *confirmation* is used to describe 'the process by which we make others feel valued, recognized and supported' (Leon, 2007: 306). Leon conducted a study to analyse teachers' language, and the participants of her study pointed out that they felt more secure and supported when teachers praised them for doing well and conveyed to them confidence in their capabilities.

Empathy may be the term that encompasses all of the above (Mercer, forthcoming). When a teacher is able to put himself/herself in the shoes of his/her students (i.e. understand what they think and perceive how they feel), a more sincere and deeper communication can be established in the FL classroom and the correct emotional climate can be fostered (Dewaele, 2015). Empathy, communicative abilities and other intra- and interpersonal factors can be developed through training programmes that are paramount to the existential development of the teacher. Actually, *to be* (how you are and behave) is one of the main characteristics of a good teacher, together with *to know* (in our case about pedagogy and language) and *to do* (curriculum and instruction classroom; based on Sartre, 1956).

Implementation based on methodology

A task that every teacher should do is control the time spent on activities centred on the teacher or the student. In many contexts, teachers still use most of their class time for teacher-centred activities, which not only limits the possibilities of oral interaction but also creates an atmosphere of intimidation, since students have the fear of being evaluated by the teacher and their classmates. A learner-centred methodology gives students the possibility to be the main agents of the learning process, so that they can explore, discover and perform tasks that lead to experiencing flow states (Rubio, 2011). This is related to having better motivational attitudes and a stronger sense of self-concept.

Cooperative work can also be used to foster a greater sense of belonging and to create a less competitive classroom climate. Casal (2007) explains that before starting group-work activity, roles have to be assigned (e.g. director, spokesperson, writer, FL and volume controller), and after completing the task students should evaluate themselves (i.e. both their work effort and duty accomplishment). Personally, I have been doing cooperative work for many years, and it is also very effective to generate flow, collaboration, intense work atmosphere, security and motivation.

The importance of being aware of the use of assessment instruments has already been touched on in this chapter. Rubio and Tamayo-Rodríguez (2012) note that written evaluation, as the only form of evaluation, is still used in many contexts, and that most activities focus on grammatical content. They also point out that a common teaching practice is to include only a written exam for summative assessment while most lessons, to a greater or lesser extent, deal with oral skills. Exams, especially oral exams, have been identified as one of the most anxiety-provoking activities in the FLC (Horwitz *et al.*, 1986) because of their importance for students. Some alleviating guidelines can be used before, during and after the exam. For example, prior to it, a tutorial should be deployed so that students have the possibility to ask questions, do a mock exam and see the basis on which they are going to be evaluated (i.e. the evaluation criteria that will be used along with a rubric to help them see how these criteria will be quantified). Transparency in the evaluation system will provide a stronger sense of security. This should not be restricted to the classroom context, but, in the case of younger learners, the tutorial could be submitted in written mode for parents or language tutors to facilitate home study.

Rubio (2002b) adds other tips that can be used in the oral exam, such as smiling just before starting the test. He found that starting the exam with interactive activities (e.g. interviews, short personal questions) instead of non-interactive ones (e.g. speaking about a topic, describing an image) can help to reduce anxiety. Also, Rubio (2002a) suggests using the *positive re-evaluation technique*, which reduces anxiety by starting the exam with asking very simple, closed-ended questions. By doing so, students should have a successful start and their sense of confidence would grow; then, the exam would gradually increase in difficulty.[3]

Implementation based on the type of activities

De Andrés and Arnold (2009) suggest that the experience of learning a language should not be confined to the development of communicative competence but also to personal development, in case the language classroom is likely to raise feelings of anxiety and other types of personal discomfort. Accordingly, many activities can be designed to learn the language and, at the same time, reduce anxiety and empower self-esteem. These can be implemented occasionally, when the topics of the lesson and the self-esteem activity are related, or as part of a programme. These activities are a good alternative for difficult teaching slots (e.g. the last hour of class, Fridays or pre-holiday sessions).

Reasoner (1983) was a pioneer in proposing self-esteem development programmes in the academic context. These were designed to enhance the perceptions of self-concept in five dimensions (security, identity, belonging, purpose and competence). Some publications with proposals for the FLC followed later (Davis & Rinvolucri, 1991; De Andrés & Arnold, 2009; Murphey, 2006; Rinvolucri, 2002; Rubio, 2007a). Two activities will be described here in order to exemplify the dimensions of security and identity. A wide range of activities can be found in the references cited above.

Dimension of security

Make groups and let the students devise rules for the FLC. If their level is low, you can give a list of rules for them to choose from. For example:

- I raise my hand before speaking in class.
- I only use English in oral tasks.
- I ask for materials in English.

Then, they write the rules on a poster and hang it on the wall for the other groups to see. Finally, the most popular rules are chosen and students discuss the consequences of breaking those rules and write these on a poster or banners, which are hung around the classroom. This will promote a higher sense of security because students, especially children, need to have clear guidelines on how to act and interact in the classroom and to incorporate them as routines.[4]

Dimension of identity

This activity, which I always use in class, is very useful to create positive identity labels regarding personality, physical appearance, competence and work profile (Rubio, 2007b):[5]

(1) Ask students to write their names in the centre of half a sheet of paper. Tell them to write the following information in the four corners and to keep it secret (you may need to do a pre-task to review vocabulary related to it):
   - At the upper left-hand corner: a positive personality trait.
   - At the upper right-hand corner: something they like about their body.
   - At the lower left-hand corner: a talent/hobby or a positive aspect of their working profile.
   - At the lower right-hand corner: a feature of their personality that they would like to improve (grown-ups could instead write an aspect of language learning they need to improve).
(2) Collect students' products, shuffle, select one and start describing the content for students to guess who the product belongs to: 'This person is friendly ... and likes her eyes ... is hard-working ... and would like to improve her pronunciation'. Let students guess who it is, and repeat the process with a new one. A positive aspect of the game is that when students do not name the correct person, they are actually providing other students with positive attributions.
(3) Hand out the products randomly and tell students to add more positive features and write a description. For example, 'David is friendly and cheerful. He likes his nose and I like his hair, and his favourite hobby is swimming, but he is also good at basketball...'.
(4) Finally, ask a student to read the description and then return it to the owner, and form a chain accordingly. Also, tell students to stand in a circle and choose one (especially one who most needs it) to stand in the middle for the others to say positive aspects about him/her.

Conclusion

This chapter has acknowledged the influence that anxiety and self-esteem exert in the process of learning an FL. Related terms were clarified, namely anxiety, stress, fear, self-esteem, self-concept and self-efficacy, and the relationship between anxiety and self-esteem was also analysed in order to conclude that a high level of anxiety is related to low self-esteem. The sources (mainly fear of negative evaluation and communicative inhibition), symptoms (physical, cognitive, psychological, communicative and behavioural) and effects of anxiety (passive attitude and disruptive behaviour) were described. Finally, suggestions about coping strategies and classroom implementation programmes and activities were given.

Classroom applications should not be conceived of as a way to inflate the students' ego, such as giving false feedback for the sake of providing students with positive feelings; neither should they be employed as a way to overprotect students, but, on the contrary, they should be the tools that empower students to cope with difficult situations so that they can develop competences and learn content in an appropriate learning atmosphere.

For many years, language learning has been a mechanical exercise, depersonalised, impractical and even intimidating in many contexts. I hope this chapter may contribute to a change.

Notes

(1) Clément and Kruidenier (1985) and Schumann (1976) mainly studied anxiety and self-esteem in multicultural settings and social contexts.
(2) Please note that in some cultures it is polite to avoid eye contact with the teacher.
(3) This occurs because, before the exam takes place, students tend to have multiple visualisations of themselves performing the exam, sometimes anticipating success or failure. When they cope with the situation, they compare the actual situation with the one previously envisaged, and when it is perceived positively the anxiety symptoms disappear.
(4) For further information on this rule-generating activity in relation to group dynamics and the setting of 'norms' of behaviour, see Dörnyei and Murphey (2003).
(5) A version for learners of Spanish is available at http://cvc.cervantes.es/aula/didactired/anteriores/mayo_07/07052007b.htm.

References

Aida, Y. (1994) Examination of Horwitz, Horwitz and Cope's construct of foreign language anxiety: The case of students of Japanese. *The Modern Language Journal* 78, 155–168.
Arnold, J. (ed.) (1999) *Affect in Language Learning*. Cambridge: Cambridge University Press.
Arnold, J. and Brown, H.D. (1999) A map of the terrain. In J. Arnold (ed.) *Affect in Language Learning* (pp. 1–24). Cambridge: Cambridge University Press.
Bailey, K.M. (1983) Competitiveness and anxiety in adult second language learning: Looking *at* and *through* diary studies. In H.W. Seliger and M.H. Long (eds) *Classroom-Oriented Research in Second Language Acquisition* (pp. 67–103). Rowley: Newbury House.
Bandura, A. (1977) Self-efficacy: Toward a unifying theory of behavioral change. *Psychological Review* 84, 191–215.
Casal, S. (2007) The social dimension of self-esteem in the English classroom. In F.D. Rubio (ed.) *Self-Esteem and Foreign Language Learning* (pp. 91–104). Newcastle: Cambridge Scholars Publishing.
Clément, R. and Kruidenier, B.G. (1985) Aptitude, attitude and motivation in second language proficiency: A test on Clément's model. *Journal of Language and Social Psychology* 4 (1), 21–37.
Costa, P.T., McCrae, R.R. and Dye, D.A. (1991) Facet scales for agreeableness and conscientiousness: A revision of the NEO personality inventory. *Personality and Individual Differences* 12 (9), 887–898.

Daly, J.A. (1991) Understanding communication apprehension: An introduction for language educators. In E.K. Horwitz and D.J. Young (eds) *Language Anxiety: From Theory and Research to Classroom Implications* (pp. 3–13). Englewood Cliffs: Prentice Hall.

Damasio, A. (1994) *Descartes' Error: Emotion, Reason, and the Human Brain*. New York: Avon.

Davis, P. and Rinvolucri, M. (1991) *The Confidence Book*. London: Longman.

De Andrés, V. (1999) Self-esteem in the classroom or the metamorphosis of butterflies. In J. Arnold (ed.) *Affect in Language Learning* (pp. 87–102). Cambridge: Cambridge University Press.

De Andrés, V. and Arnold, J. (2009) *Seeds of Confidence. Self-Esteem Activities for the EFL Classroom*. Rum: Helbling.

Deci, E.L. and Ryan, R.M. (1985) *Intrinsic Motivation and Self-Determination in Human Behaviour*. New York: Plenum Publishing.

Deci, E.L. and Ryan, R.M. (2002) *Handbook of Self-Determination*. Rochester: University of Rochester Press.

Dewaele, J.-M. (2013) The link between foreign language classroom anxiety and psychoticism, extraversion, and neuroticism among adult bi- and multilinguals. *The Modern Language Journal* 97 (3), 670–684.

Dewaele, J.-M. (2015) On emotions in foreign language learning and use. *The Language Teacher* 39 (3), 13–15.

Dewaele, J.-M. and Tsui Shan Ip, T. (2013) The link between Foreign Language Classroom Anxiety, Second Language Tolerance of Ambiguity and self-rated English proficiency among Chinese learners. *Studies in Second Language Learning and Teaching* 3 (1), 47–66.

Dörnyei, Z. (2005) *The Psychology of the Language Learner*. Mahwah, NJ: Lawrence Erlbaum.

Dörnyei, Z. (2009) The L2 motivational self system. In Z. Dörnyei and E. Ushioda (eds) *Motivation, Language Identity and the L2 Self* (pp. 9–42). Bristol: Multilingual Matters.

Dörnyei, Z. and Murphey, T. (2003) *Group Dynamics in the Language Classroom*. Cambridge: Cambridge University Press.

Dörnyei, Z. and Kubanyiova, M. (2014) *Motivating Learners, Motivating Teachers: Building Vision in the Language Classroom*. Cambridge: Cambridge University Press.

Ehrman, M.E. (1996) *Understanding Second Language Learning Difficulties*. London: Sage.

Eronen, S. and Nurmi, J.E. (1999) Life events, predisposing cognitive strategies and well-being. *European Journal of Personality* 13, 129–148.

Fickova, E. and Korcova, N. (2000) Psychometric relations between self-esteem measures and coping with stress. *Studia Psychologica* 42 (3), 237–242.

Folkman, S. and Lazarus, S. (1985) If it changes it must be a process: A study of emotion and coping during three stages of a college examination. *Journal of Personality and Social Psychology* 48 (1), 150–170.

Gantiva Díaz, C.A., Viveros, A.L., Dávila, A.M. and Salgado, M.J. (2010) Estrategias de afrontamiento en personas con ansiedad. *Psychologia. Avances de la Disciplina* 4 (1), 63–70.

Gardner, R.C. (1985) *Social Psychology and Second Language Learning*. London: Edward Arnold.

Gregersen, T. and Horwitz, E.K. (2002) Language learning and perfectionism: Anxious and non-anxious language learners' reactions to their own oral performance. *The Modern Language Journal* 86, 562–570.

Hadfield, J. and Dörnyei, Z. (2013) *Motivating Learning*. Harlow: Longman.

Harter, S. (1999) *The Construction of the Self: A Developmental Perspective*. New York: Guildford Press.

Higgins, E.T. (1987) Self-discrepancy: A theory relating self and affect. *Psychological Review* 94, 319–340.

Horwitz, E.K. and Young D.J. (1991). *Language Anxiety. From Theory and Research to Classroom Implications.* Englewood Cliffs, NJ: Prentice-Hall.

Horwitz, E.K., Horwitz, M.B. and Cope, J.A. (1986) Foreign language classroom anxiety. *Modern Language Journal* 70, 125–132.

Horwitz, E.K., Horwitz, M.B. and Cope, J.A. (1991) Foreign language classroom anxiety. In E.K. Horwitz and D.J. Young (eds) *Language Anxiety. From Theory and Research to Classroom Implications* (pp. 27–39). Englewood Cliffs, NJ: Prentice Hall.

Krashen, S. (1982) *Principles and Practice in Second Language Acquisition.* Oxford: Pergamon Press.

Lazarus, S. and Folkman, S. (1984) *Stress, Appraisal, and Coping.* New York: Springer.

LeDoux, J.E. (1996) *The Emotional Brain.* New York: Simon and Schuster.

Leon, I. (2007) Teacher's self-esteem: The role of confirmation. In F.D. Rubio (ed.) *Self-Esteem and Foreign Language Learning* (pp. 192–205). Newcastle: Cambridge Scholars Publishing.

Littlewood, W. (1981) *Communicative Language Teaching: An Introduction.* New York: Cambridge University Press.

MacIntyre, P.D. and Gardner, R.C. (1991) Language anxiety: Its relation to other anxieties and to processing in native and second languages. *Language Learning* 75, 513–534.

Markus, H. and Nurius, P. (1986) Possible selves. *American Psychologist* 41, 954–969.

Mercer, S. (2010) *Towards an Understanding of Language Learner Self-Concept.* Dordrecht: Springer.

Mercer, S. and Williams, M. (2014) *Multiple Perspectives on the Self in SLA.* Bristol: Multilingual Matters.

Mruk, C.J. (2006) *Self-Esteem Research, Theory, and Practice: Toward a Positive Psychology of Self-Esteem.* New York: Springer.

Murphey, T. (2006) *Language Hungry! An Introduction to Language Learning, Fun and Self-Esteem.* Rum: Helbling Languages.

Onwuegbuzie, A.J., Bailey, P. and Daley, C.E. (1999) Factors associated with foreign language anxiety. *Applied Psycholinguistics* 20, 217–239.

Ortega, A. (2007) Anxiety and self-esteem. In F.D. Rubio (ed.) *Self-Esteem and Foreign Language Learning* (pp. 105–127). Newcastle: Cambridge Scholars Publishing.

Oxford, R.L. (1999a) Anxiety and the language learner: New insights. In J. Arnold (ed.) *Affect in Language Learning* (pp. 58–67). Cambridge: Cambridge University Press.

Oxford, R.L. (1999b) 'Style wars' as a source of anxiety in the language classroom. In D.J. Young (ed.) *Affect in Second Language Learning: A Practical Guide to Dealing with Learner Anxieties* (pp. 216–237). Boston, MA: McGraw-Hill.

Pérez Paredes, P.F. and Martínez Sánchez, F. (2000) A Spanish version of the foreign language classroom anxiety scale: Revisiting Aida's factor analysis. *Resla* 14, 337–352.

Price, M.L. (1991) The subjective experience of foreign language anxiety: Interviews with highly anxious students. In E.K. Horwitz and D.J. Young (eds) *Language Anxiety: From Theory and Research to Classroom Implications* (pp. 101–108). Englewood Cliffs, NJ: Prentice-Hall.

Reasoner, R. (1983) Enhancement of self-esteem in children and adolescents. *Journal of Family and Community Health* 2, 51–64.

Rinvolucri, M. (2002) *Humanising Your Coursebook.* London: DELTA Publishing.

Rojas, E. (1989) *La Ansiedad.* Madrid: Temas de Hoy.

Rubio, F.D. (2001) El pensamiento en la clase de inglés: Fuente de poder o vulnerabilidad. *Estudios De Lingüística Inglesa Aplicada (ELIA)* 2, 49–56.

Rubio, F.D. (2002a) Una forma de reducir la ansiedad en los exámenes orales de inglés como lengua extranjera: Técnica de reevaluación positiva. *Estudios De Lingüística Inglesa Aplicada (ELIA)* 3, 173–186.

Rubio, F.D. (2002b) Making oral test more human and less anxiety generating. *Humanising Language Teaching, Year 4* (4 July 2002). See http://www.hltmag.co.uk/jul02/sart3.htm (accessed 23 September 2015).

Rubio, F.D. (2004) *La Ansiedad en el Aprendizaje de Idiomas.* Huelva: Universidad de Huelva.

Rubio, F.D. (ed.) (2007a) *Self-Esteem and Foreign Language Learning.* Newcastle: Cambridge Scholars Publishing.

Rubio, F.D. (2007b) Inteligencia intrapersonal: 'Adivina quién es'. *Didactired, Mayo,* 1–4. See http://cvc.cervantes.es/aula/didactired/anteriores/mayo_07/07052007b.htm (accessed 23 September 2015).

Rubio, F.D. (2011) Optimal experiences in the foreign language classroom: Flow states in speaking tasks. *Anglistik. International Journal of English Studies* 22 (1), 63–80.

Rubio, F.D. (2014) Self-esteem and self-concept in foreign language learning. In S. Mercer and M. Williams (eds) *Multiple Perspectives on the Self in SLA* (pp. 41–58). Bristol: Multilingual Matters.

Rubio, F.D. and Tamayo-Rodríguez, L. (2012) Estudio sobre prácticas docentes en evaluación de la lengua inglesa en la ESO. *Profesorado. Revisa de Currículum y Formación del Profesorado* 16 (1), 295–316.

Ryan, S. and Irie, K. (2014) Imagined and possible selves: Stories we tell ourselves about ourselves. In S. Mercer and M. Williams (eds) *Multiple Perspectives on the Self in SLA* (pp. 109–123). Bristol: Multilingual Matters.

Sartre, J.P. (1956) *Being and Nothingness.* New York: Philosophical Library.

Schumann, J.H. (1976) Social distance as a factor in second language acquisition. *Language Learning* 26 (1), 135–143.

Schumann, J.H. (1997) *The Neurobiology of Affect in Language.* Malden, MA: Blackwell Publishers.

Tóth, Z. (2008) A foreign language anxiety scale for Hungarian learners of English. *Working Papers in Language Pedagogy* 2, 55–78.

Tsui, A. (1996) Reticence and anxiety in second language learning. In K.M. Bailey and D. Nunan (eds) *Voices From the Language Classroom* (pp. 145–167). Cambridge: Cambridge University Press.

Underhill, A. (1999) Facilitation in language teaching. In J. Arnold (ed.) *Affect in Language Learning* (pp. 143–158). Cambridge: Cambridge University Press.

Young, D.J. (1990) An investigation of students' perspectives on anxiety and speaking. *Foreign Language Annals* 23 (6), 539–553.

Young, D.J. (1991) Creating a low-anxiety classroom environment: What does language anxiety research suggest? *The Modern Language Journal* 75, 426–439.

Zare, P. and Riasati, M.J. (2012) The relationship between language learning anxiety, self-esteem, and academic level among Iranian EFL learners. *Pertanika Journal of Social Sciences & Humanities* 20 (1), 219–225.

12 Conclusion

Christina Gkonou, Jean-Marc Dewaele and Mark Daubney

Introduction

In this final chapter, we would like to bring together the main themes emerging from all contributions to this volume in terms of recent developments in theorising about language anxiety, empirically investigating it and suggesting practical ideas for addressing it. As many authors in this anthology have acknowledged, research into language anxiety is not new to the field of second language acquisition (SLA) (cf. Horwitz, 2010). In this sense, the present volume could be viewed as a compilation of new insights into language anxiety which, taken together, are indicative of a need to broaden the agenda on three fronts: theory, research and practice. In what follows, we discuss what we feel are the most salient themes with regard to language anxiety and these three aspects.

Theorising About Language Anxiety

A common thread evident in most chapters in this volume is the recognition that language anxiety is not monolithic and unidimensional but might more usefully be conceived of as a complex construct. In his overview of language anxiety research and trends in its development, MacIntyre discusses the increasingly influential Dynamic Approach in which anxiety is conceptualised and investigated in connection with a complex set of language experiences. Additionally, strong interconnections were found to exist between anxiety and other language learning psychology constructs. For example, Horwitz suggests that language anxiety, motivation, autonomy and self-concept should be studied in tandem. Şimşek and Dörnyei propose a new, self-based conceptualisation of language anxiety which they designate the 'anxious self', thus highlighting the link between anxiety and the self. Gkonou demonstrates that learner agency and extrinsic interest in the foreign language interplay with language anxiety. Tóth found that there exists a strong, dynamic relation between high anxiety levels and self-perceived competence and ability. Mercer (2013: 376) has argued that 'at present, SLA is undergoing what could be termed a "complexity turn" [...] as researchers become increasingly aware of and sensitive to the inherent complexity and dynamism involved in learning and teaching foreign languages'. For many contributors to this volume, language anxiety is seen as an inherently complex construct which cannot be meaningfully abstracted from other psychological variables.

Another new insight into theorising about language anxiety that is evident from the chapters is that, despite being a negative emotion, anxiety could be viewed through a positive psychology lens too. Oxford establishes a link between language anxiety and a range of positive psychology constructs such as flow, hope, optimism, emotional intelligence and positive emotions (e.g. pleasure, contentment and satisfaction). She goes on to suggest a number of positive psychology interventions and activities that could help minimise language anxiety among learners such as hyper-reflection, situation analysis, signature strengths or the 'three-good-things' exercise, among others. Horwitz also discusses flow in her chapter. In particular, she questions the existence of 'facilitative' anxiety and advocates that under no circumstances should language educators exacerbate students' negative emotions in class. On the contrary, language teachers should increase their students' motivation and allow their positive emotions to flow. These points reflect current trends in the field of positive psychology in SLA (see, for example, Gregersen & MacIntyre, 2014; MacIntyre et al., 2016; MacIntyre & Mercer, 2014) and, most importantly, mirror Dewaele and MacIntyre's (2014, 2016) conclusion that positive and negative emotions should not be thought of as opposite ends of the spectrum but rather as complementary constructs.

On reflecting on the theory underpinning language anxiety, we believe it is also necessary to refer to one of Horwitz's insights which – albeit not new – the author, understandably, feels is important to clarify and reiterate in this book. In their seminal paper, Horwitz et al. (1986) described three performance-related anxieties, namely communication apprehension, fear of negative evaluation and test anxiety, in order to facilitate understanding of the nature of language anxiety. However, Horwitz et al. (1986) did not suggest that communication apprehension plus fear of negative evaluation plus test anxiety equalled language anxiety, as has been the case in a number of subsequent interpretations. We think it is important and indeed very useful to have this point clarified in this anthology. In addition, Rubio focuses on definitional concerns with reference to anxiety, stress and fear and to a range of self-beliefs, and through examples from individuals' general behaviour and language learning, he presents fine-grained conceptualisations of all relevant key terminology. It is hoped that these definitions will help clarify a number of overlapping constructs.

Researching Language Anxiety

Looking at this volume as a whole, one possible interpretation is that it marks the advent of mixed-methods research into language anxiety, mainly with a quantitative component preceding a subsequent, qualitative study. For instance, King and Smith used a structured observation instrument called the Classroom Oral Participation Scheme and collected quantitative data on students' classroom oral participation in Japan; they then selected 11 students who were interviewed twice. Şimşek and Dörnyei conducted a preliminary interview study which was followed by a survey and interviews with a purposefully selected sample. Tóth administered the Hungarian version of the Foreign Language Classroom Anxiety Scale (FLCAS; Horwitz et al., 1986) to English university students and then purposefully selected a sample for follow-up interviews. However, this collection shows that psychometric instruments also have a central role to play in delineating aspects of language anxiety. In particular, Dewaele administered different surveys to three groups of participants in order to examine the links between perfectionism and language anxiety.

In addition to language anxiety being regarded as a complex variable, contributors to this volume also see it as non-linear and dynamic. Gregersen, MacIntyre and Olson examine emotion and anxiety as a dynamic system which is in a constant state of flux. To this end, they used the idiodynamic method (Gregersen et al., 2014; MacIntyre & Gregersen, 2012) to look at moment-to-moment fluctuations in participants' language anxiety levels in real time. Therefore, their chapter is in line with current thinking and recent developments in the field of SLA in terms of Complex Dynamic Systems Theory (CDST; Larsen-Freeman & Cameron, 2008). Further, Şimşek and Dörnyei report that there were times when the highly anxious students in their study would not feel anxious at all but would instead enjoy the task being undertaken and feel relaxed. Gkonou notes that some of her participants could identify occasions that would cause little or no anxiety at all to them.

In addition to a range of methodological designs, language anxiety was empirically investigated on the basis of prominent psychology-based frameworks such as McAdams's (2006) New Big Five model (see Şimşek and Dörnyei), the Frost Multidimensional Perfectionism Scale (Frost, 1990; see Dewaele), Clark and Wells's (1995) model of social anxiety (see King and Smith) and Bronfenbrenner's (1979) nested ecosystems model (see Gkonou). The first two studies reveal strong links between language anxiety and personality traits such as neuroticism and perfectionism, respectively. Indeed, previous research has revealed significant correlations between neuroticism and language anxiety (Dewaele, 2002, 2013). The last two studies elucidate the importance of the interplay between wider contextual factors such as the education system in Japan and Greece, respectively; specific language skills, communicative tasks and situations such as speaking in a foreign language; and learner-internal variables such as language anxiety, emotions, learner agency, reticence and silence.

Ideas for Mitigating Language Anxiety

Broadly speaking, language anxiety seems to interfere with different stages of the process of acquiring and using a second language, and understandably, the potential challenges facing teachers may be varied and complex. The present volume also offers a range of classroom activities and teaching strategies which language educators and teacher trainers across the globe might wish to incorporate into their own practices. More specifically, Gregersen, MacIntyre and Olson stress the importance of raising teachers' awareness of nonverbal cues as indicators of language anxiety and of how these can be meaningfully interpreted. They conclude that body language, vocalics, emotion and their respective manifestations are closely linked. Oxford draws on suggestions from general psychology and positive psychology and suggests a series of interventions for classroom use and for independent, autonomous learning and self-awareness. Indeed, negative emotions such as language anxiety can be counterbalanced by maintaining and increasing the positive ones. Rubio suggests that teaching strategies for language anxiety should be part of school curricula and teacher training programmes. He goes on to describe three different types of classroom-based activities for reducing language anxiety and boosting students' self-esteem, namely implementation based on rapport, methodology and the type of learning activities. King and Smith also suggest useful strategies for combating social anxiety and silence, with classroom rapport and group dynamics being the main 'weapons' in this battle. Finally, Şimşek and Dörnyei suggest that teachers ask their learners or help them to produce constructive narratives about their language anxiety symptoms and episodes with a view to urging them to verbalise their negative emotions while in the classroom. We believe that introducing explicit discussions of language anxiety during lessons might not only be of help in creating a greater sense of community among students but also in bringing about a heightened awareness on the part of anxious students that they are, in fact, not alone and that other classmates may well experience similar feelings to themselves.

Final Thoughts

To conclude, this volume, as its title also suggests, could be viewed as a wide-ranging collection of chapters which offers new insights into and directions in theorising about analysing, researching and addressing language anxiety. Within SLA, this is the third anthology to tackle language anxiety (see also Horwitz & Young, 1991; Young, 1999), and we hope it has gone some way to capturing many of the recent trends and developments within the field, thus showing its wide-ranging diversity and complexity. It is hoped that this rich collection of chapters will help to encourage researchers to undertake new projects, drawing on the new theoretical and methodological frameworks discussed here, and inspire educators and teacher trainers to try out new ideas and techniques for alleviating anxiety.

Reflecting on possible future directions that language anxiety theory, research and practice could take in the field of SLA, our position is that focusing on fluctuations in language anxiety levels, by taking into account changes in time, place, teaching situations, specific skills and different groups, could be a fruitful trajectory. It would also be of interest to see action research projects conducted in a variety of geographical areas and educational contexts, depicting language learners' emotions and language anxiety in class. Another possibility concerns how and which constructs from both language learning psychology and general educational psychology might have a role to play in conceptualising language anxiety. Future research may also want to explore the intriguing and complex links among motivation, anxiety and identity. Rather than acting as a brake on motivation, Yan and Horwitz (2008) have difficulties envisaging a motivated learner, free of anxiety. Block (2007) suggests anxiety could be a 'by-product' of identity work, while Stroud and Wee (2006) discuss 'identity-based anxiety' and 'competence-based anxiety'; that is, learners are just as concerned with peer pressure and teacher reaction as they are with their language proficiency *per se*. Drawing on the 'narrative identity level' considered by Şimşek and Dörnyei in this volume, for example, could yield further insights into these areas and how anxious individuals co-construct and narrate their emotional experiences by deploying identity types in their discourse, thereby contributing to a deeper understanding of the overall experience of anxiety. Finally, the present volume, and also much of the previous research (with the exception of Bekleyen, 2009; Daubney & Araújo e Sá, 2012; Horwitz, 1996; and Tum, 2014), has only centred on anxious language learners and not on anxious language teachers. Given the high levels of teacher burnout and emotional labour reported in the literature on general education, further research could look at language teacher anxiety and professional well-being and at possible links between teacher and learner anxiety.

References

Bekleyen, N. (2009) Helping teachers become better English students: Causes, effects, and coping strategies for foreign language listening anxiety. *System* 37 (4), 664–675.
Block, D. (2007) *Second Language Identities*. London: Continuum.

Bronfenbrenner, U. (1979) *The Ecology of Human Development: Experiments by Nature and Design*. Cambridge, MA: Harvard University Press.

Clark, D.M. and Wells, A. (1995) A cognitive model of social phobia. In R.G. Heimberg, M.R. Liebowitz, D.A. Hope and F.R. Schneier (eds) *Social Phobia: Diagnosis, Assessment and Treatment* (pp. 69–93). New York: Guilford Press.

Daubney, M. and Araújo e Sá, M.H. (2012) On managing anxiety in foreign language learning: Developing emotional literacy on the practicum. *Intercompreensão* 16, 119–136.

Dewaele, J.-M. (2002) Psychological and sociodemographic correlates of communicative anxiety in L2 and L3 production. *The International Journal of Bilingualism* 6, 23–39.

Dewaele, J.-M. (2013) The link between foreign language classroom anxiety and psychoticism, extraversion, and neuroticism among adult bi- and multilinguals. *The Modern Language Journal* 97 (3), 670–684.

Dewaele, J.-M. and MacIntyre, P.D. (2014) The two faces of Janus? Anxiety and enjoyment in the foreign language classroom. *Studies in Second Language Learning and Teaching* 4 (2), 237–274.

Dewaele, J.-M. and MacIntyre, P.D. (2016) Foreign language enjoyment and foreign language classroom anxiety: The right and left feet of the language learner. In P.D. MacIntyre, T. Gregersen and S. Mercer (eds) *Positive Psychology in SLA* (pp. 215–236). Bristol: Multilingual Matters.

Frost, R.O., Marten, P., Lahart, C. and Rosenblate, R. (1990) The dimensions of perfectionism. *Cognitive Therapy and Research* 14, 449–468.

Gregersen, T. and MacIntyre, P.D. (2014) *Capitalizing on Language Learners' Individuality: From Premise to Practice*. Bristol: Multilingual Matters.

Gregersen, T., MacIntyre, P.D. and Meza, M. (2014) The motion of emotion: Idiodynamic case studies of learners' foreign language anxiety. *The Modern Language Journal* 98 (2), 574–588.

Horwitz, E.K. (1996) Even teachers get the blues: Recognizing and alleviating language teachers' feelings of foreign language anxiety. *Foreign Language Annals* 29 (3), 365–372.

Horwitz, E.K. (2010) Foreign and second language anxiety. *Language Teaching* 43 (2), 154–167.

Horwitz, E.K and Young, D.J. (eds) (1991) *Language Anxiety from Theory and Research to Classroom Implications*. Englewood Cliffs, NJ: Prentice-Hall.

Horwitz, E.K., Horwitz, M.B. and Cope, J. (1986) Foreign language classroom anxiety. *The Modern Language Journal* 70 (2), 125–132.

Larsen-Freeman, D. and Cameron, L. (2008) *Complex Systems and Applied Linguistics*. Oxford: Oxford University Press.

MacIntyre, P. and Gregersen, T. (2012) Affect: The role of language anxiety and other emotions in language learning. In S. Mercer, S. Ryan and M. Williams (eds) *Psychology for Language Learning: Insights from Research, Theory and Practice* (pp. 103–118). Basingstoke: Palgrave Macmillan.

MacIntyre, P.D. and Mercer, S. (2014) Introducing positive psychology to SLA. *Studies in Second Language Learning and Teaching* 4 (2), 153–172.

MacIntyre, P.D., Gregersen, T. and Mercer, S. (eds) (2016) *Positive Psychology in SLA*. Bristol: Multilingual Matters.

McAdams, D. (2006) The role of narrative in personality psychology today. *Narrative Inquiry* 16 (1), 11–18.

Mercer, S. (2013) A complexity-informed pedagogy. *RBLA* 13 (2), 375–398.

Stroud, C. and Wee, L. (2006) Anxiety and identity in the language classroom. *RELC Journal* 37 (3), 299–307.

Tum, D.O. (2014) Foreign language anxiety's forgotten study: The case of the anxious preservice teacher. *TESOL Quarterly*, Early View.

Yan, X.J. and Horwitz, E.K. (2008) Learners' perceptions of how anxiety interacts with personal and instructional factors to influence their achievement in English: A qualitative analysis of EFL learners in China. *Language Learning* 58 (1), 151–183.

Young, D.J. (ed.) (1999) *Affect in Foreign Language and Second Language Learning: A Practical Guide to Creating a Low-Anxiety Classroom Atmosphere*. Boston, MA: McGraw Hill.

Index

affect (also affective dimension, affective domain, affective factors, affective sphere, affective states, affective variables), 2, 4, 41, 51, 94, 110, 132, 135, 147, 199, 200, 201, 203
   negative affect (*see also* negative emotions), 113, 114, 117, 131, 165
   positive affect (see positive emotions)
affective behaviour, 150
affective decoding skills, 131
Affective Filter Hypothesis, 200
affective questionnaire, 161, 174
affective reactions, 157, 161, 162, 170
affective strategies, 186, 190
affective techniques to face fearsome situations, 180
anxiety, foreign language (also language anxiety and foreign language classroom anxiety)
   behavioural manifestations of, 53, 208
   cause or effect of performance, 20–22, 27
   cognitive/linguistic manifestations of, 53, 202, 206–207, 208
   defined, 1, 70, 111
   effects of, 1, 16–18, 25, 111, 132
   and experimental methodology, 22–23
   and learner subjective experience of conversing in TL, 157
   and listening, 43, 93–95
   measuring, 12, 15–16
   nature of, 41–42
   non-verbal manifestations of, 112–113, 131
   physiological manifestations of, 53, 57, 206
   and reading, 18, 43, 92–93
   reducing anxiety (also mitigating anxiety and strategies for reducing anxiety), 38, 44, 102, 104–105, 111–112, 183–184, 188, 191, 199, 210, 212, 221
   relation to agency, 151, 178, 182, 186–187, 188, 191–192, 218, 221
   relation to avoidance behaviour/strategies, 25, 62, 77, 98–100, 106, 111, 179, 188, 189, 208
   relation to coping behaviours, 25, 27, 43, 62, 185, 189, 208–209
   relation to gender, 71
   relation to identity, 1, 21, 41, 56–57, 61–66, 157, 168, 203, 206, 208, 212, 213, 222
   relation to learner beliefs, 21, 37, 70, 96, 98, 100, 101, 104, 105, 136, 142, 146, 147, 148, 149, 150, 157, 180, 181, 183, 184, 190, 219
   relation to motivation, 1, 4, 14, 24, 25, 26, 40, 43, 51, 55, 56, 72, 75, 95, 138, 159, 179, 183, 185, 192, 201, 206, 211, 218, 219, 222
   relation to perceived competence, 19, 26, 45, 218
   relation to perfectionism, 19, 73–88
   relation to personality, 19
   relation to positive emotions, 219
   relation to proficiency, 157–159
   relation to safety behaviours (also safety-seeking behaviours), 62, 99, 102–103, 105, 106
   relation to self-esteem, 1, 21, 41, 77, 199–214, 221
   as self-exacerbating syndrome, 114
   social manifestations of, 17
   sources of (also causes of), 4, 5, 15, 16, 20, 21, 24, 70, 130, 138, 159, 203–206
   and speaking, 93, 96–97, 104–105, 142, 145, 149, 159
   and specific language skills, 18–19
   and teacher support, 38, 42
   and teachers decoding manifestations of, 113–114
   variables linked to, 74
   and writing, 18, 43, 95–96
anxious self, 53, 52, 54–55, 63–66
Attitude Motivation Test Battery (AMTB), 14

attractor states, 25–26
authentic self-presentation, 42

Beliefs about Language Learning Inventory (BALLI), 37
Big Five Inventory (see also New Big five Model), 53

Classroom Oral Participation Scheme (COPS), 97
cognitive behavioural techniques, 105
cognitive psychology, 4
cognitive therapy, 38, 190
communication apprehension, 31, 33–36, 38, 42
complexity turn in SLA, 219
Confucian Heritage cultures (CTC) versus non-Confucian Heritage cultures, 97
context in individual differences research, 135–136

debilitating anxiety (also harmful anxiety), 5, 12–13, 27, 39–40, 53, 66
diary studies, 20, 115
Dynamic Systems Theory (DST) (also Complex dynamic systems theory [CDST]), 2, 23
dynamic turn in SLA, 2

emotional intelligence, 19, 72, 74, 118, 183, 191, 219
emotions, 5, 41, 77, 114, 117, 141, 152, 182–184, 192
  discussion of in classrooms, 210, 221
  dynamic nature of, 116, 132
  functions of, 52
  learners' self-rating of, 130
  measuring emotions, 115
  mutual interaction between positive and negative emotions, 5, 219
  negative emotions, 59, 94, 170, 182–183, 221
  positive emotions, 94, 183, 192, 219
  reducing negative emotions, 180–181, 184, 187
Ecosystemic model of human behaviour (also ecology), 138–140

facilitating/facilitative anxiety (also helpful anxiety), 5, 12–13, 27, 39–40, 42
factor analysis, 16, 35–36, 94

fear of negative evaluation, 31, 33–36, 38, 42
Flow Theory, 31, 41, 182, 184–186, 191, 192, 211, 219
Foreign Language Classroom Anxiety Scale (FLCAS), 4, 15–16, 18, 24, 33, 34–37, 42, 44, 71, 81, 82, 115, 117, 140, 160, 166, 169, 200, 220
Frost Multidimensional Perfectionism Scale (FMPS), 76, 78, 79, 80, 81, 82

idiodynamic method, 24, 116–130, 220
individual differences (also learner-internal variables), 2, 3, 4, 55, 76, 135, 136, 221
integrative motivation, 14
intrinsic motivation, 184–185

L2 motivational self-system, 55, 201
  feared self, 201
  ideal self, 66, 73, 201
  ought to self, 25, 201
L2 narrative identity, 57
learner as person in context, 136
learner diaries, 140–141
learner narratives, 65, 66, 183
learner silence, 98–103
learners' illusion of transparency, 114–115

Multidimensional Self-oriented Perfectionism Scale (MSPS), 71, 81, 82

New Big Five model, 54–57, 220

personality variables, 72
positive psychology, 179, 182–191, 219, 221
psychology of language learning, 3
public speaking anxiety, 114, 127

qualitative interviews, 25, 38, 53, 54, 57, 60, 98, 158, 161, 164, 166, 168

self-concept, 55–56, 66, 91, 138, 142, 169, 200–203, 205–209, 211–213, 218
situation-specific anxiety, 5, 15–16, 33, 51, 137–138
social turn in SLA, 27, 135
social anxiety, 91–92, 178–181, 191
  model of, 98–103, 220, 221
  relation to learner silence, 98–103

sociobiographical variables, 72, 82, 83, 84, 86, 87
Socio-Educational Model, 14, 200
state anxiety, 5, 12, 32–33, 65, 137–138
Strategy Inventory for Language Learning (SILL), 37
student-initiated talk vs teacher-initiated talk, 97

teacher anxiety, 158, 222
test anxiety, 13, 31, 33–36, 38, 42, 59
trait anxiety, 5, 12, 32–33, 51, 65, 137–138

Willingness to Communicate (WTC), 1, 19, 20, 25, 26, 43, 72, 136, 178